I0813709

TAKE HEART FOR TEENS

Daily Devotions
to Deepen Your Faith

DAVID POWLISON

newgrowthpress.com

New Growth Press, Greensboro, NC 27401
newgrowthpress.com

The text of *Take Heart for Teens* has been adapted from David Powlison, *Take Heart: Daily Devotions to Deepen Your Faith* (New Growth Press, 2022) by a team of editors including Gwenyth Powlison Ray, Aubrynn Whitted, Michael Gembola, Chanelle Gregersen, and Kim Monroe.

Cover Design: Faceout Books, faceoutstudio.com
Interior Typesetting and Ebook: Lisa Parnell, lparnellbookservices.com

ISBN: 978-1-64507-553-0 (hardback)
ISBN: 978-1-64507-554-7 (ebook)

Library of Congress Cataloging-in-Publication Data on file

Printed in Colombia

29 28 27 26 25   1 2 3 4 5

INTRODUCTION

I had the great gift of a great earthly father. David Powlison was my dad for thirty-seven years before he went to live with his heavenly Father, and I wish you could have met him. He could make anyone feel at ease and often looked for a way to bring a laugh into the conversation. Before you jump into reading his words, I thought you might like to know a little more about him. So come along and let me introduce you to my dad.

It was the end of a long, hot day of driving in Northern California when my dad decided to chase the moon. He was there to teach at a conference—I was fourteen and along for the ride. As far as I know he had no idea where he was going. There were no cell phones or internet searches to get recommendations for *amazing nature experiences in Alameda County.* On that evening in June we were driving through a flat and barren land on a back road seemingly to nowhere.

We parked in the dirt and walked up a slight rise. The sky was vastly open, reflecting in its own way the washed-out landscape. The sun in the west was finally warming to the idea of setting by glowing in softer colors—not the harsh brightness of midday, but hues of dusky peach and soft plum. The sunset itself would have been worth the wandering, but soon we turned a half circle and saw the start of a parallel light rising in the east. I remember the quietness of awe settling on us as the full moon rose to give a farewell glance to the other great light. As it emerged, the color and feel of the whole sky shifted to cooler and serene. It was a magic of mirroring with my dad and me right in the middle. We didn't know where to look, so we kept repeating the half turn over and over. We made it a game to try and catch the last glimpse of the fading sun and the moment the moon was freed from the horizon to begin its rule of the night sky. We laughed and delighted in wonder.

I only realize now how unique this quality of my dad's was. Children are naturally filled with wonder and awe. But sadly, most of us grow out of it. He never grew out of wonder and awe and it affected every area of his life. You need a sense of awe to live a life of vibrant faith. Maybe you know that by now, but maybe you've forgotten. Let me encourage you that no matter why or how you came to have this devotional book in your hand, if you continue to read past the introduction, you will find reasons to remember and grow in your own sense of wonder. And a commitment to that growth will change your life.

Because my dad lived a life of awe, he wrote and spoke a lot about reasons to delight in and live under our awesome God. As you read, you will find that he was always finding new aspects of God's character to rejoice in and be uplifted by. He was fascinated by the ways the Bible speaks into the ordinary life experiences of all people. And he was especially filled with wonder at God's care for the hurting and the suffering. My dad loved the Bible, and if he were here to write this introduction, he would certainly encourage you to ponder the Scripture references that lead off each day. Because God is alive and the words of the Bible are living and active, a life full of Scripture promises to be pretty exciting. At the end of each entry, there are a few lines to *Take with You*. These thoughts and questions were added by the editors to help you pause and grab onto one more layer of who God is and how he is speaking to you in your daily reality.

I hope that as you walk forward, one day at a time, you will grow in your own excitement and delight, your own awe and wonder of your life with the God who sees you. And don't forget to stop and look at the moon.

—Gwenyth Powlison Ray

JANUARY 1

As for me, I am poor and needy,
but the Lord takes thought for me.
You are my help and my deliverer;
do not delay, O my God! —Psalm 40:17

We don't like to be weak or let others think we are. But the truth is, we are. We are physically weak—we don't live forever, we get sick, and we face hard things. And we are spiritually weak—our hearts want their own way. We put what we want ahead of loving God. We think we are better than others or care more about what others think of us than what God thinks.

To admit weakness is not natural. We would rather hear people say, "You are STRONG!" and "You can do it!" But admitting we are weak is a good thing. *Weakness is a most unusual door into all the ways God makes us strong.*

Being unafraid to be publicly weak was true of King David. This psalm paints a picture of God's strength and rescue. Yet David describes himself this way: "As for me, I am poor and needy, but the Lord takes thought for me." David's strength grew out of his total sense of weakness and his total faith in God's strength.

My deepest hope for you is that you would be unafraid to admit you are weak and that you'd find, like David, that admitting you need help is the doorway to the strength of God himself.

Take with You: Ask God for help when you feel weak. Instead of trying to cover up and pretend you are strong, tell God all about it and maybe talk with a friend too.

JANUARY 2

"But seek first the kingdom of God and his righteousness, and all these things will be added to you." —Matthew 6:33

What are you wishing for? What are you obsessing about? What do you want most? The answers to those questions will be connected to what you're worrying about. *When your whole heart is consumed with something besides God, you're going to worry about it. Only God can be pursued wholeheartedly without worry or anxiety.*

So the biggest question you will face cuts the deepest: What do you want with your whole heart? What are you loving? Who are you loving? Are you loving pleasure, your image, or control? Are you loving being liked? Are you obsessed with wanting to escape? These questions cut deep, and your answers affect everything you feel, everything you think, how you treat people, and the way you come into a conversation.

We're called to love God with all that we are. God wants us to seek him, his kingdom, and his good way of living first. We can make pursuing God the most important thing when we trust he's going to take care of all the other things. And, as we grow in our trust in God, our worries will be opportunities to turn to him for the help we need.

> **Take with You:** When you are worried or consumed by something, stop and ask God to help you love him first and best right in the middle of your anxiety. Ask him to turn your anxiety into trust.

JANUARY 3

For God, who said, "Let light shine out of darkness," has shone in our hearts to give the light of the knowledge of the glory of God in the face of Jesus Christ. —2 Corinthians 4:6

Can people change? Can you change? Or do life experiences or personality dictate who you are? Some days it might feel like you are always going to have the same struggles. But that's not true. *The good news is that you can change when the Holy Spirit brings the love of God into your heart through the gospel.*

The things that have happened to you can shape you. But they don't have the last word on who you are and who you will become. On the contrary, disappointments can make you long to know your heavenly Father, Good Shepherd, Savior, and God! You can cry out, "Abba, Father," and he will hear and answer you (Romans 8:15).

When God lives in you, his truth becomes clearer and brighter than your troubles, failures, and sins. You will change as you hear and see what God tells you about himself (Psalm 103:10–13; Isaiah 49:13–16).

God is in the business of changing people's minds; he is not hindered by wrong thinking. He can reveal himself, "[shining] in our hearts to give us the light of the knowledge of the glory of God in the face of Christ" (2 Corinthians 4:6). Life experience or the lies people believe don't trump everything. God is supreme, and he alone can change your heart, your mind, and your actions.

Take with You: What is one thing you would like God to change about you today? Change begins with knowing God. Ask him to show you specific ways he cares for you.

JANUARY 4

Jesus said to her, "I am the resurrection and the life. Whoever believes in me, though he die, yet shall he live, and everyone who lives and believes in me shall never die. Do you believe this?" —John 11:25–26

How do you know that the promises God makes to you are true? How do you know that the living God gives true, concrete hope? Because Jesus defeated death. As a willing and sinless substitute, he died in our place on the cross. And God raised him to life and joy. He is alive! Peter explains it this way: "Praise be to the God and Father of our Lord Jesus Christ! In his great mercy he has given us new birth into a living hope through the resurrection of Jesus Christ from the dead, and into an inheritance that can never perish, spoil, or fade. This inheritance is kept in heaven for you" (1 Peter 1:3–4 NIV). Your Father in heaven has great mercy. He makes us alive. He gives us realistic joy and hope.

Jesus is alive! His resurrection is his guarantee that you can live in real hope. *Your hope is not based on a pipe dream that changed circumstances, the passing of time, a new set of friends, or even giving up will somehow cure how you feel. God gives living hope based on the physical reality of the resurrection of Jesus Christ.* Because the resurrection happened and Jesus is alive, well, and at work, your story can end in life.

Take with You: Today when you're sad, disappointed, or hopeless, ask God to give you hope based on Jesus's resurrection. What difference does Jesus's resurrection make to how you feel right now?

JANUARY 5

Even though I walk through the valley of the shadow of death,
I will fear no evil,
for you are with me;
your rod and your staff,
they comfort me. —Psalm 23:4

What will give you the most happiness in life? What pleasure will not dim through life's changes? It's the pleasure of knowing God and being known by him. You step into that pleasure by coming to Jesus for mercy and grace. You grow in your relationship with him by asking for mercy as a daily, lifelong habit. *Your own inability to deal with your everyday sins is God's mercy to you. It forces you to go to God for the help you need.* As you go to God, let his Word guide you.

In Psalm 23, God is speaking to you, and you can speak these words back to God. Praying through it is one way to experience the pleasure of a growing relationship with God.

Start by reading it out loud. Do you notice how the psalmist takes hold of suffering? He looks the shadow of death right in the eye: "I will fear no evil" (v. 4). He knows the Lord is with him. Notice how he switches from talking about God in the third person ("he") to the second person ("you"), remembering his intimacy with God. The last two lines say that goodness and lovingkindness are literally chasing him! "I am being pursued by your goodness and mercy all my life, and then I will live with you forever." This is the supreme pleasure.

Take with You: What are some words or phrases from Psalm 23 you can use today to talk to God? What words might God be speaking to you today from Psalm 23?

JANUARY 6

"A new commandment I give to you, that you love one another:
just as I have loved you, you also are to love one another.
By this all people will know that you are my disciples,
if you have love for one another." —John 13:34–35

In heaven you will see the One you love face-to-face. But heaven will also be full of other relationships you enjoy—your closest friends and family, the people who love you without pretense, competition, or manipulation. We don't wait for heaven to express love. We are to love now—even though it may be hard. Love for others is how we make God visible around us.

The Bible calls us to get out of our comfort zone and love enemies, strangers, people who are different from us, and those who are needy, sinful, and broken. This is a harder call, isn't it? We are also to love these people right now—even though it might seem impossible.

This call tests whether we are turning the gift of a close relationship into something that shuts others out. Are you and the people you enjoy turning into a clique? Are you willing to widen the circle of intimacy so enemies become friends, strangers become like family, and someone you don't know becomes like a dear brother or sister?

The goal is simple, joyous relationships with others—the mutual caring and honest give-and-take. *God calls you to widen the circle of your friendships and to avoid making a god out of those who bring you the greatest pleasure.*

Take with You: Who might God be calling you to love today from your close circle? And who might God be calling you to love today who is outside your circle? What's one small kindness you can show others?

JANUARY 7

The Lord is near. Do not be anxious about anything, but in every situation, by prayer and petition, with thanksgiving, present your requests to God. And the peace of God, which transcends all understanding, will guard your hearts and your minds in Christ Jesus. —Philippians 4:5–7 NIV

The Lord has something to say about what you are going through every single day. Scripture has been designed by God himself to connect to the reality of human experience. But how do you make those connections? Start with the short, straightforward passages of Scripture. Philippians 4:6, for example, says, "Do not be anxious about anything, but in everything by prayer and supplication with thanksgiving let your requests be made known to God."

But it's hard to think straight when we are anxious. What promise could anchor you so you can make such a response? One of them is tucked in verse 5: "the Lord is near." Anxiety is the experience that you're all alone in a world that's too big for you. You feel anxious because you can't control your circumstances. But if the Lord is near, everything changes. You aren't alone. The one who is in control, who orders and provides, is near. He cares for you and he is involved.

Starting with these basic promises reminds you in the midst of your day that the Lord is with you. *Simple promises, taken to heart, get you and God on the same page with each other.*

Take with You: Throughout your day, when you are worried or anxious, what can you do to remind yourself that the Lord is near? Try holding your one hand with your other hand and remember that the Lord is holding you.

JANUARY 8

"Pray then like this: 'Our Father in heaven, hallowed be your name. Your kingdom come, your will be done, on earth as it is in heaven. Give us this day our daily bread, and forgive us our debts, as we also have forgiven our debtors. And lead us not into temptation, but deliver us from evil.'" —Matthew 6:9–13

In the Bible, prayer lands in three main categories: prayers for physical circumstances, prayers for personal change, and prayers focused on God's glory and power.

Sometimes we ask God to *change our circumstances*: heal a sick family member, help me do well in school and sports, keep me safe on a trip, help my friend who is depressed, provide a new job for my mom or dad.

Sometimes we ask God to *change us*: teach me to love hard people, deepen my faith, give me peace about the future, help me to be wise and honor you with my choices, show me how to understand Scripture and hold truth in my heart, teach me to encourage others and not gossip.

Sometimes we ask God to *change everything by revealing himself* in glory and power. Your kingdom come! Your will be done! Let your glory fill the earth! Come, Lord Jesus!

The Lord's Prayer intertwines all three types of prayer. In God's kingdom, sins and sufferings are no more. His rule brings perfect wisdom and a wealth of situational blessing. *Prayers for God to change me and my circumstances are requests that he show his glory and mercy on the stage of this world.*

Take with You: Ask God for his will to be done in your specific circumstance today. Where do you need his help, forgiveness, and deliverance today?

JANUARY 9

His divine power has granted to us all things that pertain to life and godliness, through the knowledge of him who called us to his own glory and excellence, by which he has granted to us his precious and very great promises, so that through them you may become partakers of the divine nature, having escaped from the corruption that is in the world because of sinful desire. —2 Peter 1:3–4

God already knows we are a tangled web. We are slow to change. We have darkness within ourselves. Every one of us has stubborn inconsistencies and blind spots. *The only one who completely understands us is God. Sometimes he helps us to change rapidly. But he usually intervenes slowly—to transform how we think, love, fear, want, and trust on a scale of years, over a lifetime.*

Reorienting our hearts is a slow road. Our outward behaviors and speech matter and the deep, stirring waters of our inner person also matter. To attend to both the inner and outer workings of our lives, we need humility, patience, and an awareness of our need for divine help. We will only be made wholly right when we see Jesus face-to-face.

Our Abba Father is always reminding us of his love for us in Christ. We change as we believe his great and precious promises that are ours because of Jesus (2 Peter 1:4). God's powerful, patient love brings clarity to the challenges of hard life circumstances and our internal struggles.

Take with You: It takes great courage to acknowledge true need, but you are in a grand story. Ask for God's powerful, patient love to turn your heart to him today and trust him to write the next page of your grand story.

JANUARY 10

If your law had not been my delight,
I would have perished in my affliction.
I will never forget your precepts,
for by them you have given me life. —Psalm 119:92–93

Psalm 119 is personal prayer. It's talking *to* God, not teaching *about* God. We get to hear what a man says out loud in God's presence: his joyous pleasure, open adoration, blunt requests, deep struggles, and fiercely good intentions. The synonyms for the Word of God (law, precepts, statutes) appear once in each verse, but I-you (relationship) words appear about four times in each verse.

So the topic of Psalm 119 isn't about getting Scripture into your life. Instead, it's the honest response that overflows when the truth of what God says about his world gets deeply into you. The words of Psalm 119 show a real life interacting with the real God. They are the words of someone who has listened to God and then opens his heart to God. That may sound simplistic, but the model of listening and responding holds the power to change a whole life.

How did the psalmist learn to be so outspoken to God? He listened to what God said in the rest of the Bible and lived it. *The Lord says who he is and is who he says. The Lord says what he does and does what he says. A life of faith is one of listening, experiencing what is true, and talking back in simple sentences.*

> **Take with You:** We can be busy, noisy, distractible people in a busy, noisy, distracting world. Find a time today to quiet your space and your mind. Read a few more verses on Psalm 119. What is God saying? What do you want to say back to him?

JANUARY 11

And he answered, "You shall love the Lord your God with all your heart and with all your soul and with all your strength and with all your mind, and your neighbor as yourself." —Luke 10:27

Jesus summarized the Bible's goal in this way: Love God with your whole heart. Love your neighbor as yourself. God's law is a picture of how a human being becomes truly human (Galatians 5:6; 1 Timothy 1:5).

The wholeness that comes by abiding in this law is the way life is meant to be experienced. The God of the universe calls us to love him with complete dedication. When I forget my Good Shepherd, I arrange my life around another god and I love some good gift more than the Giver of the gift. God, who made people in his image, calls us to love each other with the same fierce concern that we look out for our own interests. When I forget to live in the light of this truth, I get frustrated and hateful, or fearful and withdrawn. When I remember, I get boldly caring and outwardly focused. Will I primarily love myself and my own goals and preferences? Will I become wholly indifferent and blind to the needs of my friends, family, and community? I am commanded to the sanity of this whole, selfless love, and it lays my heart bare.

The law of love is a mirror showing us who we are. It is also a lamp, lighting the way to where we ought to be.

Take with You: Has anyone ever loved you in a way that you felt seen in your need? Ask God to show you one small way that you can practice love today.

JANUARY 12

Rock of ages, cleft for me
Let me hide myself in Thee
Let the water and the blood
From Thy riven side which flowed
Oh, be of sin the double cure
Cleanse me from its guilt and power
—Augustus Toplady, "Rock of Ages"

Every part of the grace of God is meant to make us new. Anger, criticism, fear, and pride deform our lives until we find shelter and healing in the glorious forgiveness of Jesus. His blood poured out on the cross gives us a "double cure" from both the guilt and the power of sin.

His forgiveness cures us. James 4:6–10 captures the two simple actions that are needed on our part: *turning* from our way and *seeking* God's way. In our need, we turn to the Person willing and able to help and we see that repentance in faith is rooted in relationship. These verses begin with a gift, "But he gives more grace." In light of that gift of grace, we are called to action in the face of multiple expressions of sin. Life serves us big problems, but God is at the center of every solution.

God is *present.* When we seek, we find that Someone moves toward us with grace. Someone whose power freely helps us. To heal our hearts of internal and external conflict, we must seek God's mercy. *Our strivings and struggles are fueled by trying to take God's place. The grace of Jesus Christ forgives and reinstates God's rule in our hearts.*

Take with You: Read James 4:6–10. Notice the words that describe our actions and the phrases that describe God's action. Take a moment to thank God for the wild gift of grace.

JANUARY 13

The LORD passed before him and proclaimed, "The LORD, the LORD, a God merciful and gracious, slow to anger, and abounding in steadfast love and faithfulness, keeping steadfast love for thousands, forgiving iniquity and transgression and sin, but who will by no means clear the guilty, visiting the iniquity of the fathers on the children and the children's children, to the third and the fourth generation." —Exodus 34:6–7

God consistently reveals who he is in the incredibly wonderful dance of mercy and justice. It's hard to understand how mercy and justice can exist together perfectly in God, but one of the most vivid expressions of this in the Bible is when God reveals himself to Moses on Mount Sinai.

Even though we go wrong daily, we are still invited into God's life-giving goodness. But he does not ignore unacknowledged and unrepentant wrong. This can be confusing. Is God patient, or is he impatient? Does God forgive, or is he unforgiving? Does he show love, or not? His mercy creates a conflict with our sins as we do not receive what we do deserve. His mercy is not niceness. His mercy is not blanket acceptance of any and all. *Mercy to us costs him—the blood of the Lamb.* His steadfast love and faithfulness welcomes us to turn to him in repentance. We are needy, and mercy is given through Christ. God repeatedly invites us to faith as a response to his abounding mercy.

Take with You: It's okay to have questions about God's intricate and infinite character. As you seek answers throughout your life, remember that *because* of your brother, Jesus, you have full access to God the Father and to his love, wisdom, and welcome.

JANUARY 14

"If I tell the truth, why do you not believe me? Whoever is of God hears the words of God." —John 8:46–47

In his life, death, and resurrection, Jesus triumphed over the powers of darkness. He knew the ugly reality of the world, the weakness of the flesh, and the tempting deceit of the devil better than any human before or since. *In the midst of his real enemies, he trusted in his heavenly Father to bring light out of darkness. He continually called everyone he encountered to the same living, active dependence on his heavenly Father.*

Jesus recognizes that the Evil One plays a significant role in adding to human misery. But he continually speaks to the human heart and how the state of the heart informs the whole person. In John 8 when Jesus describes the devil, he is speaking to a group of people right in front of him (John 8:44–47). The devil's influence is real, but Jesus directly asks questions about life or death to his listeners and expands on the conversation. These can be the same questions we ask of ourselves and others to uncover the deepest reasons for joy or sorrow in life:

- Who are you allowing to guide you?
- Whose words are catching your ears and repeating in your mind?
- Whose desires and examples are you following?
- Who do you say Jesus is?

Take with You: In John 1:5, it says, "The light shines in the darkness, and the darkness has not overcome it." This is a promise to you. There is no darkness in your life that the light of Christ cannot reach. Take heart. You are not alone.

JANUARY 15

When my anxious thoughts multiply within me,
Your comfort delights my soul. —Psalm 94:19 NASB

Because there's trouble in this world, we have good reasons to be anxious. In the midst of trouble our hearts forget God, and we get attached to other masters—to all kinds of desires, needs, beliefs, and quick comforts. We get anxious for bad reasons, and we overreact even to the good reasons we have to be anxious. Living in a world where there is trouble, with hearts that quickly stray, means we will always be tempted to lose sight of God. When we lose sight of God, we try to control our world on our own, and we become filled with worry.

But don't despair: God, in his Word, gives you better and never-ending reasons for responding to the troubles of life in faith. His comfort can and will delight your soul when you turn to him. You can learn to remember God instead of forgetting him. God wants us to know him so intimately and trust him so completely that our desire to fix our troubles in our own way will no longer consume us. As we grow in our love for God and our knowledge of his character, we will experience the right kind of concern in the midst of our troubles.

Take with You: In moments of anxiety, try having some go-to prayers and statements to remind you of who you are in God's kingdom. "I am not alone." "I am loved with an everlasting love." "I am seen and known right now." "I have a friend who is always near."

JANUARY 16

Incline your ear, O LORD, for I am poor and needy.
—Psalm 86:1

Faith always shows itself in practical love for other people. As you go to God and tell him your needs, your sorrows, and your joys, your faith will branch out into loving concern and awareness for the people in your life (Galatians 5:6). Loving others may seem like an impossible wall to climb when you are in the midst of your own struggle physically, emotionally, and spiritually. But you will start to love even in the way you struggle. For example, *loving those around you in the midst of your weakness can be as simple as sharing your own needs and concerns with someone else.* Guys sometimes have a harder time than girls being honest about weakness and talking about it with others. But a show of having it all together all the time and never being sad or hurt is not just a guy thing. The truth is that most people don't really like needing help. But the Bible is honest about our weakness. King David wrote many psalms out of his sense of weakness and need. Jesus asked his disciples to watch and pray with him in his own pressing need. Paul often shared his personal need with the church—pressures that almost overwhelmed him, his thorn in the flesh, and the sorrows God had spared him.

Take with You: It can be hard to honestly share a sensitive need with someone. But the more you practice, the easier it becomes. Find someone you trust this week and practice sharing a personal struggle through a lens of love. Ask for specific prayer and see how God awakens you to look out and care for others.

JANUARY 17

What then shall we say to these things? If God is for us, who can be against us? He who did not spare his own Son but gave him up for us all, how will he not also with him graciously give us all things? Who shall bring any charge against God's elect? It is God who justifies. Who is to condemn? Christ Jesus is the one who died—more than that, who was raised—who is at the right hand of God, who indeed is interceding for us. —Romans 8:31–34

God's past grace to sinners shows that he is for us. How do you know God is for you? He did not spare his own Son. This good news isn't just for your early Christian life. What Jesus did once continues to reshape what we do. In 2 Corinthians 5:14–15, past grace is described as the power working to change our present Christian life: "The love of Christ controls us, having concluded this, that one died for all, therefore all died; and He died for all, so that they who live might no longer live for themselves, but for Him who died and rose again on their behalf" (NASB).

Do you want to honestly look at yourself and change? *Past grace gives you the ability to fearlessly see yourself in the mirror of God's loving gaze and gives you a reason to become different.* You don't have to obsess or avoid looking at your failures. Past grace never lets you forget that the merciful Father is for you.

Take with You: This term *past grace* might be new to you. As you think about it, enjoy it as an invitation to fully trust God. His forgiveness will help you change now and every day until eternity.

JANUARY 18

I will instruct you and teach you in the way you should go;
I will counsel you with my eye upon you.
Be not like a horse or a mule, without understanding,
which must be curbed with bit and bridle,
or it will not stay near you. —Psalm 32:8–9

We live in a day when saying your opinion matters more than listening intently. But Christ wants listeners. He wants whole hearts. How does he gain this audience? He tells us to listen and then tells us about himself. He communicates a rational, solid, bluntly historical message and offers us a firm foundation. As we hear the gospel story accurately, emotions may swell: deep regret over sin, utter gratitude, melting sorrow. Listening well to the best story leads to wise action.

Are you listening?

People who will not stop talking have an actual problem. A sharp proverb notes, "Too much talk leads to sin" (Proverbs 10:19 NLT). Another comments ironically, "Even a fool who keeps silent is considered wise" (17:28).

The Bible says repeatedly that we grow and change only by listening, not by talking. With good reason Jesus says, "He who has ears to hear, let him hear." With good reason King David utters God's call for us to hear personal counsel: "I will instruct you and teach you in the way which you should go; I will counsel you with my eye upon you" (Psalm 32:8). Willingness to listen is itself a significant aspect of repentance and renewal.

Take with You: What is a situation today where you could practice active listening? Ask God for help to hear his voice and to love others well by listening.

JANUARY 19

Blessed be the God and Father of our Lord Jesus Christ, the Father of mercies and God of all comfort, who comforts us in all our affliction, so that we may be able to comfort those who are in any affliction, with the comfort with which we ourselves are comforted by God. —2 Corinthians 1:3–4

You have a story to tell of how God has worked in you. It's personal and specific, and it reaches out to other people. As you process your life, you have something to give away to others. I need your story, and you need mine. This is the "one-anothering" the Bible speaks about. You need other people to help the story of the Bible come to life. This dynamic runs throughout Scripture, enabling you to give away what you're getting.

When you look through the book of 2 Corinthians, you see that Paul is deeply encouraged not only by God but also by people. *Paul received comfort so that he could comfort, strengthen, encourage, guide, lead, challenge, and support others, and that's the way it's meant to be for every one of us.* When the Bible comes to life for me, I'm given something worth sharing.

Every Christian has three callings: Pray for one another, give practically, and speak words of wisdom and encouragement. To accomplish these calls, you must be connected both to God and to what's really going on with the people God placed in your right-now life.

Take with You: Is there an experience you've had, either good or bad, that has helped you to build a deeper relationship with someone in your life? Give thanks! God is using your personal story in a divine way.

JANUARY 20

For the wages of sin is death, but the free gift of God is eternal life in Christ Jesus our Lord.
—Romans 6:23

For those who know Jesus, death doesn't have the last word; it has the next-to-last word. *The last word for the Christian is the resurrection. The last word is life. The last word is mercy. The last word is that God will take us to be with him forever.* God's gift of eternal life stands in stark contrast to "the wages of sin is death" (Romans 6:23). Jesus stands in contrast to the killer, the murderer, the slayer. He, the only innocent person who ever lived, who faced death not for his own sins, but for the sins of his people (John 3:16). Jesus faced death for you to give you a gift instead of a punishment.

On the cross, he died in multiple dimensions. He was killed by asphyxiation and torture, but this was only the physical cause of his death. As he died, he bore the full cost of sin and rebellion, suffered the hateful intentions of Satan, and experienced the holy wrath of God. He, the innocent one, willingly died for the guilty.

When Jesus, our brother, freely gave up his life, death was destroyed by God through the resurrection. Because of Jesus, life has the last word. Because of Jesus, you don't have to experience death as he did. He has already paid for your sins. You will die physically, but you will rise to life eternal (John 3:16).

Take with You: The life-giving beauty of these truths is hard to comprehend, but the simple posture of gratitude can renew an hour, a day, a whole life. Take a minute to thank God for the gift of eternal life.

JANUARY 21

Be strong and take heart,
all you who hope in the LORD. —Psalm 31:24 NIV

King David's life, like yours, is full of disappointment, troubles, and layers of discouragement. Yet because God is with him, he has hope. He says, "You heard my cry for mercy when I called to you for help" (Psalm 31:22 NIV). And he ends Psalm 31 with this encouragement: "Be strong and take heart, all you who hope in the LORD" (v. 24 NIV). David is able to endure with courage because God is with him.

God is always calling you to press on in your suffering, but not by simply gritting your teeth. Persevering through suffering is only possible when you put your hope in the living God. *He promises to come near to you, be present with you, and let you see his goodness right in the middle of your pain and difficulty.* Jesus was able to persevere through the greatest time of suffering that any human has ever faced. He endured death on the cross "for the joy set before him" (Hebrews 12:2 NIV). And what was the joy that motivated Jesus in the face of such horrors? Doing his Father's will and saving our eternal lives. As you look to Jesus, who is always writing a new page of your story, he will give you strength to persevere through suffering and find joy in living for God.

Take with You: Suffering is as personal as your unique fingerprints. What bothers you or makes you cringe or makes you cry is a part of your specific journey. Jesus knows all these layers. He loves you. How can that truth change you today?

JANUARY 22

The aim of our charge is love that issues from a pure heart and a good conscience and a sincere faith. —1 Timothy 1:5

Everything about a human being operates either for God or against him. Every desire and belief is either true or twisted. Every hope or fear is either realistic or imaginary. Every attitude of our hearts and every interaction with other people comes weighted. We either tilt toward the kingdom of God or bend toward the kingdom of selfishness.

Wisdom refreshes our understanding of what it's like to be fully human. *Here is the true definition of human flourishing: love from a pure heart, a good conscience, and a sincere faith (1 Timothy 1:5).* A "pure heart" means you are turning toward the living God. You're resisting the madness in your heart's desires and fears. A "good conscience" means you're learning to evaluate all things as they truly are. You are turning toward God's own definition of himself and you. You're letting God clarify what's right and wrong, true and false, worthy and worthless. A "sincere faith" means you are placing your full confidence in the mercies of Jesus Christ. You are turning away from trusting in yourself, in others, in admiration, and in achievements.

Human beings are dependent on the God who creates and sustains. He has come in person to save us from ourselves. This reality of rescue addresses each person's deepest problems. Christ alone sheds light on what's wrong and begins the most wonderful work of making all things right.

Take with You: When you feel stuck in a friendship, take comfort that God knows all the layers of every person. Ask God for help to answer the question, "What does love look like in this situation?"

JANUARY 23

Blessed be the God and Father of our Lord Jesus Christ, the Father of mercies and God of all comfort, who comforts us in all our affliction, so that we may be able to comfort those who are in any affliction, with the comfort with which we ourselves are comforted by God. —2 Corinthians 1:3–4

Praise God for the in-person directness of his mercies and how his comforts rush from him to us, from us to one another. In 2 Corinthians 1:3–4, Paul talks about what afflicts us, what it means to be comforted, and how God comforts us.

First, "all our affliction" and "any affliction" point to human troubles without naming specifics. Affliction (*thlipsis*) is a catch-all. So 2 Corinthians 1:4 invites you to read into it whatever pressures you, distresses you, tests you or troubles you, hurts you or burdens you. Whatever come our way, we can see ourselves, others, and what we each face within these verses.

Second, what does it mean to be comforted in your troubles? God's comfort is not passive. He doesn't make life easy. He doesn't take struggle and hardship away. He even adds the pain of caring. *But our Father's comfort actively strengthens you in the midst of weakness, pain, and need—so you can take heart and take action.* "The Father of mercies and God of all comfort" encourages us so we can encourage others. God's comfort deepens your faith, anchors your hope, nourishes your love, and brings about your joy.

Take with You: Look around. Who in your life could use a big hug or a word of encouragement today? You are more than able to take part in the comforting of the world with simple actions.

JANUARY 24

For this is the will of God, your sanctification.
—1 Thessalonians 4:3a

What is God's will for you? *Where should I go to college? What sport should I play? What friend group will I join?* These might seem like the biggest life decisions, the places we most need direct guidance. These questions are important, and the decisions have consequences. There may be better or worse reasons to choose one commitment over another, and we do need wisdom. Yet such items are not on God's written list of what he wills for us. He never promises to give us "fortune cookie" guidance.

A wise professor once said to me as I entered my last year of seminary, "It may be relatively unimportant whether you eventually become a pastor in Kalamazoo or a missionary in Timbuktu. . . . But it may be a matter of life or death whether or not you decide to cross the street, if you spot an old friend from whom you've been estranged walking on the other side. God really cares what you do next."

God urgently calls us to seek peace with people. My professor pointed out that loving my neighbor well is more important than which city I move to. If you remain angry, judgmental, and avoidant, you will certainly perish. God opposes the proud but gives grace to the humble. He gives tools to become peaceable and constructive humans in a broken world.

God's will is your sanctification. He calls us to become more like him over our lifetime.

Take with You: God's will for you is simple and complex at the same time. Instead of feeling frustrated by all the unknowns, shift your focus to what is known and walk forward one step at a time. Love God. Love people.

JANUARY 25

As a father shows compassion to his children,
so the LORD shows compassion to those who fear him.
—Psalm 103:13

Our Lord is trustworthy. He is protective. He is generous. He nurtures. He hears our cry for help. He corrects wisely. He freely forgives when we turn. He is highly communicative—telling us about himself and quickly hearing us. He pursues. He is patient. He knows us—he really, truly, always "gets us." And he gets down on our level. Like a truly good father, he has compassion on his children, and never forgets our limitations (Psalm 103:13–14). His instruction is always good, his correction is always for our future best.

So he gives us every reason to trust, even though we struggle amid all the limitations, betrayals, and sins that go against trust. You see this matured trust in the Psalms. It is totally childlike, and yet fully adult. It is entirely aware of every dark thing in life, and yet it voices both the unhappy cry of need and the happy heart of contentment or joy.

How does such trust grow in us? We learn to take specific Scripture to heart. God is not vaguely all-present. He is immediately, personally, specifically, and relevantly in each scene of our day. He is paying attention, caring, and helping. He has something to say that makes a difference. We can know he is true because he has shown himself again and again.

Take with You: Breathe in. Breathe out. Read these words one more time. Rejoice and thank God for how he tends to your every need. Trust him today with your real concerns, hopes, and sorrows.

JANUARY 26

But he answered, "It is written, 'Man shall not live by bread alone, but by every word that comes from the mouth of God.'" —Matthew 4:4

We don't live by bread alone but by every word from the mouth of God. That's not just a noble-sounding religious statement. It's true in the details of life lived. So slow down and notice what's going on with you. It will help you see that the Bible is relevant because it's exactly in tune with your daily struggles.

- Feel dull and distant? Psalm 119's cries come alive.
- Feel the hurt of someone's unkindness toward you? Psalm 10 has been there and walks with you.
- Feel your insignificance in the eyes of other people? Jesus's approach in Luke 18:15–17 speaks warmly.
- Feel the sting of your sins? Romans 8:31–34 and Psalm 51 show you the way of repentance.
- Feel your insecurity when walking into a difficult interaction? James 1:5 and 3:17–18 come alive.
- Feel anxiety because many hard things are coming at you all at once? Jeremiah 17:7–8 sparkles with hope.
- Feel the approach of death? Psalm 23 is right there beside you.
- Feel your own doubts about your faith? Jesus comes true to life as you watch Matthew, Mark, Luke, or John proclaim their own faith. "You are the Christ, the Son of the Living God. I believe, help my unbelief."

As you become aware of your need, you awaken to where God intersects your life. Speak up about exactly the help you need.

Take with You: Where are you feeling unsettled today? Make your prayer small and specific. God knows your deepest need and wants you to talk to him about your deepest need. He is near.

JANUARY 27

But he said to me, "My grace is sufficient for you,
for my power is made perfect in weakness." Therefore I will
boast all the more gladly of my weaknesses, so that the power
of Christ may rest upon me. —2 Corinthians 12:9

When Scripture connects in a new way to your life, it's the mark of a living relationship with the God of the Bible. *The God who speaks wishes to speak intimately to you.* Who you are and what you are facing always connects to what God reveals in the Bible.

Take a look at your life: the good things about you, the bad things you struggle with, and the hard things you face. They open doors to the mercies of God. As you know yourself more accurately, you'll see how your life and Scripture intersect.

There's something you need today that only God can give you. This is also true of your friends and family. You and I need something from the living God that will make a difference in our lives.

Take 2 Corinthians 12:9, for example. Everyone could look at the thorn in the flesh passage and the promise of God in a somewhat different way. We would think of different details, weaknesses, hardships, and heartaches. It's not just head knowledge we come away with. It's real, lived, personal knowledge, and we end up with joy, love for God, and love for other people.

Take with You: The message being promised here is completely upside down from the messages you hear everywhere else. What a relief that we do not have to be strong and have it all together! Where might God be wanting you to come to him in weakness today?

JANUARY 28

Be angry and do not sin; do not let the sun go down on your anger, and give no opportunity to the devil.

Be kind to one another, tenderhearted, forgiving one another, as God in Christ forgave you. —Ephesians 4:26–27, 32

Our earthly fight against dark spiritual forces is not just about ourselves and our relationship with God. It's about the people around us. Who benefits when we have strength to stand up against the world, the flesh, and the devil? Yes, God is glorified when we stand. Yes, we are blessed when we stand. But other people also benefit. When we live as children of light, the light of the glory of God shines in our dark world. Standing against evil is not a separate topic from the one-anothering passages in Ephesians 4 and 5. *We stand against evil and shine light into darkness as we live out Paul's call to "Be kind to one another, tenderhearted, forgiving one another, as God in Christ forgave you" (Ephesians 4:32).*

We each have a part to play in the body of Christ. When Paul says in Ephesians 4:27 not to give the devil a foothold, he is referring to relationships breaking within the body of Christ. Ephesians is about union with Christ and union with each other in Christ. Spiritual warfare is a direct stand against the forces that would divide and break our fellowship with Christ and with one another in community and family.

Take with You: You do not have to understand all the details of the fight between good and evil. Small acts of love in building relationships create a big glow in a dark world.

JANUARY 29

"Blessed are the poor in spirit, for theirs is the kingdom of heaven."
—Matthew 5:3

Do you have a serious problem with anger?

Yes.

How do you react to this statement?

Try turning this sentence over in your mind: "I do have a serious problem with anger." What comes to mind? Do you agree or disagree? Are you not quite sure? How is that statement true or partly true? Do you think it's not true at all? Pause and collect your thoughts into words and specific examples from your inner and outer life.

I can confidently write that you have a serious problem with anger because I do, because we all do.

With an all-humankind problem like anger, there is a sweet paradox in how God works. He blesses those who admit they need help: "Blessed are the poor in spirit" (Matthew 5:3). True sanity has a deep awareness that we were created for dependency on God. *I need help. I can't do life right on my own. Someone outside of myself must intervene and come to my rescue. The sanity of honest humility finds mercy, life, peace, and strength.* By contrast, saying we don't ever need help keeps us stuck in making excuses and blaming others. The end result isn't life and peace; it's anger, self-righteousness, self-justification, isolation, and bitterness.

Take with You: Even though you don't have tantrums anymore, the heart of "I want it my way" is in all of us. One description of God is *a very present help in trouble.* When you run into the trouble of angrily grasping for control, ask God to turn you toward himself.

JANUARY 30

You desire and do not have, so you murder. You covet and cannot obtain, so you fight and quarrel. You do not have, because you do not ask. You ask and do not receive, because you ask wrongly, to spend it on your passions. —James 4:2–3

Anger goes bad because of a demand. A simple desire (and the pain that comes when we do not get what we want) becomes magnified into something we must have. The wrong in our desires is often not what we want, but that we want it too much. Desires become needs. We must be perfect. We must fit in. We insist that you understand us. We get twisted into believing that what we want is right; therefore, we are right to be angry when it doesn't happen! Even if it's a good thing, sometimes we want it so much that it devours us.

There's something high and mighty about anger when it's broken down into its basic elements. Anger goes wrong when you act like the ruler of your own life. When anger goes right, there's some higher purpose or person who puts a cap on it, who sets a limit on bitterness, who gives reasons not to whine and complain. The most high God, his loving mercies, and his higher purposes transform anger. *Something miraculous happens when I stop saying, "My kingdom come, my will be done on earth." My motives no longer attempt to take over God's place. The mercy that humbles us begins to master us, and my universe returns to reality.*

Take with You: Try opening your hands while you pray today. Ask God to help you release the desires in your life that you are holding onto with a death grip.

JANUARY 31

For the righteous falls seven times and rises again.
—Proverbs 24:16

When your heart becomes fearful, and you wonder how God could ever love you, take a moment to remember this: Jesus took your sins upon himself. The innocent was killed in place of the guilty. When God considers you and your failings, he remembers his mercy.

When you feel discouraged and weak and that you have no strength to fight all that is proud, chaotic, and forgetful inside you, take a moment to remember. The Holy Spirit hates evil, loves good, and he will not quit working in your heart. He will complete the good work he began in you.

When you feel overwhelmed by all the heartache, unfairness, disappointment, and betrayal that you experience, take a moment to remember. The Lord will destroy every cause of pain, confusion, and tears. Because God loves those he has befriended, he will ultimately defend them from every enemy: death, sin, Satan, and unfriendly people.

When you're tempted to pack it in and give up, plunging back into the darkness, take a moment to remember: The Lord is a holy fire, and he firmly instructs those he loves that we might share his holiness. "The righteous falls seven times and rises again" (Proverbs 24:16). He will not let you go fatally astray.

Take with You: Remembering is a powerful tool for a life well lived. Read these sweet reminders through one more time. Find someone today who needs to be reminded of God's mercy, or the Holy Spirit's commitment, or the Lord's eternal dedication to his loved ones. Give them a hug and delight in the Truth together.

FEBRUARY 1

"Are not five sparrows sold for two pennies? And not one of them is forgotten before God. Why, even the hairs of your head are all numbered. Fear not; you are of more value than many sparrows."
—Luke 12:6–7

"The Lord is near" (Philippians 4:5 NIV). If you think about your anxiety—the unhealthy worry, fretting, and churning—you will notice you have always forgotten that the Lord is near. When you worry and obsess, you're living as if just you and your struggles are going back and forth. *If you remember, in even the worst circumstances, that the Lord is near, then you will have a rock on which your heart can rest.* You have a hope that's bigger than any threat, even death. You are invited to draw near to the Lord who's already close.

After all, this Lord created the whole universe and controls every moment of your life. He counts the hairs on your head and notices each one that falls. You're living in his world. And this Lord is not only the all-powerful Creator, but he has also experienced firsthand the anxiety-producing fragility of life on earth.

This Lord is near to you. He is raised from the dead. He will raise you with him. When you know this is true, then you have hope bigger than any loss. What you have today in this Lord and what you will be given on the day you see his face is greater, weighs more, and has more lasting power than anything you might lose here on earth.

Take with You: When you know that Jesus is near, obsessive anxiety slows down and care and trust grow. Let this nearness and presence of Jesus grow you in faith and love today.

FEBRUARY 2

But I call to God, and the LORD will save me.
Evening and morning and at noon I utter my complaint and moan,
and he hears my voice. —Psalm 55:16–17

In the Psalms, relationship with God is happening out loud. More than 95 percent of the Psalms express or invite audible words. Most are spoken directly to God. Quite often psalms speak to other people, inviting them to join in. And sometimes a psalm even speaks of the "voice" of the natural world.

Prayer is a verbal interaction. In the mere handful of psalms that have no obvious verbal cue, a psalm might speak about human destiny in relation to God (e.g., Psalm 1), or God himself might be the one speaking (e.g., Psalm 110). Our audible response is the most natural thing in the world.

The spoken action of the Psalms show that we're talking to someone. There's rejoicing in who God is, asking for help, and expressing heartfelt thanks. *It's fair to say having a "quiet time" may not be very accurate. It's more of an out loud, "noisy time"! When you talk aloud you express the reality that you're talking with someone else, not simply talking to yourself inside your own head.* "Silent prayers" are not wrong, but they are the exception. Prayer is essentially verbal in nature and expresses blunt, head-on, heartfelt need, gladness, and gratitude.

You and I can learn much from the Psalms. Our relationship with God is not meant to be so quiet that we lose the words of direct speech.

Take with You: If this idea of talking aloud to God feels uncomfortable, start small. Close the door, take a walk, get in the car—and speak up a few words at a time.

FEBRUARY 3

For we are his workmanship, created in Christ Jesus for good works, which God prepared beforehand, that we should walk in them.
—Ephesians 2:10

Our Father works personally and purposefully in each one of his children. Each of us is handmade, one-of-a-kind. Our existence is evidence of Christ's dedicated creativity and craftsmanship. We are not mass-produced. We are not clones or spare, interchangeable parts. We are individual members in one intricate living body of Christ, every one of us playing a part.

You have been made alive by the Holy Spirit with particular purposes. He places you on location. You live here and now—not anywhere, anytime. You are on call for particular people—not anyone and everyone. Your story, sorrows, personality, temptations, the things you know, your abilities and limitations, your experiences, choices, and feelings . . . they are beautifully personal. Every detail happens in a specific way. Nothing happens in general. *God's redemption acts to gather up every experience and characteristic into his purpose for you.*

So each day, in each situation, you have the opportunity to do and say constructive things that no other human being could do or say. In the loving hands of God, your life is custom-designed and custom-built. And we will all fit together in the end. Every hand will do its work. Every voice will sing its part.

This is your calling.

Take with You: Don't let the concept of *finding your calling* be bigger than it needs to be. Let your calling today be love. Love God by expressing gratitude and loving the people right in front of you.

FEBRUARY 4

Even though I walk through the valley of the shadow of death,
I will fear no evil,
for you are with me. —Psalm 23:4

Our reactions to serious wrongs are messy, not tidy. Reactions in life rarely appear like the primary colors, sharply separated from each other. Reactions come in hues, shades, mixtures, and combinations. Sometimes you might get a "pure" color—for a moment. But most often, you will live out some swirling of "all of the above."

It is extremely significant that the Bible, Jesus, and the mercies of God directly speak to "all of the above." The loving kindnesses of God are exactly in line with what is wrong and hard. When life goes easy, Christian faith sometimes seems irrelevant. But when life is hard (and life always ends up very hard), the true God sparkles. But making the connection isn't always easy. How on earth does "You are with me" (Psalm 23:4) connect with "Right now I am walking through a dark valley. I feel vulnerable. I am scared." How does the promise that, "You are with me" make progress in my life, so that I am changed and become unafraid?

God meets us in our need. He enters our circumstances in person. He shares in our troubles. *Suffering is the place in our lives where Christ shows himself. It's where faith awakens. It is through suffering that our love becomes wise. We learn faith and love when life goes wrong.*

Take with You: God places us in families and communities to help us grow. Is there an older Christian in your life who might be able to encourage you in a hard time? When you share burdens with others, they truly get lighter.

FEBRUARY 5

Love is patient and kind; love does not envy or boast; it is not arrogant or rude. It does not insist on its own way; it is not irritable or resentful; it does not rejoice at wrongdoing, but rejoices with the truth. Love bears all things, believes all things, hopes all things, endures all things. —1 Corinthians 13:4–7

You have probably heard that "love is patient; love is kind." You can translate those first two words describing love in 1 Corinthians 13:4 in this way: love is in it for good.

Love is in it for good: patient. God is patience. He's committed for as long as it takes, whatever is going on, however hard the process. Patience is not passive. Our Father, Savior, and the Holy Spirit work with purposeful patience. He walks with his children intentionally, through all time, to accomplish something. In his great patience, he will complete what he has begun, to his glory and to our joy.

Love is in it for good: kind. God is kindness. He freely gives every good gift, doing and saying what's helpful. Kindness is not sentimental. *Our God works a fiercely realistic kindness. He is always holy and constructive, always merciful and firm, always generous and inquiring. He knows what we are; he gives more grace.* He gives what we need. In his great kindness, he will complete what he has begun, to our glory and to his joy.

God is love; therefore he is in it for good.

Take with You: This is the best news! And because every promise of God is "Yes" in the Son of God, Jesus is in it for good too. Who's one friend who would benefit from being reminded that God is in it for good with them?

FEBRUARY 6

So then you are no longer strangers and aliens, but you are fellow citizens with the saints and members of the household of God.
—Ephesians 2:19

You are one of the Lord's "saints." Today the word "saint" has been reduced to describe only extraordinary, individual spiritual achievements. But in the Bible—where God defines sainthood—the word describes ordinary people who belong to an extraordinary Savior and Lord. Our Redeemer pulls off all the extraordinary things. At our best (and too often we are at our worst, or bumping along in the middle!), "we have done only that which we ought to have done" (Luke 17:10 NASB). *God calls you a saint to point out who owns you, not to honor you for going above and beyond.* It's not a Medal of Honor. It's your birth certificate and ID. When God has written his name on you, how you face suffering changes. Pain, loss, and weakness are no longer the end of the world and the death of your hopes.

God calls you "his chosen ones, holy and beloved" (Colossians 3:12). You will dwell in his house forever. This truth gives you full freedom to grow more childlike toward him and more helpful toward others. Your hopes will come true beyond your wildest dreams. You have been given an eternal future that cannot be destroyed. Our path as Christians is like the light of dawn, shining brighter and brighter until full day.

Take with You: Make a list of the ways in which you are just like everyone else. Doesn't that feel weird? Most often, we want to stand out and be special, but a whole life of seeking that is exhausting. You can rest in the fact that you're an ordinary person with an extraordinary God.

FEBRUARY 7

For the word of God is living and active, sharper than any two-edged sword, piercing to the division of soul and of spirit, of joints and of marrow, and discerning the thoughts and intentions of the heart. And no creature is hidden from his sight, but all are naked and exposed to the eyes of him to whom we must give account.
—Hebrews 4:12–13

Hebrews 4:12–13 could be paraphrased like this: *The Word of God clearly sees the map of your reality, and it clearly sees the set of purposes that you pursue.* It describes both how you see and what you are about as you face the world. These words reveal the thoughts that control who you are. One of the roles of Scripture is to show us what's in our hearts. Verse 13 says we are laid bare, which means God sees what makes you most yourself. Verse 12 says Scripture searches us so we can understand ourselves and others, like having the chance to look in a mirror of reality.

Jeremiah 17:9 says "The heart is deceitful above all things, and desperately sick; who can understand it?" Who can understand himself? Why do we do what we do? We don't always know. The human heart doesn't tell the whole truth, and it can change like a shifting shadow. Scripture, under the power of the Spirit, helps us see how we are coming at the world and the intentions that rule what we do.

Take with You: Ask God to give you wisdom and courage to see your heart as it is. He will not be silent. Remember your need for Jesus and know that he sees the perfection of Jesus when he looks on you.

FEBRUARY 8

As for me, I am poor and needy,
but the Lord takes thought for me.
You are my help and my deliverer;
do not delay, O my God! —Psalm 40:17

The Psalms are the place to land when you face hardships and struggles. The Psalms go first through David but primarily through Jesus Christ, who was surrounded by evils and evildoers. As we read the Psalms, they become patterns for our experience. In the historical parts of Scripture the story is the main point. In the Psalms, the story is left at the door.

Many details of circumstance are intentionally left out of the Psalms. Instead you're given templates for relationship with God in many different contexts. You're invited to personalize each template with your particular situation—your own struggles, fears, shame, sorrows, and joys. *The Psalms ask to be made personal, because they are real prayers, written by real people going through the ups and downs of life just like us.* But praying the Psalms isn't just about us pouring our hearts out. We get to be renewed by reminders of God's character and the clarity and power of his promises. Psalm 40 proclaims: "You will not restrain your mercy from me; your steadfast love and your faithfulness will ever preserve me! . . . Be pleased, O Lord, to deliver me! O Lord, make haste to help me! . . . I am poor and needy, but the Lord takes thought for me. You are my help and my deliverer" (vv. 11, 13, 17).

Take with You: Our needs are met by God's promises to think of us, help us, and deliver us. Turn to a psalm and be refreshed by his truth for your specific needs, sorrows, hopes, or fears.

FEBRUARY 9

Watch over your heart with all diligence,
For from it flow the springs of life. —Proverbs 4:23 NASB

The way you find meaning in hard things reveals the human heart. The Bible does not present people in isolated circumstances, and we do not live on blank pages either. Hardships hit, and you find out things about yourself. Do you whine and complain? Do you run to your phone and escape? Do you gossip about someone to make yourself feel better? Do you get gripped by fear and anxiety or anger and insecurity? Without the pressure, you would never see where your struggle is.

The human heart is the wellspring of the kind of life that we actually live. In whatever circumstance we are put under, we bear fruit of one sort or another. But when Jesus makes his home in your heart, the fruit we produce begins to change.

The foundation of your specific environment and personal circumstance on earth is the living God. We live in God's world. We breathe God's air. Our heart beats because he sustains us. He searches every thought; every careless word is evaluated by him. As we think about any aspect of life, God is purposefully in it, and he's up to something good in the lives of his children. *Christ's voice focuses our hearts to God's purposes—to value what's meaningful, to reject what's false, and to remember that we live in God's world with Jesus at work in us for good.*

Take with You: How can the truth of God's bigger purpose *in all things* change your day today? He is able. Listen for his voice and notice what fruit grows.

FEBRUARY 10

No temptation has overtaken you that is not common to man. God is faithful, and he will not let you be tempted beyond your ability, but with the temptation he will also provide the way of escape, that you may be able to endure it. —1 Corinthians 10:13

The Bible makes this point: There's no struggle you face that isn't common to all people. We each face the same temptations—everyday life brings frustration and disappointment, and we react with irritation and complaining. We're all more alike than different. Whether my problems appear large or small, I have the same kind of struggle as everyone else. Obviously, not all of us are ruled by explosive anger or hostility. But all of us are tempted to grumble. Like the tiny cone and seedling from which giant redwood trees grow, major sins are only minor sins grown up. Complaining has the same DNA as violent rage.

So it makes sense that the life-changing solution for complaining has the same DNA as the solution to bitterness or an explosive temper. The discussion in 1 Corinthians 10 helps us see how we're all in the same boat. *In Paul's writing, he leads us by the hand onto solid ground. He says, "God is faithful, and he will not let you to be tempted beyond your ability, but with the temptation he will also provide the way of escape, that you may be able to endure it."* When you and I encounter challenging circumstances, we're tempted to spin into big reactions or rebellion. But here's a way out and a way forward: We are promised provision and endurance from an ever-faithful God.

Take with You: We are all more alike than different. How can this truth help you to love well today?

FEBRUARY 11

Who is wise and understanding among you? By his good conduct let him show his works in the meekness of wisdom.

But the wisdom from above is first pure, then peaceable, gentle, open to reason, full of mercy and good fruits, impartial and sincere. And a harvest of righteousness is sown in peace by those who make peace. —James 3:13, 17–18

The essence of living faith is something different from any one particular experience. Seek the true God who speaks truth and offers true help. *Faith takes God at his word and acts on it.* The power in a life of faith is not mystical or focused on feelings or sentiment, instead it is robust, straightforward, and simple. Relate your life to God in Christ, and he will rearrange your life. Take God at his word. When looking to get to the heart of conflict you must seek God. And if you seek, you will be changed. Living faith can never be fruitless: "The fruit of righteousness is sown in peace by those who make peace" (James 3:18 NASB).

On the day we see Christ, all who are in him will be like him. From that day on there will be no more stumbling, no more "quarrels and conflicts." The process of getting to the heart of conflict will one day be finished. Simple and pure devotion will replace double-mindedness forever.

Take with You: James 3:13, 17–18 describe good conduct and wisdom from above as peaceable and constructive. Where do you need to work *peace* into your relationships? Where do you need to build up? How could you move toward those goals practically today?

FEBRUARY 12

Praying at all times in the Spirit, with all prayer and supplication. To that end, keep alert with all perseverance, making supplication for all the saints. —Ephesians 6:18

Because prayer is a vital part of how we fight against the powers of darkness, Paul ends his discussion of spiritual warfare in Ephesians in prayer. His prayers are wondrously normal. *These "warfare prayers" do not speak of or to Satan, but instead address our deepest need for Christ's presence and help.* What Paul asks for is very simple: "May God strengthen you to know him." There is no binding of evil spirits or proclaiming truth with "special" words or phrases. He tells us to keep on "praying at all times in the Spirit, with all prayer and supplication" and to pray for "all the saints" (v. 18). He also asks for prayer for himself (v. 19).

Here are some ideas on how to pray at all times for every saint:

- Pray for friends and family. The people you're most connected to need the Lord to directly strengthen them to be able to walk in faith and love. Pray that the Spirit would make them like Christ. Pray that their eyes would be open to their need for Christ.
- Take the truth that has stood out the most as you've been reading and pray for the Spirit to make this truth alive in your life.
- Ask others to pray for you. Paul knew he needed God to give him the words to say with boldness. What do you need that only the Lord can give?

Take with You: As you have been encouraged, take a moment to pray for the Spirit to encourage your pastor or youth leader. Leadership is a very hard calling, and your leaders need much grace!

FEBRUARY 13

"Do not be afraid of them,
for I am with you to deliver you,
declares the LORD." —Jeremiah 1:8

"When he has brought out all his own, he goes before them, and the sheep follow him, for they know his voice." —John 10:4

Anxiety, like anger, is often seen as a purely mental health or emotional problem. But anxiety also keeps us from caring about other people and reaching out of our own world toward others. When we are afraid, the lies we believe isolate us from others. In the action of withdrawal, we are set in the middle of the fight between light and dark and are called to move toward love and faith.

How do you talk to someone gripped by fear? You speak truth to them. The central promise of the Bible to fearful people is "I am with you." *Do not fear is a command that doesn't come with a warning; it comes with a promise of God's help and presence.* This is a gift that we can ask for.* We don't have to listen to the lies of the Evil One. We can see the dark for what it is and turn to God for help in our time of need. We can learn to hear the voice of the Good Shepherd and move toward him and out toward others with him (John 10:4, 9).

Take with You: Ask the Lord to show you how to grow in a living dependency on him, our Good Shepherd. How can you be reminded throughout your day that you aren't alone?

---

* See, for example, Deuteronomy 31:6–8; Jeremiah 1:8; Matthew 14:27; Philippians 4:4–7.

FEBRUARY 14

Prove me, O LORD, and try me;
test my heart and my mind. —Psalm 26:2

Anger occurs not only in your body, emotions, thoughts, and actions. It comes from your deepest motives. Underlying desires and beliefs are at work—always. Motives run far deeper than our conscious thoughts. We often feel, think, act, and react without being aware of what's driving us. But motives are the organizing center of who you are and what you live for. The smallest incident of irritation or the slight lingering of bitterness reveals big truths about you—if you're willing to look.

To see the motives underneath anger, ask, "What are my expectations?" That simple question helps you stop and think. And the answer often comes in layers, not all at once. *Self-knowledge is both a simple gift and a hard-won achievement.* You might be aware of your expectations at one level, but gradually come to understand deeper levels. It's really hard to accurately see our motives for what they are. Part of the problem comes because anger can feel so "righteous." "I'm so right, because you are so wrong." That same desire to think well of ourselves gets in the way of seeing and facing our motives.

When anger goes astray, it says something about how we are going astray inside, about who's the center of the universe. But when God's larger purposes are in control, the evil of anger is balanced out. Anger can be a servant of goodness. Anger can be just and merciful to all who turn, trust, and become more like Christ. He changes our motives.

Take with You: *What are my expectations?* It's one of the most clarifying questions you can ask. Try it and see how God gently shows you your own heart.

FEBRUARY 15

I have stored up your word in my heart,
that I might not sin against you. . . .
Your word is a lamp to my feet and a light to my path.
—Psalm 119:11, 105

How does Scripture get personal? How does the God of the Bible actually connect to you? What's happening when you take it personally? What's going on when his words map onto your life? They fit your life. They take hold of your life. They speak into your life. And how does that happen?

God himself makes his words connect right to you. He awakens you. He gives you ears to hear and a heart to be open. He gives the desire to take to heart the things you hear. The more you know yourself as you truly are, the more relevant Scripture is. As your self-knowledge deepens, Scripture will just explode off the page. You will understand yourself in more profound ways.

Where are you feeling troubled? What pressures are you under—what's coming at you? What are you feeling guilty about? Answering these questions honestly for yourself become open doors to hear what God says about you in your real life. There are things that are tailored by God himself everywhere in Scripture that speak into our need.

Scripture becomes relevant as you stop and think about God's words. As you stop and think, your troubles and God's mercies connect and start to get into conversation. Who you are and who he is begin to cross paths so that what you need and how he meets you come together.

Take with You: There is great comfort in being fully known. Praise God today that he knows you perfectly and will speak right to you from the Bible.

FEBRUARY 16

Trust in the LORD with all your heart,
and do not lean on your own understanding.
In all your ways acknowledge him,
and he will make straight your paths. —Proverbs 3:5–6

Your troubles do not rest on your shoulders. You're living in a really big, confusing world where there's trouble, but you're in relationship with an even bigger God who's in charge of his world. He has a purpose for you in every situation where there is trouble: God is calling you to be useful and productive in a very small corner of his world. Have you ever heard this motto? "Think globally, act locally." You can apply this to your day-to-day life. *Think globally by remembering every day that God is in charge of the whole world, and he's watching over every person. And then act locally by asking God each day to show you what small, constructive thing he's calling you to do.*

Remember, your step of obedience will always be smaller than the problem. In every area of your life where there's trouble, God is calling you to a small step of faith and love. He isn't calling you to solve what's wrong. Your call to love will never be as big as what's wrong. Go through your entire list of worries. Notice that what God is calling you to do is always less than the bad things that might happen. Just knowing that will bring peace and sanity back into your life.

Take with You: What is your small corner of the world? Name it specifically. God has placed you with purpose in that very corner. You can shine a light in the darkness of that corner.

FEBRUARY 17

For the word of God is living and active, sharper than any two-edged sword, piercing to the division of soul and of spirit, of joints and of marrow, and discerning the thoughts and intentions of the heart. —Hebrews 4:12

The words "I feel" have become a key phrase in a lot of communication. What we feel affects decisions we make and the advice we give and take. "I feel" creates a potent and fuzzy cloud of "what's true for me" around a dozen questionable statements. It's tough to argue with feelings, but they need a closer look. When feelings are dragged into the light, what meaning do you find among the layers?

"Feelings" are often used to communicate four very different things: experience, emotions, thinking, and desires. When "I feel" a certain way about something, I'm adding a weight of personal control to my statement. Those little words cast a different power over my wants, plans, choices, expectations, and fears.

How do you use the words "I feel"? Are your feelings about something your personal truth? Do you leave room for analysis with the lens of God's Truth? Are your feelings the "real you" who needs to be taken seriously without question and given a voice? Or do they show how we drift toward our own desires? A biblical understanding of feelings lets us look behind the often-misleading language of daily life. *The Bible exposes and judges the darkness that can hide within the "I feel that" and "I feel like" language that we so often use.*

Take with You: We have been given a wonderful alternative to living with too much trust in our flighty feelings. We have a firm foundation in our identity in Christ. Take hold of this good news today.

FEBRUARY 18

Take care, brothers, lest there be in any of you an evil, unbelieving heart, leading you to fall away from the living God. But exhort one another every day, as long as it is called "today," that none of you may be hardened by the deceitfulness of sin. For we have come to share in Christ, if indeed we hold our original confidence firm to the end. —Hebrews 3:12–14

What do you ask people to pray for? What do others ask you to pray for? We each look at life outwardly, as though through a camera lens, asking for changes in everything we see without looking back at the selfie image. The picture taker is never in view. The "wisdom-in-action" needs of the photographer are rarely talked about. We pray for good grades with friends with high expectations; we rarely pray they find peace in the midst of worry or rest in a perfect Jesus. We pray for the girl nervous in social situations; we rarely ask God to show her his love in the face of fear of what others will think of her. We pray for family members to know Jesus; we rarely pray we would grow more patient and loving toward them.

As we pray at this heart level, we have reasons to offer meaningful advice. They enter into life as a disciple whose calling is to learn. *A lifelong learner knows the importance of giving and receive counsel every day (Hebrews 3:12–14) to grow into the image of Jesus.*

Take with You: Our Perfect Counselor made you in his image. You are a counselor whenever you speak into someone else's life. Ask God to give you courage and wisdom to use your voice and help build up your community.

FEBRUARY 19

Blessed is the one whose transgression is forgiven,
whose sin is covered.
Blessed is the man against whom the LORD counts no iniquity,
and in whose spirit there is no deceit. —Psalm 32:1–2

Someone who knows his sinfulness, but also knows God's mercy, can be called worthy by the grace and mercy of God. You, too, can experience what King David experienced, but you must seek this Lord. In Psalm 32, David describes how he felt after his sin was exposed, when he hadn't yet confessed his sins to God. His life drains away; he feels hopeless. If that is you, then do what David did—go to God with your sins and failures. *Your Savior is who he says he is: merciful. He does what he says he does; he forgives.*

Here is a wonderful description of seeking God in the midst of guilt: David says, "I acknowledged my sin to you and did not cover up my iniquity. I said, 'I will confess my transgressions to the LORD.' And you forgave the guilt of my sin" (Psalm 32:5 NIV). Notice that David is turning to God and laying out his failures. He isn't turning inward. He isn't turning to those around him. He isn't ashamed. He's forgiven. He can hold up his head and write about it in the Bible, recording his sins for all time. This is because he knows God is with him.

And then David gives the key to having God with him: "Therefore let everyone who is godly pray to You" (Psalm 32:6 NASB). Prayer is the key.

Take with You: Daily asking for help in prayer brings you into God's presence where you are safe from trouble—even the trouble you bring upon yourself. What a comfort!

FEBRUARY 20

Jesus said to them, "I am the bread of life; whoever comes to me shall not hunger, and whoever believes in me shall never thirst." —John 6:35

All good gifts, beginning with life itself, come from God. You will never be independent. The Lord sustains our lives physically, every word from the mouth of God gives life, and, above all, Jesus Christ is the bread of life. *Faith knows and embraces this core identity: "I am his dependent."*

Our dependency as created beings is complicated and increased by sins and sufferings. To know ourselves is to know our need for help. Faith knows and embraces this core identity: "I am poor and weak."

The Lord is merciful to the rebellious. He redeems the naturally sinful, forgetful, and blind. Faith knows and embraces this core identity: "I am sinful—and I am forgiven."

God is our Father. He adopts us in Christ and re-creates us with a childlike heart by the power of the Spirit. We need parenting every day. We need tender care, patient instruction, and helpful discipline. Faith knows and embraces this core identity: "I am God's child."

The Lord is our refuge. Our lives are filled with a variety of troubles, threats, and disappointments. We aren't strong enough to stand up to what we face. God's presence is the only safe place. Faith knows and embraces this core identity: "I am a refugee."

The Lord is our shepherd. He laid down his life for the sheep. He watches over our going out and coming in. Faith knows and embraces this core identity: "I am a sheep in his flock."

Take with You: How would your thoughts change toward yourself if you embraced these core identity words today? *Dependent, weak, sinful, forgiven, refugee, God's child.*

FEBRUARY 21

I have learned in whatever situation I am to be content. I know how to be brought low, and I know how to abound. In any and every circumstance, I have learned the secret of facing plenty and hunger, abundance and need. I can do all things through him who strengthens me. —Philippians 4:11–13

Our loving Father wills that we learn to live with no complaining about the present, no regrets about the past, and no worrying about the future. This is a high, hard calling! We fail. But our failures, honestly seen, open a wide door into new mercies every morning. Christ freely commits to teaching us the secret of contentment amid a world filled with stress. Most of us are in the pre-K class of learning contentment, but any progress in the direction of such life-wisdom is worth more than silver, gold, and jewels. "Nothing you desire can compare," as Proverbs 3:14–15 says.

Christ is forgiving and Christ is working to make your life beautiful. When you see him face-to-face, you will be like the Savior we have trusted over a lifetime.

First Thessalonians 5:16–18 says: "Rejoice always, pray without ceasing, give thanks in all circumstances, for this is the will of God in Christ Jesus for you." *Candid joy, honest need, and open gratitude are three voices of faith—and faith is God's will for you.*

Take with You: It's hard to be content. Where might God be nudging you to accept something that's not exactly what you want? In Christ is fullness of joy. Pray for help to be content in your hard situation.

FEBRUARY 22

The Father of mercies and God of all comfort who comforts us in all our affliction, so that we may be able to comfort those who are in any affliction. —2 Corinthians 1:3–4

"Sanctification" is a big word that can describe your whole experience as a Christian. It's your life-growth story of becoming more like Christ. It's common for people to view sanctification as a moral self-help project that gets rid of your bad habits and replaces them with good habits. Under Christ's mentoring, we do "improve," of course. But it's not exactly in the ways we might expect. It's easy to think God's goal is simply to make you a better, happier, and more self-confident person. The Lord's vision, however, is not simply a "better you" living your best life now as someone who has found a sense of inner peace and gotten your act together. *His goal for you is to learn love by taking to heart the troubles and struggles of others. He does it by first taking to heart your troubles and struggles.*

When you find the hope and encouragement of Christ in your own troubles, you're receiving a dynamic gift that you can bring to other people in whatever troubles and unhappiness they experience. The welfare of others and your welfare are knit together. This means the hardships of your friends, family, teachers, and peers become yours to enter into with the powerful comfort of Christ. God is making you into a person who is more connected to others.

Take with You: The process of sanctification is not about making you a "better person." You grow to be more like Christ in your community as you learn to ask and answer the question, "What does love look like?"

FEBRUARY 23

The unfolding of your words gives light; it imparts understanding to the simple. —Psalm 119:130

There's a big difference between knowing something because you memorized the facts and actually understanding how it works. You think more deeply and creatively when you understand something. Likewise, there's a big difference between doing something as routine habit and being fully oriented. You make skillful decisions when you're oriented. For example, your Maps app offers mechanical guidance to get from point A to point B. So when you lose the cell signal in a strange neighborhood, you have no idea where you are. You're disoriented! But when you're driving in your own neighborhood and a road is closed, you have a half dozen different ways to get from where you are to wherever you need to go. You're oriented. You understand.

It's the same with how Scripture works in our lives. *Merely having Psalm 23 memorized won't persuade you that someone strong and caring is watching out for you. If you're to find any help in dark, vulnerable times, you need to understand what Psalm 23 means.* And saying the Lord's Prayer from memory will never convince you that God actually is your Father or that he'll provide what you need to live in his will today. But when you become oriented, then you mean the words you say. You understand how Jesus's teaching captures what you most need—strength for today, mercy for your sins, protection from what afflicts you.

Take with You: As you take this moment of quiet, what fears and concerns rise to the surface of your mind and heart? What is one small thought you could reposition before your loving Abba Father?

FEBRUARY 24

For we are his workmanship, created in Christ Jesus for good works, which God prepared beforehand, that we should walk in them. —Ephesians 2:10

The idea of calling provides a perspective on all of life and all of Scripture. The concept springs from the One who calls: God speaks. And because he's vocal, he calls forth all that exists. Because he's vocal, he proclaims who he is. Because he's vocal, when he comes in person, he's the Word becoming flesh.

And because he's vocal, your life has a vocation, a calling. *Vocation is not just a word for a professional career. Vocation is not restricted to those in "vocational ministry": pastors, missionaries, monks, and nuns. God's calling is personal with each of his children.*

How do we get clarity about our calling? It gets hammered out gradually in the process of living your Christian life honestly. As the different seasons of your life unfold and you come to moments of decision-making about your future, reflect on these five questions.

What are your gifts? What is your life experience? What are your opportunities? How have you grown? What do you thrive doing? You will understand your calling as you understand the intermingling of these five things about you and about the corner of the world you've been placed in. This calling is your true "vocation": what you are called to do in your life situation. What are those specific good works God has prepared beforehand for you to walk in (Ephesians 2:10)? Your understanding grows as you bring together these five strands of self-knowledge.

Take with You: Don't be overwhelmed by figuring out your calling. Ask the Lord to show you one good work to do today with the people in your actual life.

FEBRUARY 25

O LORD, you have searched me and known me!
You know when I sit down and when I rise up;
you discern my thoughts from afar.
You search out my path and my lying down
and are acquainted with all my ways. —Psalm 139:1–3

Because no two people and no two situations are exactly alike, God personalizes the way he acts and speaks. When we describe characteristics of our God, the words might sound stiff and unmoving. But he is dynamically connected to each of his people in real time. It might sound like he was the Creator long ago. But he's also continually creating and recreating a people for himself. It might sound like he will become the Judge at the end of time. But he's also continually judging and working so his plan for the safety and glory of his people prevails. It might sound like he was once the Savior when he died and was raised long ago and that he will again save when he returns in the future. But he's also continually saving his sons and daughters by changing them into the image of the Son. *He gets personal—with everyone, with those who long for him and with those who wish they could wish him away.*

God answers. He involves himself in the details of our lives, and life makes sense.

When he takes hold, everything moves at the right speed, not a mad scramble. We become our right size. The pressures on us become their right size. Our God becomes his right size.

Take with You: A truth for you to hold in your back pocket today: We are small. Pressures in our lives are big. God is bigger.

FEBRUARY 26

And behold, there were two blind men sitting by the roadside, and when they heard that Jesus was passing by, they cried out, "Lord, have mercy on us, Son of David!" The crowd rebuked them, telling them to be silent, but they cried out all the more, "Lord, have mercy on us, Son of David!" And stopping, Jesus called them and said, "What do you want me to do for you?" —Matthew 20:30–32

When something is so wrong that you will never get over it, your reaction will either make you wise or will poison you. Great suffering puts a fork in the road. You will need to choose. It's no accident that "Lord, have mercy" is the core prayer of the man or woman who looks at the facts honestly. *A deep inner sense of need for help from outside yourself is the essential step of living a sane life.* It's this faith—"I am poor and needy. Help me."—that Jesus admires so often. Faith is not a leap in the dark. Faith is honestly looking at your need for help and then stepping toward the person who can help you.

Our culture usually talks about suffering, anger, despair, or anxiety as things with "how to" solutions. But the things that cause the deepest angers, fears, and despairs are betrayals at a soul level. You need more than boxes to check to solve these hurts. You must learn to live honestly in the face of evils that don't necessarily go away. Learn to honestly face your own evil in light of bigger mercies.

Take with You: What does it look like for you to embrace this mercy today? It may be as simple as acknowledging, "I am selfish and sinful, but God put his hands on me, that is all."

FEBRUARY 27

And you were dead in the trespasses and sins in which you once walked, following the course of this world, following the prince of the power of the air. . . . But God, being rich in mercy, because of the great love with which he loved us, even when we were dead in our trespasses, made us alive together with Christ—by grace you have been saved. —Ephesians 2:1–2, 4–5

Everyone knows "sin" means bad behavior. But our actions, attitudes, words, thoughts, and emotions aren't isolated or existing by themselves. The Bible identifies the obvious sin behaviors in an intricate, intertwined web of dark forces. Wise Christians have named three forces that tangle us up: the flesh, the world, and the devil.

The flesh describes the personal side of sinfulness. Sins of your own flesh work in outward ways, destroying relationships, but this type of sin is also deeply internal. We can be constantly self-centered, self-willed, and self-deceived. Our ego seizes God and self-destructs. We are tempted by our own desires, which birth sins, which result in death (James 1:14–15).

The world describes the situational side of sinfulness. Our time and place in our society and culture meet with our heart's listening to a buzz of deceitful voices, values, promises, pains, and pleasures. We not only sin against others; we also are drawn into sin by the influence of others.

The devil adds a false-father, false-lord dimension of sinfulness. An active enemy lies, tempts, enslaves, accuses, and murders.

O merciful Father, lead us not into temptation. Deliver us from evil.

Take with You: You are safe in Christ. This changes everything about our fight with sin in all its forms. Thank God for his rich mercies.

FEBRUARY 28

"Cursed is the man who trusts in man and makes flesh his strength, whose heart turns away from the LORD."

"Blessed is the man who trusts in the LORD, whose trust is the LORD. He is like a tree planted by water, that sends out its roots by the stream." —Jeremiah 17:5, 7–8

When you are angry, anxious, or want to escape from hard things, where do you choose to turn? Jeremiah describes a person turning away from God: "cursed is the man who trusts in man and makes flesh his strength, whose heart turns away from the LORD" (17:5). This picture is the opposite of true repentance, which is characterized by turning toward God. Jeremiah is describing someone turning away from the fountain of living water and becoming like a dried-up bush that lives in the desert. That accurately describes those who are caught up in anger, anxiety, and escapism.

Usually when you feel stuck in anger, anxiety, or escapist behavior, you don't think you can choose to feel, think, and act differently. But those in Christ still have the power of Christ. They have Christ's strength, truth, and righteousness. They have the Word of Christ and the power of prayer. Because of Christ, they can choose Christ. Because of the Spirit, they can keep in step with the Spirit.

Turning to Christ and away from our own strength is to win spiritual warfare.

Take with You: Is there a pattern of thoughts or actions that you can turn away from today? Often, very small shifts are what make the biggest impact on our lives being lived for light or darkness.

FEBRUARY 29

Again he entered the synagogue, and a man was there with a withered hand. And they watched Jesus, to see whether he would heal him on the Sabbath, so that they might accuse him. And he said to the man with the withered hand, "Come here." And he said to them, "Is it lawful on the Sabbath to do good or to do harm, to save life or to kill?" But they were silent. And he looked around at them with anger, grieved at their hardness of heart, and said to the man, "Stretch out your hand." He stretched it out, and his hand was restored. —Mark 3:1–5

It's possible to say, "That's wrong!" and show that we're upset in constructive, loving ways. Jesus saw wrong and called it out. His purpose is described here: "God did not send his Son into the world to condemn the world, but in order that the world might be saved through him" (John 3:17).

Good anger has a name: the constructive displeasure of mercy. Each of those three words matters. Good anger works as one aspect of mercy. It brings good into bad situations. It stands up for helpless victims. It calls out wrongdoers while holding out promises of forgiveness and new life at the same time.

Our anger can be remade into God's image. Strong, clear-minded mercy is the foundation of the Bible's redemption story with Jesus at the very center. *Jesus gathers up our anger, not to cut down our sensitivity to evil, but to redeem how we respond. Strong, clear-minded mercy is the way we're meant to transform feeling upset by what is.*

Take with You: Mercy always builds up. It shows up to help solve problems. It gives you a new way to see and act.

MARCH 1

But I am poor and needy; hasten to me, O God! You are my help and my deliverer; O LORD, do not delay! —Psalm 70:5

Why do you pray? I suspect your answer is the same as mine. The reason I pray is I need to pray. It is the door of life, and if I don't pray, I can't live.

A good definition of prayer is that it's real talk with the real God about what's really going on and what really matters. In prayer you find a deep honesty about the things that really matter. You need a certain kind of help, and you need things that God himself must give or you waste away. When he gives them, you rejoice with gladness of heart.

What do we need? We cannot fix what's wrong in and around us without help from outside, and prayer recognizes this reality. We need everyday wisdom and understanding about how life actually works and what we are to do with our lives. We need strength and power to live within the sufferings and afflictions of human life in this world and to live well with courage, humility, hope, faith, and love. And we need protection God alone can provide.

When you become aware of what you really need and who God really is, you pray for one reason—you need to.

Take with You: What do you really need today that only God can give you? Peace? Joy? Hope? If you aren't sure, ask God to show you your need of him. He will meet you there.

MARCH 2

Likewise the Spirit helps us in our weakness. For we do not know what to pray for as we ought, but the Spirit himself intercedes for us with groanings too deep for words. —Romans 8:26

Why do we pray? We need hope. We need to know that the King will come and wipe away every tear from our eyes, that there will be no more death or mourning or crying or pain. We need unbreakable friendship. We need the presence of God himself in our lives. *We pray real prayers because we know what we most need is to know him.*

So how do we pray? You must get down to your core need and God's core promises. When you bring those together, you speak honestly to the one who can help you. Our needs line up with the qualities of who God is—his character, what he does, what he thinks, what he promises.

We pray about things Psalms portrays: Protect me—I'm vulnerable, and you're strong (72:4). Make me alive—I'm dying, and you are life (119:50). Give me wisdom—write your words on my heart (119:34). Don't let go of me (38:21). Watch over me (16:1). Give me strength (119:28). Have mercy on me (51:1).

As we pray prayers of need, they lead to prayers of praise for his goodness and mercy (1 Chronicles 16:34; Psalm 23:6). As we pray, the Holy Spirit steps in to turn our confusion into something beautiful and fruitful.

Take with You: Ask the Lord to show you his face and teach you more of his character and promises so that you would be transformed from one degree of glory to another (2 Corinthians 3:18).

MARCH 3

Then Jesus told his disciples, "If anyone would come after me, let him deny himself and take up his cross and follow me."
—Matthew 16:24

Jesus's amazing grace comes to sinners with everything needed to create children of glory. But the soul, driven by self-love, doesn't want to embrace the central activity of the Christian life: true change. What gets in the way of living fully dependent on Christ's comfort and love? What gets in the way of loving God with all that you are? What gets in the way of looking out for what other people need? *Something in you doesn't want to be seen for what it is. Yet the power and instruction of the Bible and the Holy Spirit intend to remake you. God willingly and faithfully teaches you to love, fear, trust, and serve him.*

The Bible calls this life of change by many names. Jesus says, "Become a disciple." A disciple actively engages in becoming different and seeking out ways to grow. Jesus says, "Follow me." Follower, deny yourself, taking up your cross daily. Jesus says, "First take the log out of your own eye." Without the heavy weight of sin, you will treat other people very differently.

The war against selfishness comes paired with the peace of God that passes all understanding. The price is high: yourself. The reward staggers: God himself.

Take with You: What area of your inner life or outer life might God be nudging you to change? He walks slowly and patiently with us. He is a trustworthy leader.

MARCH 4

"Blessed are the peacemakers, for they shall be called sons of God."
—Matthew 5:9

A Prayer for Us to Become Peacemakers

Our God and Father, we thank you that you have given to us Christ Jesus, fully God, fully a man. Thank you for his honest suffering, sweat, and blood. Thank you that he entered our troubled world, was genuinely tempted, faced death itself, and yet did not recoil in the face of horrors. Help us to see and hear the Prince of Peace. Lord, you say peacemakers are blessed, and you yourself are the peacemaker of the world. We are so often war-makers, or we are peace lovers who avoid necessary conflict. *Make us men and women who are workers of peace in our world at war, who repent quickly when we are aggressive or when we are fearful, who learn to go forward with our heads held high and to love people. We ask that we would enter into difficult situations courageously, recognizing that this is a world that needs redemption and that means stepping into hard places.* Help us not be lovers of comfort or protectors of our reputations who only want life on our own terms. Help us not to create little private kingdoms of peace and our own control, but let us live freely within the real world, the one that cries out for peacemakers. Lord, thank you that this is exactly what you are doing in our lives, one and all. Give us your own wisdom. Fill us with the Holy Spirit, who is the instrument of a peaceable wisdom. Amen.

Take with You: Take a moment to make this prayer your own. How would you speak these truths to God? God is listening and on the move.

MARCH 5

And because you are sons, God has sent the Spirit of his Son into our hearts, crying, "Abba! Father!" So you are no longer a slave, but a son, and if a son, then an heir through God. —Galatians 4:6–7

Who are you really? What defines you? You're not defined by your place in your family, whether you are single or dating, whether you got the starring role or are captain of the team. You're not defined by your grades or your college acceptance. You're not defined by your friendships. You're not defined by your local church or your school. You're not defined by your ethnic background.

If you were, you'd be cursed if you got a C+, a wreck if your best friend betrayed you or you had a breakup, in despair if you happened to be sick for the championship game, or hopeless if your ethnic background was mocked.

You're defined by your relationship with the living God. Getting that straight is the one thing that lets you actually engage in the right way with all of these other roles, embracing the joys and positives and the blessings. And it lets you face whatever evils, darkness, or disappointment is there. Whatever your family history, current ranking, friendship situation—whatever the future brings in gains or losses—your most true identity stands.

Here's who you are: You belong to Jesus Christ. You have been bought with his blood. You belong to your Father. You've been given the identity of a child who says, "Abba, Father." Your God is gracious to you. He is always gracious.

Take with You: God is always up to something good in your life. That is what defines you. Thank him for your identity in Christ.

MARCH 6

For we do not have a high priest who is unable to sympathize with our weaknesses, but one who in every respect has been tempted as we are, yet without sin. Let us then with confidence draw near to the throne of grace, that we may receive mercy and find grace to help in time of need. —Hebrews 4:15–16

A Prayer to Our Redeemer

Our Father, it is very good to know you. *And we thank you that Jesus helps us. We thank you that Jesus forgives us. We thank you for mercy and grace to help in moments of need.* Your understanding of the struggles of the human condition brings us to seek you. We thank you that Christ Jesus, the Lord of life, the Prince of Peace, the Lord of love, wears many crowns. All that you are speaks to the concerns, needs, and struggles of people who need redeeming. We want to grow into your image.

We pray that the significance of the mercies of God in Christ would change our hearts. These mercies are vast. His dying love on the cross for us, his gift of the Holy Spirit, his modeling of the life he works to shape in us, his choosing us before the foundation of the world, his interceding for us on our own behalf. Would you make these truths run down deep into the places in life where we grumble, get bad attitudes, or get caught up in fear, anxiety, or bitterness? We ask this for your name's sake. Amen.

Take with You: Our God hears you and sees you right where you are today. Draw near to him in full confidence and you will find grace.

MARCH 7

Well might the sun in darkness hide and shut his glories in,
When Christ, the mighty Maker, died for man the creature's sin.

Thus might I hide my blushing face while his dear cross appears;
Dissolve my heart in thankfulness, and melt mine eyes in tears.

But drops of grief can ne'er repay the debt of love I owe;
Here, Lord, I give myself away, 'tis all that I can do.
— Isaac Watts, "Alas! and Did My Savior Bleed"

We live in a world of laid-back, carefully measured commitments. We live in a world of halfhearted loyalties. We're loyal and committed, but only to a point. What gets our full devotion is self-interest, private addiction, self-pity, and self-righteousness. But Christ wants whole hearts. He wants hearts fully believing, poured out, engaged, given away. How does he win us to his vision? He tells us about himself and says, *Listen.*

Isaac Watts listened. He heard Jesus's message and his response was, "Here, Lord, I give myself away." What moved him so deeply? One supreme truth: Christ, the mighty Maker, died for the sins of his very own created beings. One truth pierced his heart, soul, mind, and strength. *One decisive truth made him respond with self-forgetting love: Christ, the mighty Maker, died for the sins of his very own created beings.*

Are you listening? What do you need to stop and hear? The same message that Isaac Watts heard: Christ died for all, that they who live should no longer live for themselves, but for him who died and rose again on their behalf (2 Corinthians 5:15).

Take with You: We're all created beings, but we're all specifically unique. Ask God for help to know where and what you are holding back from him. He wants your whole heart.

MARCH 8

If any of you lacks wisdom, let him ask God, who gives generously to all without reproach, and it will be given him. —James 1:5

A Prayer for Wisdom

Our Father, will you grant us nothing less than divine wisdom? We thank you that you have mercifully promised to shine light in our lives. Open the eyes of our hearts that we might know you and see you as you are. Give us clarity about ourselves. Let us understand our world more and more the way you understand it. Above all else, will you shield us from all evil and strengthen us in all good? *Lord, through our lives, be honored. And would our lives, by your mercy, become fruitful, wise, and good.* Give us your wisdom, that we might become full of peace and gentleness, open to reason, full of mercy and good fruits and sincere in love. Give us your wisdom that we would become men and women who delight that a God who is so spectacularly beautiful has done such wondrous things. May your wisdom lead us to see and consider others more important than ourselves instead of seeing them as a problem to fix or a hassle we don't like. Help us see practically how to move in your direction and learn to love and not be gripped by fear, or hate, or confusion. Make it so. And we ask it in Jesus's name. Amen.

Take with You: God wants to hear from you. Not just at a meal or before bed, but all day long. A prayer like this puts you in the right position to face your life with humility and courage. What line can you take with you and pray again and again today?

MARCH 9

Stand therefore, having fastened on the belt of truth, and having put on the breastplate of righteousness, and, as shoes for your feet, having put on the readiness given by the gospel of peace. In all circumstances take up the shield of faith, with which you can extinguish all the flaming darts of the evil one; and take the helmet of salvation, and the sword of the Spirit, which is the word of God, praying at all times in the Spirit, with all prayer and supplication.
—Ephesians 6:14–18

In Ephesians 6, Paul describes the Christian life in simple terms. If we strip the metaphor of armor out, he is telling us what seven basic elements we need to be strong in the Lord and in his might. *What will make you able to stand against the hard circumstances and deceit in the world, the personal fight with your own flesh, and the dark deliberate spiritual realm of the devil? Truth, righteousness, the gospel of peace, faith, salvation, the Word of God, and prayer.* These elements are not set aside for Sunday morning or for a special spiritual experience. They are what you and I need every day in normal Christian life. It's what we have been given through Christ to live in the strength of Christ. It's what we have to offer others in the middle of their everyday struggles with anger, fear, and escapism. There's hope for them and for you because Christ has provided specifically for us to live in his strength.

Take with You: There's great comfort in being provided for. Thank God for his strength that works all the more perfectly in our weakness and dependence on him alone.

MARCH 10

Be kind to one another, tenderhearted, forgiving one another, as God in Christ forgave you. Therefore be imitators of God, as beloved children. And walk in love, as Christ loved us and gave himself up for us, a fragrant offering and sacrifice to God.
—Ephesians 4:32–5:2

God's way of dealing with what's wrong in this world is wonderful and surprising, combining firmness with gentleness, honesty with forgiveness. But how do you make his way your way? How do you learn to let go of your wrong anger and express your just anger constructively to build up and not tear down?

Paul gives you practical help in Ephesians 4:29–5:2. He starts by telling us how *not* to express our anger. First, he says we are not to keep to ourselves and brood ("bitterness"). Second, he says we are not to go to the other person and dump our anger ("wrath"). Finally, we shouldn't go to others who aren't involved and gossip ("slander").

You have to go to God for help. As you go to him, you will learn how to think through your angry reactions and slow down. You will learn how to approach other people in such a way that you're actually asking for help. You will learn how to be positive and constructive. *Your anger will be transformed when you understand deep in your heart how God, in Christ, treats you.* God's patience, mercy, forgiveness, and loving confrontation will only become real in your life as your relationship with him grows and you see his heart for his people and his world.

Take with You: Christ has set out for us a perfect example of love. May we grow as imitators of him! Ask God to show you his heart for those around you.

MARCH 11

But the fruit of the Spirit is love, joy, peace, patience, kindness, goodness, faithfulness, gentleness, self-control; against such things there is no law. And those who belong to Christ Jesus have crucified the flesh with its passions and desires. —Galatians 5:22–24

How does God respond when something important in the world is wrong? He responds redemptively. Is God angry when people act like little gods of their own kingdoms and bring grief to themselves and others? Yes. But how did he express that anger? By sending his very own Son to this broken world to be broken on the cross. He sacrificed his Son so his people can be forgiven, changed, and restored to a right relationship with him and others.

Your anger can also result in redemption. As you turn to God and find forgiveness, you will be filled with God's Spirit. Because of his Spirit in you, it will be possible for you also to respond redemptively when you are angry. You can learn to say, "That's wrong," without ranting, exaggerating, cursing, or name-calling.

Being filled with the Spirit means everything about you will start to resemble God. Instead of reacting with sinful anger to unimportant things, God's perspective on your life will overtake your own perspective.

When Jesus was on earth, he was not a stoic. No one cared more than he did about things that were wrong in this world. But his upset was driven by faith and love, not by pettiness, hostility, and aggression.

Take with You: Becoming more like Christ over a lifetime means you will care about the things closest to God's heart—the only things that truly matter in his world.

MARCH 12

Beloved, let us love one another, for love is from God, and whoever loves has been born of God and knows God. Anyone who does not love does not know God, because God is love. —1 John 4:7–8

How do you seek to be close with God? Spend time thinking about the way he treats you. *Love for others will come as you experience the love of your Father in heaven.* God's love for us is the most wonderful thing in this world—his love is at the core of what makes life bright and hopeful. Read these Bible verses and make them your own:

- You're never out of sight or out of mind to God (Psalm 139:7–10).
- He creates closeness with you by the way he treats you (Isaiah 42:3).
- He notices and cares about everything that happens to you (Luke 12:6–7).
- He speaks openly about himself (John 15:15).
- He listens to you (Psalm 6:8–9).
- He's a refuge in the midst of your sufferings (Psalm 46).
- He hangs in there over the long haul (Isaiah 49:14–16).
- He laid down his life for you (John 3:16; Romans 5:6–8).
- He forgives all your sins (Psalm 103:1–5).
- His mercies are new every morning (Lamentations 3:21–24).

God wants you to respond to his love by trusting him with your whole life. He's closed the distance between you and him through the life, death, and resurrection of his Son. Now he's making you like him and walking with you every step of the way. He's helping you step-by-step to love others the way he loves you.

Take with You: As you take time to read these verses, delight in drawing closer to God as you learn about his character and specific care.

MARCH 13

For I am sure that neither death nor life, nor angels nor rulers, nor things present nor things to come, nor powers, nor height nor depth, nor anything else in all creation, will be able to separate us from the love of God in Christ Jesus our Lord. —Romans 8:38–39

As you read through Romans 8, notice Paul doesn't say we won't have hardships. Instead he acknowledges the "trouble . . . hardship . . . persecution . . . famine . . . nakedness, [and] danger" (v. 35 NIV). *But he does promise that not one of these things "will be able to separate us from the love of God that is in Christ Jesus our Lord" (v. 39 NIV). Cling to this promise.* Cling to Jesus. Invite him into your struggles, sorrows, and questions. Fill your mind with his words.

When you read the Gospel of Luke, you read a very unusual story of the life of Jesus. Luke doesn't talk much about famous, smart, successful people. He focuses on little people: those who are powerless, grieving, ignored, and neglected. Right now, maybe you fall into one of those categories. You may be going through something far bigger than your ability to control or fix. As you read Luke, watch Jesus in action. Notice how he treats people with wisdom, love, and tenderness. He's content to do and say only one thing, or a few things. Take to heart that this is also the way he treats you.

Take with You: You are seen and known in your very own life right now. This Jesus that you trust has words of life, words of comfort, words of wisdom, and delight for you today. Ask him to make his presence known to you.

MARCH 14

The secret things belong to the LORD our God, but the things that are revealed belong to us and to our children forever, that we may do all the words of this law. —Deuteronomy 29:29

Edith Schaeffer once used the image of a cloth tapestry to talk about the difficult things in life. She pointed out that the front of the tapestry was a beautiful pattern, but the back was a mass of knots and tangled threads. Even in life's broken knots and tangled experiences, the promises and presence of your God and Savior are real. One day, you will see the front side of your life tapestry and an image of beauty and order will be on display. One part of the beauty of the tapestry will be the way you learn to know God and love others by going through difficult experiences. But is that the whole answer to why God lets hard things happen in your life? No. Parts of his will and purposes are beyond us. The Bible says, "The secret things belong to the LORD our God" (Deuteronomy 29:29).

What has been revealed is given so you can live. What has not been revealed to you is meant to be hidden, so you can actually find peace even when all of your questions cannot be answered. *Instead of trusting in your own strength and knowledge, trust in God's love and goodness.* This is a lesson you get to learn and relearn over a lifetime.

Take with You: Often when we don't know the answers, we get nervous. Learning to rest in God's knowledge of the "big picture" of your life is hard, but it brings deep peace. Ask him to help you trust more today.

MARCH 15

But he said to me, "My grace is sufficient for you, for my power is made perfect in weakness." Therefore I will boast all the more gladly of my weaknesses, so that the power of Christ may rest upon me.
—2 Corinthians 12:9

Turn to God in suffering. He will change the way you think about your life. Instead of despising your weakness, notice that weakness reveals God's power. Pour out your heart to God just as Paul did in 2 Corinthians 12. He had a weakness he called a "thorn in my flesh" (v. 7 NIV). He begged God to take his weakness away more than once.

Paul received from God this response: "My grace is sufficient for you, for my power is made perfect in weakness" (v. 9). God's power is perfectly revealed in our weakness. God uses your weakness to show you that what drives your life is not you but the power and mercy of Another.

Paul responded to God by saying, "I will boast all the more gladly about my weaknesses, so that Christ's power may rest on me" (v. 9 NIV). The world despises weakness, but as Paul embraces it, he gets to see the power of Christ on display. He finds contentment: "For Christ's sake, I delight in weaknesses, in insults, in hardships, in persecutions, in difficulties" (v. 10 NIV).

People value being strong and independent. But weakness and dependency make Christ matter more in your life. When Christ matters, he shines through your life. People see the evidence of something wonderful—the hand of a loving God at work in you.

Take with You: Where are you strong? Where are you weak? Our lives glow as we invite God to use both our strengths and weaknesses. He is able.

MARCH 16

Do not be overcome by evil, but overcome evil with good.
—Romans 12:21

How you treat your enemies is a measure of where your heart is with the Lord. Romans 12:14–21 talks about how you deal with your enemies—-whether you seek to take revenge or whether you are able to do courageous good in the context of evil. Whatever pours out of our hearts reveals our very selves. There's a major strand in the Bible about how we deal with the enemy-like behavior of other people. How will you react? Evil for evil, good for good? Two dominant themes are on display here. One theme is refuge. The other is repentance.

We are transformed by repentance—turning from the natural way we show displeasure, unhappiness, and anger—to the constructive displeasure that actually glorifies God. Being upset in a productive way in the face of evil expresses the character of Christ and demonstrates a hope bigger than our situation. Revelation 21:4 reminds us that one day there will be a righting of all wrongs, no more sorrow, no more sighing, no more dying, no more tears. Every cause of stumbling, every cause of evil, heartache, and heartbreak will be gone. And what will be left is joy and full freedom from sin. The hope of heaven and all that means for those in Christ reframes how we see and respond to being sinned against.

Take with You: Is there someone in your life that sins against you over and over again? As you acknowledge your genuine suffering, ask the Lord to give you courage in that relationship. And then keep asking. God's timing is perfect. He will open a door for you.

MARCH 17

"I the LORD search the heart
and test the mind, to give every man according to his ways,
according to the fruit of his deeds."
—Jeremiah 17:10

No one but God can see, explain, or change the human heart. We do not see anyone's heart. We cannot explain why anyone has the specific behavior patterns they do. And we have no power to change another person's motives. But we can describe the human heart with the words of the Bible in clear categories like fear of man, pride, lust of the flesh, and selfishness. In Jeremiah 17, it says the human heart is unsearchable in terms of who can see it, explain it, and change it. It also gives examples of hearts that have gone off track. Having accurate words to describe what goes on at the heart level to disrupt, distract, and destroy us is helpful as we talk with people and seek to understand ourselves.

Can you change what you want? Can your desires change? Of course they can. That's the very heart of the Christian message. By the grace of God, weak people can actually learn to care about other people and seek to reach outward instead of inward. It's a long, hard fight to actually learn to love, but this learning is exactly what redemption is about. Is it easy? No. Is it hard? Yes. Is that what redemption is about? Yes. And that redemptive change is actually at the center of God's purposes for you.

Take with You: You are not in control. God is. He is trustworthy and will complete the good work he began in you. Take a deep breath and rejoice!

MARCH 18

To put off your old self, which belongs to your former manner of life and is corrupt through deceitful desires, and to be renewed in the spirit of your minds, and to put on the new self, created after the likeness of God in true righteousness and holiness.
—Ephesians 4:22–24

In the New Testament, desire language is the summary term for the sin nature. The Old Testament shows physical idolatry through outward desires with idols. The New Testament shows more of a heart idolatry with words like "desire," "lust," and "craving," which all refer to the same idea. It answers the "why" question. What motivates us?

When you desperately want something, it becomes your master. It's a desire that has become an evil lord over your life. Often with Christians, the thing someone wants is a good thing. What's wrong with wanting a good thing? *But the evil in our desires is often not what we want—the object—it's that we want it too much.* The desires themselves can become extreme and excessive—our thoughts and lives revolve completely around them. Desires that get out of control lead to anxiety, anger, fears, escapism, aggression, obsession, and so on.

Our world today views desires as needs that must be met no matter the cost. Or we see them as drives within us that must get trained for good or bad. These views will always fall short. As we listen to God in his Word, we can grow to truly understand our desires.

Take with You: Our life as Christians is marked by what we are embracing to look more like Christ. Ask your good Father to help you put off desires gone wrong and to put on Christ.

MARCH 19

Remember that you were at that time separated from Christ, alienated from the commonwealth of Israel and strangers to the covenants of promise, having no hope and without God in the world. But now in Christ Jesus you who once were far off have been brought near by the blood of Christ. —Ephesians 2:12–13

We usually try to measure our self-esteem and self-worth by sizing ourselves up against what we value the most and by comparing ourselves to others. In comparing myself to another person in any arena of life, I'm ranking myself by a system I call the "ladders to nowhere." If you are on the sixth rung of the ladder and I'm below on the fourth, you're better than me. But if I am above on the sixth rung and you are only on the fourth, I'm better than you. It's so sad. But there's good news. Scripture knocks down these ladders to nowhere when we learn about God and his kingdom. God, in his power and design over all things, creates differences between people. We could wish we were more athletic, prettier, smarter, or richer—like that other person—but God chooses to make us different from one another.

Before the living God, however, all of us are poor. We are all strangers needing to be brought in. We are all weak, disabled, dying. We're all children. We all need a safe refuge and deliverer. *One of the ways the Bible reverses the false worldly ranking systems is by taking lowly meanings and making them signs of relationship with God.* Being called a sheep is the perfect example of this.

Take with You: God's value system is radically different. "Ladders to nowhere" do what they promise. They get you nowhere.

MARCH 20

"Blessed are the meek, for they shall inherit the earth."
—Matthew 5:5

What qualities most define the Christian life? We usually (and rightly) say faith and love. But you can equally say that at the very center of the Christian life is meekness. What is meekness? It's not weakness. Meekness is simply the knowledge that your life is completely under somebody else's control. When you're meek, you're acknowledging your dependence and your need for grace from the One who's bigger than you. You seek his voice and his will. The opposite of being meek is to be self-centered and focused only on getting what you want.

Thinking of ourselves first comes naturally, but it doesn't lead to a blessed life. Think of the first beatitude: "Blessed are the poor in spirit" (Matthew 5:3). *Blessed are those who know their need. Blessed are those who are aware of the living God in the midst of life's sins and sufferings.*

Think of how so many of the Psalms display this attitude of neediness, even though the word "meekness" it not used: "Hear me, hear my cry, help me, be merciful to me" (Psalms 4:1; 57:1; 61:1–3, author's paraphrase). That's meekness.

The opposite of meekness is to be self-exalting. You don't listen. You're a traitor and you want what you want, like Satan. Meekness is to die to itself. It's life from the dead.

Take with You: Where do you need God's help today? Consider what it might look like to practice meekness by taking your neediness to God.

MARCH 21

Even though I walk through the valley of the shadow of death,
I will fear no evil, for you are with me;
your rod and your staff, they comfort me. —Psalm 23:4

He has said, "I will never leave you nor forsake you."
So we can confidently say,
"The Lord is my helper; I will not fear;
what can man do to me?" —Hebrews 13:5–6

The most frequently repeated command in the entire Bible is "Don't fear." It's everywhere. It's interesting that the way Scripture deals with "Don't fear" is different from how it deals with "Don't steal" or "Don't lie." In those sins, Scripture calls you to stop, to turn and repent.

But with "Don't fear," the Bible consistently gives you comfort. It says, "Don't be afraid, I'm with you." "Come to me." "Don't be afraid, I will never leave you or forsake you. You're not alone." In our fears, we feel alone, and we're afraid of something bigger than us that's out to get us—like embarrassment, rejection, failure, or even death.

But when you know you're not alone, your fears don't seem so strong. We get tastes of God's comforting presence now. One day we will see him face-to-face, and on the last day, all fear will be gone forever.

Take with You: What is something you're afraid of? Take one of the Bible verses mentioned here and pray that back to God, telling him all about your fears and asking for him to be with you. Ask God to remind you when you are afraid to ask him for his help and presence.

MARCH 22

Your words were found, and I ate them,
and your words became to me a joy
and the delight of my heart,
for I am called by your name,
O LORD, God of hosts. —Jeremiah 15:16

When Jesus changes people, it's usually through the truth of a particular passage of Scripture and the trustworthy love of a person who reflected Christ.

When people think about how God has changed them, I ask them two sets of questions. The first set considers how God works through the Bible.

1. What part of the Bible has been most important in your life? What passage is most meaningful to you? Why? Why do these particular words from God have such an impact on you? How do these words make a difference in your life?

The second set of questions considers how God works through his people.

2. Who do you trust the most? What about this person makes you trust them? What changed in you because of that person's influence? What are you able to talk about because you trust that person?

When God changes us, he works through the Bible and through people. People who genuinely love us can speak God's truth to us and reflect him in how they live.

Take with You: Identify one Christian who has had a big impact on your faith: a parent, teacher, youth group leader, or someone else. Ask that person how they have seen God change them. Do they talk about how God used his Word and his people?

MARCH 23

This is love: not that we loved God, but that he loved us and sent his Son as an atoning sacrifice for our sins. —1 John 4:10 NIV

When what you hope for doesn't happen, there is one hope that can never be destroyed: "This is love: not that we loved God, but that he loved us and sent his Son as an atoning sacrifice for our sins" (1 John 4:10). *These words aren't just what we say at church. These are God's words to us when we face suffering and sin in our lives.*

When you believe this, you learn how to live well even when things go wrong: "Dear friends, since God so loved us, we also ought to love one another" (1 John 4:11 NIV). We were made to love God and love others. You can be thankful. You can consider others and put their wants before your own. You can do small things gladly. You learn that you can make some difference in others' lives, not to save them but to simply help them. You don't think that you are better than any other human being. You don't think your actions can make everything right. You learn not to hate or fear or give up hope, because Jesus loves you. You learn to care about others.

Take with You: How does the truth that God loves you and sent his Son to save you give you hope when life is hard? Think of one way you can share God's love by doing something kind for a friend, family member, neighbor, or even someone you don't know well.

MARCH 24

I do not cease to give thanks for you, remembering you in my prayers, that the God of our Lord Jesus Christ, the Father of glory, may give you the Spirit of wisdom and of revelation in the knowledge of him, having the eyes of your hearts enlightened, that you may know what is the hope to which he has called you, what are the riches of his glorious inheritance in the saints.
—Ephesians 1:16–18

Our God is personal with his children. As Christians, we say we know and serve a "personal God" because we believe God revealed himself in the Bible as a person—in fact, "one God in three persons." He's not just an idea but a real person. He acts. He speaks. As humans we cannot fully understand him, but he invites us to know him better. He thinks and tells us what he thinks, but we can't know all his thoughts. He is wise. He is in control of everything, and he gives grace and always does what's right. He gives life. He builds up and feeds. He tears down and destroys. He does things a person does.

Our personal God is close to us, he knows what's going on in our lives, and he cares. Isn't it amazing that we get to know him in personal ways we normally only know with family? *He is our Father. He is our Savior and our Lord. He is our Holy Spirit. Our God is personal with us.*

Take with You: Spend some time thinking about what it means that God is personal with you. Write down one way you have seen God's personal care for you this week.

MARCH 25

With my voice I cry out to the LORD;
with my voice I plead for mercy to the LORD.
I pour out my complaint before him;
I tell my trouble before him. —Psalm 142:1–2

In relationships, we speak and are listened to. The reason we pray is to be heard by the Person we're talking with. Prayer isn't just thinking, and it isn't just feeling. It uses words. It's an honest conversation about things that matter with someone you know, need, and love.

I've known many people (myself included) whose relationship with God was transformed as they learned to really speak to their Father. It's easy for prayer to become just thinking, talking to yourself, or listing off requests, with little connection to who the Lord is and what he's doing. It is easy to think that prayer is just about having certain religious feelings or spiritual thoughts or having a vague sense of comfort. Sometimes prayer can sound just like anxiety and overthinking! Sometimes we confuse prayer with stopping to quietly reflect or calm ourselves. Sometimes prayer becomes a superstition, a ritual to keep bad things away and to make sure good things happen.

Instead, try being quiet so you can notice and listen—so you can find your own words to speak to God. The living God uses words to speak with his children because that's how relationships work. He invites you to speak to him, and he listens to you.

Take with You: Practice talking to God. Tell him what's going on in your life right now—not because he doesn't know, but because he wants to hear from you. Tell him what you're excited, anxious, or uncertain about. Ask for his help.

MARCH 26

Such is the confidence that we have through Christ toward God. Not that we are sufficient in ourselves to claim anything as coming from us, but our sufficiency is from God, who has made us sufficient to be ministers of a new covenant, not of the letter but of the Spirit. —2 Corinthians 3:4–6

Being forgiven doesn't make you confident in yourself. Instead your confidence is in what Jesus has done for you. Your sins and shame are covered, and you now have Christ's goodness and mercy to show to others. You are God's beloved child . . . so now you are able to love, to give your life away for others.

Your trust and confidence is not in yourself, but in the One who has loved you by saving you from trusting in yourself. Your life will continue to be stressful. You are still only human. You still live in a world of disappointments and dangers. You still fail. You still need the mercy of your King and Savior. As you serve this King and Savior, sometimes he pulls you out of your comfort zone. He shows you that you cannot control people and events. He doesn't let you create a safe zone where you don't need to care about other people who need him. *Your confidence rests outside of yourself and in God. So your life purpose is to love people who need Jesus to save them.* You are only giving away a bit of what God has generously given you.

Take with You: Ask God to show you his love for you today, then consider one person whom God may be calling you to share his great love with—such as a classmate, a sibling, or a neighbor.

MARCH 27

Come now, you who say, "Today or tomorrow we will go into such and such a town and spend a year there and trade and make a profit"—yet you do not know what tomorrow will bring. What is your life? For you are a mist that appears for a little time and then vanishes. Instead you ought to say, "If the Lord wills, we will live and do this or that." —James 4:13–15

You don't know how either your big decisions or your daily decisions will turn out. But you can trust your God. He is in control over your entire life. You don't need to try to figure out what you can't know. No need to look for signs or coincidences. No need for magical thinking. No need for repetitive praying to try to get a specific answer. *We often come to know God's will, what he meant for our lives, only afterward when we're looking back. Today, ask for wisdom and make decisions about school, activities, and friendships. You can make mature choices and have childlike trust at the same time.*

How he tells us to live and how he chooses to work meet in the mind and heart of God. Everything our Savior commands describes our sanctification, how we become more like him: a life of wisdom, self-giving love, self-control, gratitude, and joy. And our Savior God is in control, always working to grow us in these ways. He gives wisdom, love, self-control, and all other fruits of the Spirit—but often in ways we never would've imagined or planned.

Take with You: Think about one fruit of the Spirit. How is God growing you in that? Where do you see your need to make wise choices *and* trust his work?

MARCH 28

Blessed be the God and Father of our Lord Jesus Christ, the Father of mercies and God of all comfort, who comforts us in all our affliction, so that we may be able to comfort those who are in any affliction, with the comfort with which we ourselves are comforted by God. —2 Corinthians 1:3–4

God uses suffering to grow your character, to grow your trust in him and your love for others. Paul begins his second letter to the Corinthians by talking about how he saw God's love better when he went through suffering. *His suffering caused him to have compassion for others, and it can cause us to have compassion for others too. Then, when others suffer, we are able to express genuine love and reflect the love of God, because we know what suffering is like.* This truth is so important to understanding how life works that Paul talks about it throughout 2 Corinthians.

Our comfort comes from what Jesus did. God kept his promises through Jesus. He delivered us from sin and death. Jesus embodied the Father's grace. And God's promises and action are not only about what happened two thousand years ago, but every day he gives us grace through the presence and strength of the Holy Spirit. And he promises to give us new life and resurrection. If you live in him, you will never die; if you die in him, you will still live. The gift of Christ—past, present, and future grace—is the comfort God gives in suffering.

Take with You: How does God's grace—what Jesus did on the cross, the presence of his Holy Spirit now, and what he promises for eternity—give you comfort today?

MARCH 29

But you are a chosen people, a royal priesthood, a holy nation, God's special possession, that you may declare the praises of him who called you out of darkness into his wonderful light. —1 Peter 2:9 NIV

Your true identity is who God says you are. *You will never find out who you are by looking inside yourself or listening to what others say about you. The Lord gets to say who you are because he made you, he knows you, and his view of you is the only one that matters.*

Your true identity connects you to God. Everything you ever learn about who God is—his identity—tells you something about who you are. For example, "Your Father knows your need" means you're always a dependent child. "Jesus Christ is your Lord" means you're always a servant.

God's attributes tell you something about how you can become like him as you grow. For example, "The Lord's compassion for you is like a father with his children." You will always be a dependent child, but as Jesus changes you to reflect him, you can become better at caring for others like a loving parent would.

In his grace, Jesus gives you a new identity. You share his identity. Then the Holy Spirit makes you more like him over time. When you finally see him face-to-face, you will know him as he truly is, and you will fully know who you are.

You're also connected to God's other children who have the same identity. You're not alone. We're all members in the family of God.

Take with You: Write down one thing the Bible says about who God is. Then write down what that says about who you are.

MARCH 30

I have been crucified with Christ. It is no longer I who live, but Christ who lives in me. And the life I now live in the flesh I live by faith in the Son of God, who loved me and gave himself for me. —Galatians 2:20

God gave his only Son's life for you. Your life has meaning because of this. Your life is much bigger than your suffering, failures, and disappointments. *Living by faith in God and knowing that he has a plan for you will protect you from hopelessness. God wants to use your personality, skills, life situation, and even your struggles to bring hope to others.*

He has already prepared good things for you to do. The apostle Paul says in the Bible, "For we are God's workmanship, created in Christ Jesus to do good works, which God prepared in advance for us to do" (Ephesians 2:10). As you desire to do good in whatever situation you're in, wherever God places you, you will find meaning and joy. Until that time, may Jesus bless you, keep you, make his heavenly Father's face shine upon you, and give you peace.

Take with You: Think about one area of your life that you are discouraged about. Is there a way you can love another person by sharing your hopefulness because of Jesus?

MARCH 31

Because God's children are human beings—made of flesh and blood—the Son also became flesh and blood. For only as a human being could he die, and only by dying could he break the power of the devil, who had the power of death. Only in this way could he set free all who have lived their lives as slaves to the fear of dying.
—Hebrews 2:14–15 NLT

Adam and Eve believed Satan's lie: "You will not surely die" (Genesis 3:4). When they ate the fruit, death entered our world. Adam and Eve did die, and ever since then we have lived our lives as slaves because of our fear of death.

How amazing is the good news that Jesus is alive! Hebrews 2 explains how Jesus freed us from our fear of death: Jesus became flesh and blood so that he could fully enter into our life and fully enter into our death. When the Innocent One died for the sins of the world, the power of death was broken. Jesus's life, death, and resurrection destroyed the one who has the power of death—the devil—and set free everyone who has faith in Jesus.

When we face death, we make the same choice that we must make in every area of life: Who will be our shepherd? Those who trust in Jesus have a Good Shepherd, and he will lead us through the valley of the shadow of death until we live in the house of the Lord forever (Psalm 23).

Take with You: Are you ever scared of dying? How does Hebrews 2 encourage you that you don't have to be afraid to die?

APRIL 1

Lord, hear my prayer! Listen to my plea!
Don't turn away from me in my time of distress.
Bend down to listen, and answer me quickly when I call to you.
—Psalm 102:1–2 NLT

The Psalms are meant to speak for us. We're meant to make them our own. As you read them, fill them in with your own experiences. This is exactly what God's people have done for thousands of years. The Psalms give general patterns of experience that you can put the details of your own life into.

Psalm 102, for example, is labeled, "A prayer of one afflicted, when he is faint and pours out his complaint before the Lord." You can put areas of your life into these categories. You can put your life into this prayer: "Hear my prayer . . . let my cry come to you! Do not hide your face from me in the day of my distress! . . . answer me speedily in the day when I call!" (vv. 1–2). Many circumstances can make you cry for help like this and make you feel afraid, upset, and overwhelmed.

There are both psalms of sorrow and psalms of joy and gratitude. We're meant to pray both types of psalms. The Psalms are written to move through sorrow to joy, which is how life actually moves.

You have reason for joy, and you have reason for heartache, and the Psalms show you how to be honest with God in both situations.

> **Take with You:** Read Psalm 102, noticing how it moves from sorrow to joy. Where are you experiencing either sorrow or joy in life? What would it look like to talk to God honestly about both experiences?

APRIL 2

Count it all joy, my brothers, when you meet trials of various kinds, for you know that the testing of your faith produces steadfastness. And let steadfastness have its full effect, that you may be perfect and complete, lacking in nothing. —James 1:2–4

The testing of your faith produces something wonderful: steadfastness, courage, and a mature faith. Whatever you're facing, whether hard things or good things, God is doing something. Everything is a test and a trial to help you figure out what's wrong or needs to grow.

Every one of us is an imperfect version of what we will be. Corrections are needed, and God uses all sorts of things to fix what's going on inside of us. A test is something that reveals to you where you need God's transformation. One example of a test is what happens when you open your mouth. What will come out? How do you respond to the suffering of others? Do you care? How will you help? Every good and bad situation you're in, whether it's happening to you or others, is a test that reveals where you need to grow and mature.

As you see these things, keep in mind that the Father gives more grace. Ask God for help. Why ask him? Because you're missing something you need; you need more of what he only can give. He's not going to scold you. We're supposed to need him. We're made to need him and lean upon his grace.

Take with You: Think about one situation recently where you needed God's help—maybe in the way you treated a parent, sibling, friend, or classmate. Tell God about it and ask for his help. He gives you grace!

APRIL 3

"Therefore do not be anxious, saying, 'What shall we eat?' or 'What shall we drink?' or 'What shall we wear?' For the Gentiles seek after all these things, and your heavenly Father knows that you need them all. But seek first the kingdom of God and his righteousness, and all these things will be added to you." —Matthew 6:31–33

We must pay attention to our fears. We must do something with them. We tend to try to ignore them to try to get through life without paying attention to them. When worries and stresses come, we don't want to simply wait for the fear to get worse—we want to do something about it.

We want to stop. We want to speak to the Lord. We want to listen. Notice your worries that pop up today, tomorrow, and this coming week. When we recognize our limits and weakness, we are able to learn more about the Lord and speak about him in new ways. Weaknesses and fears are an opportunity to see what's true about Jesus Christ.

Focus on today because the One who loves you will be the One who cares about tomorrow. You don't have to worry about tomorrow because he will worry about tomorrow for you. And if the One of compassion and strength is the One worrying about tomorrow, then you in your human limitedness can simply focus on today. That's the beauty we have in knowing Christ.

Take with You: What is one way you worry about the future? Be honest with the Lord about it. Let him worry about tomorrow. Ask him to help you love him and others better today.

APRIL 4

In him you also, when you heard the word of truth, the gospel of your salvation, and believed in him, were sealed with the promised Holy Spirit. —Ephesians 1:13

Who is God? Everything we learn about him makes a difference.

- *God makes us know him.* "Oh, continue your steadfast love to those who know you" (Psalm 36:10).
- *God acts according to his plan.* "Whatever the LORD pleases, he does" (Psalm 135:6).
- *God gives grace.* "Surely goodness and mercy shall follow me all the days of my life" (Psalm 23:6).
- *God shows his power.* "Once God has spoken; twice I have heard this: that power belongs to God" (Psalm 62:11).
- *Christ comes to make peace between God and all nations.* "Praise the LORD, all nations! Extol him, all peoples!" (Psalm 117:1).
- *God's anger will fall on enemies.* "Kiss the Son, lest he be angry, and you perish in the way, for his wrath is quickly kindled" (Psalm 2:12).
- *God has bought us, and we belong to him.* "'You are my Lord; I have no good apart from you.' . . . The LORD is my chosen portion and my cup" (Psalm 16:2, 5).

We will be with God and will share together in his glory. We live in this hope. In the fullness of time, when Christ comes back, all shall be well and all manner of things shall be well. The Holy Spirit seals Christ into your heart now, and he promises that we will have every good gift forever (Ephesians 1:13).

Take with You: Everything about God changes how we live. Which quality of God listed above surprises you the most? How do you think it could change your life now?

APRIL 5

For the word of God is living and active, sharper than any two-edged sword, piercing to the division of soul and of spirit, of joints and of marrow, and discerning the thoughts and intentions of the heart. —Hebrews 4:12

The Word of God is living and active: it strikes home, convicting you of sin and convincing you of the grace of God in Christ Jesus. This Word transforms who or what you love and serve; powerfully changes how you see things; and wisely guides, guards, and shepherds you as you go through life.

Why is the Word so powerful? It's powerful because it is God's Word. The Word isn't a man-made idea. It isn't a magic charm. *The Word is what God says: about himself, you, the world you live in, his plan. The Word reveals the Person who speaks it, a Person who tells you what you need to repent and learn to trust, love, and obey him.* If you receive the Word, it changes you and causes you to bear good fruit. If you reject or ignore the Word, it also changes you; your heart becomes increasingly hard, blind, and deaf.

Applying the Word to your real life is work—hard, prayerful, thoughtful work. The first few verses of Proverbs 2 say you need to listen hard; you need to cry out for help; you need to search and dig. Listen to the Lord who speaks. Love him and what he says.

Take with You: Choose one passage of Scripture and think through what it says about God, you, and the world. Write the verse on a piece of paper or memorize it so you can carry it with you throughout the day.

APRIL 6

All of us used to live that way, following the passionate desires and inclinations of our sinful nature. . . . But God is so rich in mercy, and he loved us so much, that even though we were dead because of our sins, he gave us life when he raised Christ from the dead. (It is only by God's grace that you have been saved!)
—Ephesians 2:3–5 NLT

Sometimes we're right to be angry because we're experiencing true wrong. It's not right when your sibling cares more about what they want than you. It's not right if your friend treats you unfairly or your classmate says something unkind. It's not right when you're bullied or made fun of.

Anger is a way to say, "That's not right and that matters." In our broken world, you will have many good reasons to be angry. But because we are part of the broken world, sometimes we express our anger at true wrongs in the wrong way. We yell. We get irritated. We talk unkindly about people. We complain. We refuse to forgive. We ignore others. We give payback. Something really wrong happened . . . and we react by becoming really wrong.

Anger doesn't show grace. Anger punishes. *But God has chosen to show mercy to those who do wrong, including you (Ephesians 2:1–5).* God's mercy brings life to you. If you struggle with not wanting to forgive, you grumble, or you yell and argue, then you need God's mercy. You will receive mercy and help when you confess your sinful reactions to God.

Take with You: Who do you need to show grace to today? Ask God to help you give grace instead of punishment to someone who has wronged you.

APRIL 7

Be angry and do not sin; do not let the sun go down on your anger and give no opportunity to the devil. —Ephesians 4:26–27

Anger is a common response to living in a broken world where things can and do go wrong all the time. God does care about what makes you angry, but he also cares about how you express that anger. If you don't learn how to deal with your anger, you will become bitter and struggle in relationships with God and people.

Anger is our response to a wrong we think is important. God also gets angry at wrong in this world. Your capacity to be angry is one part of being made in his image.

God knows well that stuffing your anger deep inside isn't good. It will only come out in wrong ways. And learning tricks for keeping calm never gets to the heart of why God designed anger. Anger needs to be recognized and shown in a positive way, as a form of doing what's good and right.

God wants for you to express your anger in a way that actually brings good out of difficult situations and relationships. How does this happen? It starts with understanding what anger is, where it comes from, and how a right relationship with God will actually change the way you view and express your anger.

Take with You: When are you angry by how someone treated you or someone you love? God is also angry when people are treated unfairly. Be honest with him about your anger and ask him to help you to do what's right instead of what's wrong.

APRIL 8

For you did not receive the spirit of slavery to fall back into fear, but you have received the Spirit of adoption as sons, by whom we cry, "Abba! Father!" —Romans 8:15

People change when the Holy Spirit pours the love of God into their hearts through the gospel. Whoever is adopted as God's child is able to call him Father. People change when they pay attention to what they believe about God. Even with horrible experiences, we can't believe lies from the world and the devil. We must confess the lies we believe and hold onto the truth. *People change when biblical truth becomes clearer and louder than what they've experienced in life. People change when they have ears to hear and eyes to see what God tells us about himself.* God the Father is faithful and full of grace. God promises to be with his children, to teach, bless, and transform (John 15:2; Hebrews 12:1–14).

How do you grow in the knowledge of God your Father? Identify and confess where you have allowed specific lies, false beliefs, desires, and fears to control you and harm your relationship with God. Find specific truths in the Bible that speak against these lies. Turn to God for mercy and help, that his Spirit would encourage you in his love. Name the ways others have sinned against you. The love of God gives us courage to be honest about evil, which helps us forgive. Find wise Christians who can pray for you, listen, and encourage you.

Take with You: Who is one trusted person you can talk to today? Tell them about the lies you're tempted to believe about God and ask them to pray with you.

APRIL 9

Jesus said to her, "I am the resurrection and the life. Whoever believes in me, though he die, yet shall he live, and everyone who lives and believes in me shall never die. Do you believe this?" —John 11:25–26

The fear of death controls people's lives. How do we know? Because we live in a culture that doesn't want to think about death. We believe that life has meaning because of things we've done or because of things we own. Those may be all good things, but they aren't good enough to give us hope after death.

What makes your life meaningful? As we face the fact of death, we must also face the fact that Jesus is "the resurrection and the life." Jesus is the door out of the darkness of death.

Where do you put your trust? What do you actually live for? *Your hope is either in the one person who has defeated death, who is the resurrection and the life, or your hope is in something which may be a perfectly good thing but is not good enough and will die with you.* There's a hope that stands up to death. Be encouraged (and encourage others) with these promises of God:

- "I am the resurrection and the life" (John 11:25).
- "I will never forsake you" (Hebrews 13:5).
- "Your life is hidden with Christ in God" (Colossians 3:3).
- You have "an inheritance that can never perish, spoil or fade. This inheritance is kept in heaven for you" (1 Peter 1:4 NIV).

Take with You: The world convinces us that our life is meaningful because of what we do or have, but Jesus changes that. How does the fact that he's the resurrection and the life give you hope today?

APRIL 10

Now Jesus was praying in a certain place, and when he finished, one of his disciples said to him, "Lord, teach us to pray." —Luke 11:1

Praying is hard. Sometimes we can ask a friend we trust for something we need. But somehow when this same thing is called "praying" and the friend is called "God," it becomes harder.

But if your understanding and practice of prayer changes, then you will change, and so will your relationship with God and his people.

There are often three parts of a biblical prayer.

Sometimes we ask God to *change our circumstances*. Heal the sick. Give us daily bread.

Sometimes we ask God to *change us*: Deepen our faith. Teach us to love each other. Forgive our sins.

Sometimes we ask God to *change everything* by showing us more of who he is. Your kingdom come. Your will be done on earth as it is in heaven.

When we focus on any of these three and ignore the other two, prayer tends to be unbalanced. If you just pray for better circumstances, then God becomes the genie—no sanctifying purposes, no higher glory. If you only pray for personal change, then your focus could be on your own spiritual life that isn't concerned about other people and obeying God. If you only pray for the growth of God's kingdom, then your prayers may be impersonal and not specific.

Learn to pray with the three-stranded braid of your real need.

Take with You: Speak or write out a pray to God, asking him for something you need like you'd ask a good friend or family member. He is your Father, and he loves to hear from you.

APRIL 11

Blessed be the LORD!
For he has heard the voice of my pleas for mercy.
The LORD is my strength and my shield;
in him my heart trusts, and I am helped;
my heart exults,
and with my song I give thanks to him. —Psalm 28:6–7

It is uncomfortable to *need* help. Even when it ends up joyous and peaceful, neediness often doesn't feel very good in the process. You must cast your cares on God, who cares for you, because you're helpless in yourself (1 Peter 5:7). Your needs are bigger than you. You are under pressures. You are vulnerable, and you know it. You are burdened with things you cannot control or fix. Life is hard. You feel discouraged and threatened. You come as a refugee, not boasting of what you can bring, but bringing your cares. And your Father cares for you. He is strong and good. Safe at last! In the end, you rest peacefully.

Psalm 28 captures the whole cycle in a short space. David basically cries out, "Help! If you won't listen to me, I will die." This is not a comfortable feeling. He is threatened, wounded, and vulnerable. He is powerless, with nowhere else to turn. The Lord does listen, and it changes David's experience. His need turns into joy: "You are so good!" His cry for help becomes a shout of gratitude: "Thank you!" *It's not pleasant to need help. But it's a joy to find help.*

Take with You: Where are you trying to do things on your own when you're really in need? Tell God about your need. He stands eager to help you.

APRIL 12

[I pray] that the God of our Lord Jesus Christ, the Father of glory, may give you the Spirit of wisdom and of revelation in the knowledge of him, having the eyes of your hearts enlightened, that you may know what is the hope to which he has called you, what are the riches of his glorious inheritance in the saints, and what is the immeasurable greatness of his power toward us who believe.
—Ephesians 1:17–19a

Sometimes when people think about God, they ask the wrong questions. Will he meet my desires and needs? Will he help me get through life? Can I get him to make my day, my homework, and my friendships work out? If I do this for God, will he do this for me? Is it possible he might disappoint me?

What does God want you to know? Himself. His glory. Nothing less than the Lord who's at the center of the universe and history. Jesus Christ. God wants you to know right relationship between yourself and him. His light poured out into every nation: the mystery now revealed. He wants us to share in his mission to invade darkness. People who were once outcast are now welcomed into the community of promise. He wants you to know how to have peace and wisdom in all your relationships.

The letter to the Ephesians tears the doors off mysteries. The love of Christ was once beyond knowing and is now known. The endless riches of Christ, now seen. Things so far beyond all you can ask or imagine, now revealed in front of your eyes through Jesus.

Take with You: He wants you to know him. Which of the promises and truths above amaze you the most about God? Reflect on his goodness.

APRIL 13

Open my eyes, that I may behold
wondrous things out of your law. —Psalm 119:18

How do you connect your life to God's Words in the Bible? I write in my Bible all the time—I underline, highlight, and mark it up. I jot down things I might hear someone else say or my own thoughts.

When you're feeling sad, hurt, or scared, do you see Scripture as nice words to slap on to your day like a sticker? God's Word isn't like a bandage on an open wound. God's Word is alive, and it's more like a healing balm when we connect what's going on in our lives to who God is and what he says.

A simple sentence from the Bible can make a difference in your life. When you're stressed or in a difficult situation, it's there, and it reminds you God speaks to us and promises to be with us.

Philippians 4:5–6 comes to life when I can say, "Lord, here are the things I am worried about today," or "Here are the places where I'm stressed or out of my comfort zone." I need God's help. I'm wanting to bring who I am to who he is.

I have been so struck by Psalm 119. In its 176 verses about the God of Scripture, *the three most common requests are: "Teach me," "Help me to understand," and "Make me alive to this." I can read the words on the page, but God must make it alive to me and make me alive to who he is.*

Take with You: Consider one area of your life where you feel confused or stuck. Even there, God has good words to say, and he's not distant or irrelevant.

APRIL 14

If we confess our sins, he is faithful and just to forgive us our sins and to cleanse us from all unrighteousness. —1 John 1:9

The beauty of the gospel is that our confession is always connected with God's promise of good. What are God's promises to you? Here are a few specific promises to take to heart. What would it mean for you to truly believe and trust this? How does this promise change how you think about your failures and sins? Think about these promises. Say them aloud. Turn to God, confident in these promises.

I will never leave you or forsake you (Deuteronomy 31:6–8). Imagine—you will never be left alone. He will not walk away or abandon you.

The Lord make his face shine on you and be gracious to you (Numbers 6:25). Imagine—the Lord promises to turn a smiling face toward you. He will treat you with true kindness. Grace means undeserved kindness, and God is willingly gracious.

The Lord turn his face toward you and give you peace (Numbers 6:26). Imagine—he promises to never turn away from you. He gives peace. He does not get disgusted and give up. He does not leave you in worry, pain, and confusion.

All the promises of God are YES in Jesus Christ (2 Corinthians 1:20). Jesus fulfills all these promises and more, giving you true hope. He personally took your shame and guilt onto himself. Because of Jesus's death for you and his resurrection to life, you can bring your darkest sins into his bright light.

Take with You: For each of the promises above, take a few minutes to stop and consider them. God is faithful to keep his promises!

APRIL 15

And the peace of God, which surpasses all understanding, will guard your hearts and your minds in Christ Jesus.

What you have learned and received and heard and seen in me—practice these things, and the God of peace will be with you.
—Philippians 4:7, 9

The peace of God guards and watches over us, which is a comfort when we're afraid. This is a theme that runs through the entire Bible. In Psalm 121, for example, David says seven different times that God is watching over you. Who is watching over you? The Lord, the Creator of the whole universe, and the one who has ultimate power over everything. And when is he watching? During the day and during the night. Nothing that happens during the day or night can harm you, because the Lord, your Good Shepherd, is on guard.

When the Good Shepherd is present, his peace is present. Paul says, "The God of peace will be with you." When you read about David in the Bible, you constantly see that the Lord was *with* him. His life was blessed because the Lord was *with* him. He failed, he sinned big, he often blew it, and yet the Lord was *with* him. He grew very weak, and yet the Lord was *with* him. His life was a picture of living faith—a faith that faced trouble and still knew the peace of God because he knew that God was *with* him.

When you're afraid, remember your God is guarding you with his peace.

Take with You: What do you think it means that God's peace is with you? Where do you see God's presence in your life, or even this last week?

APRIL 16

Stand therefore, having fastened on the belt of truth.
—Ephesians 6:14a

Before Paul talks about spiritual warfare, he starts with the topic of truth. The truth that is in Jesus, which Paul has been speaking about throughout Ephesians, is beyond our imagination or experience. No one could have made this up. It's too good to be true—Christ died for sinners! Christ is raised to life by the power of God. We have life in him. We are raised with him. God lives with his people. Most important to the book of Ephesians is the truth of who Jesus is, and it is this truth that holds everything together.

We wrap ourselves in Christ. Just like a belt holds us together, so the truth of who Christ is and his saving work hold us together. This Christ who was crushed and humbled to the point of death, even death on a cross, has triumphed over sin, death, and the grave. The belt of truth must come first. If Christ is not real and he was not raised, then our faith is pointless. We are still in our sins, and the darkness wins. But if Christ is real and his story is true, then all the old rules and rulers are overthrown. Death and darkness lose. All that is wrong now will one day become untrue. Christ is true. And by speaking truth in love, we become more like him.

Take with You: How can the truth of who Jesus is comfort and help you today? How might you speak the truth in love to those around you?

APRIL 17

Stand therefore . . . having put on the breastplate of righteousness. —Ephesians 6:14

For at one time you were darkness, but now you are light in the Lord. Walk as children of light (for the fruit of light is found in all that is good and right and true), and try to discern what is pleasing to the Lord. —Ephesians 5:8–10

If you think about a breastplate, you might think it's only defensive and protective. And it's true; the righteousness of Christ does protect us. Because Christ's righteousness is now ours, we are protected from the death that we deserve for our sins. But in Ephesians, Paul also wants us to see Christ's righteousness in action. He is describing the goodness, love, faith, and humility that Jesus lived while he was on earth. The same righteousness that Jesus gave to us we can now show others by how we treat them. It protects us because it's the opposite of hate and pride and unbelief—which hurts us and others.

Throughout Ephesians, Paul calls us to the simple beauty of righteousness. "Walk as children of light (for the fruit of light is found in all that is good and right and true), and try to discern what is pleasing to the Lord" (Ephesians 5:8–10). *Righteousness is the way to stand up to all that is hurtful and false. Christ's battle strategy is to do what is right and good, and to say what is true and helpful.*

Take with You: Walking as children of light means the righteousness of Christ is ours. Think about one way today that you can do what is right and good and say what is true and helpful.

APRIL 18

He restores my soul. He leads me in paths of righteousness for his name's sake. —Psalm 23:3

What is your hope? I'm talking about your hope that it's all going to turn out okay in the end. The Bible is clear: He who began a good work in you will complete it (Philippians 1:6). Jesus came. God sent his only Son. How does that give you a hope that can never be broken?

In Psalm 25:7, David talks about his sins: "Remember not the sins of my youth or my transgressions; according to your steadfast love remember me, for the sake of your goodness, O Lord!"

It's a phrase we all know: "for your name's sake." God is at work because of who he is. You receive it like a gift. God is acting to complete the work because of who he is.

We see those four words again in Psalm 25:11: "For your name's sake, O Lord, pardon my guilt, for it is great."

These words so clearly show our dependence on God's grace—complete dependence on something other than ourselves. Why does David have hope? "For your name's sake."

You could say it this way: "Lord, when you think of me, think of yourself." When you remember me, remember who you are. When you think about my sinfulness and my failings, remember your grace. You are good, compassionate, faithful, loving, kind, and forgiving. Our forgiveness is all based on the fact that God is true to who he is. That is the deepest root of any confidence we have.

Take with You: God forgives you because that is who he is. How does that comfort you and give you more confidence to be honest with him about your sins?

APRIL 19

Therefore let anyone who thinks that he stands take heed lest he fall. No temptation has overtaken you that is not common to man. God is faithful, and he will not let you be tempted beyond your ability, but with the temptation he will also provide the way of escape, that you may be able to endure it. —1 Corinthians 10:12–13

As a Christian, you know you have all the same weaknesses and struggles as the rest of the people in your life. You, like me, struggle with pride. You, like me, struggle to be generous. You, like me, struggle with the fear of man, worrying what others think. It looks different for each of us, but pride, fear of man, love of pleasure—this is human nature 101, isn't it? You and I deal with all the same kinds of sufferings, to different degrees. People may treat you wrongly, there's human weakness and death, hard things and ways you're tempted, and voices in the culture that try to lead you away from the true God. These struggles are common to all of us.

Because we all face the same things, we can have gentleness toward others. We're all in the same boat. We're all in need of grace. Bible passages like Hebrews 4 and 5 tell about how Jesus, who was without sin, became a human, cried out to God and needed God to be his Savior, and trusted his Father even in the face of death. So he can help us, and we can help one another.

Take with You: Think about one temptation you face. How does knowing Jesus faced a similar temptation help you say no to what's wrong and obey God?

APRIL 20

And whatever you do, in word or deed, do everything in the name of the Lord Jesus, giving thanks to God the Father through him.
—Colossians 3:17

Have you ever realized that the events of your life actually serve the purpose of glorifying God? *As Jesus changes you, you start to understand all the events of your life—whether it's a small thing or a big hardship—as a chance to know and love the Lord more.* You can also learn how to care for someone else in a difficult situation because that's exactly how the living God in Christ cared for you. So even the way you respond to a small disagreement with a friend can help you know how to care for others going through really hard things.

Father, please help us. We don't pay attention to how you use even the little things to grow us. Sometimes we see, as though our head bobs above the ocean. And then we sink again for a long time. Please help us float, make us see how you're working. Help us to follow you, who called us out of darkness into light. Help us see the ways you are changing us so we would become people who share your light in a dark world, instead of acting as though we are lost in the darkness. Forgive us, your people. Make us beautiful. Help us to keep following you. Amen.

Take with You: Think about a time from last week where you were annoyed about a small thing. How do you think the Lord might be using that to grow you in patience, love, or another fruit of the Spirit?

APRIL 21

"Be merciful, even as your Father is merciful." —Luke 6:36

Goodness and steadfast love walked among us, took on flesh, was tempted as we are yet without sin, and felt the hardships we face. He's gentle with those who don't know any better and with those who rebel against him on purpose.

Such love is a part of God's character that we can also grow in. He commands us to learn to be patient and kind. We are often impatient and unkind. Yet in coming to us and making us look more like Jesus, the Holy Spirit will make us patient and kind. He will teach us to be "in it for good" with other people, amid the ups and downs. This is the lifelong goal for any Christian.

This is the Lord's heart: "The Lord, the Lord, a God merciful and gracious, slow to anger [in the Greek, "patient"], and abounding in steadfast love and faithfulness, keeping steadfast love for thousands, forgiving iniquity and transgression and sin" (Exodus 34:6–7). He's in it for good with all who believe that this great gift is God himself, our greatest need, the goal of our transformation.

When the Lord revealed his glory and goodness, he chose to reveal parts of his character we can imitate. He could have mentioned that he was all-knowing, all-powerful, eternal—things infinitely beyond us creatures. But he chose to reveal his mercy, which we can experience and grasp, by grace. We, too, learn to become merciful and gracious, slow to anger, abounding in steadfast love and faithfulness, and forgiving.

Take with You: Anything God calls us to do, he has done first! Consider how gracious God is to invite us to become more like him. How does this truth encourage you?

APRIL 22

O LORD, you have searched me and known me!
You know when I sit down and when I rise up;
you discern my thoughts from afar.
You search out my path and my lying down
and are acquainted with all my ways. —Psalm 139:1–3

The Psalms show how to have a personal relationship with God: honesty, gratitude, confusion, crying out, hope, trust, and the rest. But what do all these things mean? Consider with me the following wonderful truths.

God watches you and watches over you. He sees everything, inside and out. The Christian life can be lived out in the open, without hiding from him. God also protects and looks out for his children. You're never out of sight of the One who loves you with a steadfast love.

God's hand is involved in everything. God is present in every trouble. There are no accidents in the lives of God's children. He's up to something good. God's providence means that his guiding hand is over everything.

God's voice speaks to you in everything. The Holy Spirit is the author of the Bible, and the Bible speaks to all of life. Jesus himself lived by the Bible, so we as Christians must live by it too. To be a Christian is to be a sheep who hears Jesus's voice, which means that we hear the Bible.

God pours out his love in your heart through the Holy Spirit. He makes you understand the message of grace in Jesus. The Spirit's power makes the Spirit's message a joy to our hearts.

Take with You: To see and know God's redemptive love is something worth shouting about. Think of someone you can share God's amazing love with today.

APRIL 23

Refrain from anger, and forsake wrath!
Fret not yourself; it tends only to evil. —Psalm 37:8

To be made new means dying to what is old. To be made new means waking up to new life. We could say it this way: You and I must be made new with how we handle our anger. We must learn to stop complaining, arguing, and being unforgiving and unkind. To do that, we need the grace of Christ—and Christ freely gives himself to us when we're needy. Because it's normal for us to get angry and go back to our old ways of doing things, we need the Lord's work to change us. The Christian life begins when we wake up to new life, and it continues with a daily process of change. It will continue until you see Jesus face-to-face. You and I are in process.

I know many people whose anger has been completely transformed. Each of them shows us that God is actively working through his grace. And each of them shows us the perseverance of humility. It takes courage. You must honestly and patiently fight your anger. You must choose to become a different kind of person. You must keep growing over a lifetime. *No one is perfect in this life. But each of us can grow. When you make progress in fighting your anger, that's worth more than any amount of money: "nothing you desire can compare" (Proverbs 3:13–15).*

The goal is to keep changing in the right direction.

Take with You: What is one way you can say no to your anger (or another sin) today and say yes to God instead? Remember, God loves you and is committed to changing you over your lifetime.

APRIL 24

"But I say to you who hear, Love your enemies, do good to those who hate you, bless those who curse you, pray for those who abuse you."

"If you love those who love you, what benefit is that to you? For even sinners love those who love them." —Luke 6:27–28, 32

It's easy to hear "Love your enemies, do good to those who hate you," without it really impacting you. It's easy to ignore what Jesus says, as if he doesn't really mean it, as if he's not in touch with reality. Does Jesus hope that people can "just be nicer to each other"? Is Jesus unaware that this sounds like "Let people walk all over you"? Not at all! The love and goodness he is talking about has more courage than cowardice, more strength than weakness. You can't separate what he did for us—his sacrifice—from what he calls us to do, to sacrifice for others. He means what he says.

To do good to someone who does wrong, who has hurt you or others—this is a marvel. It's so much easier to give it right back to others. Someone deserves payback because they did you or others wrong. But you give grace instead.

Anger holds onto a wrong act, points it out, and punishes it. Grace acts generously toward a wrongdoer, rather than giving payback. Anger thinks this way: "I've been wronged, so I will give fair punishment." But grace, like patience and forgiveness, is "unfair." When someone treats you or others badly, you treat them with purposeful kindness.

Take with You: Think of a time recently when someone treated you or another person badly. What would it look like to repay them with kindness instead of sinful anger?

APRIL 25

Trust in him at all times, O people;
pour out your heart before him;
God is a refuge for us. —Psalm 62:8

Search me, O God, and know my heart!
Try me and know my thoughts! —Psalm 139:23

God wants to know what's on your heart. He wants you to need him, to go to him, and to cry out to him about your real problems. He wants you to tell him all about your troubles—your frustrations, your confusion, your embarrassments, and your worries. He wants you to confess to him the sins that drive your sinful fear—the false gods that rule your life. He wants you to ask for his forgiveness for your lack of trust and faith, and for times you've desired his good gifts more than him.

Start with total honesty and say, "Lord, I don't understand. Help me to understand you." Admit to him that although you can say you believe he's in control, you are still anxious and desire to be in control. Ask God to take what you say you believe and teach you how to live that out every day. God will use your honest confession to build a relationship with him that will give you true and lasting peace. Your growing and deepening relationship with God is what will transform your fearful thoughts into humble faith and trust.

Take with You: Practice pouring out your heart to God. Tell him everything you've been thinking this last day or week—be honest with him about your frustrations, sadness, or worries.

APRIL 26

"The secret things belong to the LORD our God, but the things that are revealed belong to us and to our children forever, that we may do all the words of this law." —Deuteronomy 29:29

The things God has revealed to us are for us—and they are relevant for every generation. The Bible isn't just about ideas that aren't connected to life. The Bible tells us a lot about what people are like and our relationship to God. The Bible teaches us who God is, and it also tells us how God sees us, cares for us, and works in us. This truth means many things. Here's one thing worth taking to heart and thinking about long and hard: *Anything God reveals about himself, whether in his words or actions, at the same time reveals something about us.*

Here are some simple examples:

- God makes and provides for everything that exists. This means you and I depend on him for life, whether we recognize it or not.
- God clearly sees and fairly judges everything we do. This means that whatever you want, fear, think, do, feel, or say matters, and you're accountable for it. And it means we have a problem. We often wander into sin that destroys us.
- God is merciful. This means we need grace and gifts of many kinds—rescue, forgiveness, protection, strength, help, hope, wisdom, a new heart, a new life. Every promise and gift of God is reflected in Christ.

To be a human being is to live, move, and exist under his care, under his eye, and in need of his grace.

Take with You: Can you think of another example in the Bible of how what God says about himself also says something about us?

APRIL 27

The steadfast love of the LORD never ceases;
his mercies never come to an end; they are new every morning;
great is your faithfulness. —Lamentations 3:22–23

Learning how to live well is the most complicated skill we can imagine. It's the work of a lifetime. But isn't it odd that a musician doesn't bring the same intentional learning, emotion, and skill-building into her personal life as she does to playing violin? And isn't it odd that a man who knows how much learning, experience, observation, trial and error, and heart go into crafting fine furniture will not intentionally battle his sin? And isn't it odd that a Christian would assume that a simple theological answer and a quick fix of behavior is enough to live the Christian life, when it's obvious that our struggle with failures, mistakes, pain, and weakness will not totally disappear during this life?

We are meant to stop and think purposefully. Wisdom is a way of seeing and understanding the world, ourselves, other people, and the Lord God.

We are meant to continue to grow our skills. Wisdom is a way of engaging the world, ourselves, others, and the Lord. We are meant to seek out mentors, role models, and wise friends. Whoever walks with the wise becomes wise.

We are meant to learn how to confess and grow from failures. What hides in the dark grows darker; what comes to the light becomes bright as day. We are meant to face suffering instead of ignoring it or running away. Mercies are new every morning because mercies are needed.

Take with You: Consider how you can live purposefully. Who is one person you can talk to about how to grow in living the Christian life well?

APRIL 28

Fear not, for I am with you;
be not dismayed, for I am your God;
I will strengthen you, I will help you,
I will uphold you with my righteous right hand. —Isaiah 41:10

Why do you feel afraid? There are often two reasons, and they're connected. The first reason is true no matter what you're experiencing. You live in a world that you cannot control. You face things that are threatening. You are weak and vulnerable. The second reason you feel afraid is because your heart tells you that in this world of dangers, threats, and things you can't control, you are all alone. That second reason is a lie.

God tells us all throughout Scripture to not be afraid. He says this with comfort and a promise of his presence with us: "Don't be afraid; I'm with you. I'm here. I will never leave. I began a good work, and I won't give up on you. I am yours. You are not alone."

God speaks directly to the heart of our fear with the reality of his presence. Your heart is speaking half-truth. We are indeed in a very vulnerable world. But think twice about the claim that you're all alone to face it, and you'll find that to be a lie. There's Someone who is here, and he will never leave. You have God's past, present, and future grace. You're not alone.

Take with You: What is one thing you're afraid of today? How does God's presence with you change your experience of fear?

APRIL 29

The LORD your God is in your midst,
a mighty one who will save;
he will rejoice over you with gladness;
he will quiet you by his love;
he will exult over you with loud singing. —Zephaniah 3:17

All relationships have a purpose. God himself is purposeful in his relationships. *His relationship with you did not happen by accident—it happened on purpose. He went after you to make you his own.* It is an on-purpose relationship with you. At the beginning of Philippians, Paul reminds us that he who began a good work in you will bring it to completion on the day of Christ Jesus (Philippians 1:6). This shows an intentional beginning, middle, and end to his work in you. This is a powerful reminder that you are not alone, no matter what's happening.

What do you need the most? You need strength from outside yourself, his ear to listen to you when you're in need—someone who will listen when you cry to him. You need protection and wisdom and help. To this end, you're loved by the God of creation, the God of redemption, the God who made all things, and the God who redeems all things—the Father who's compassionate toward his children, the Word of God who became a man for us, full of grace and truth.

God knows each of us by name. He knows us by heart, and his thoughts toward every single person are more than the grains of sand on the seashore. As you grow in this understanding, you begin to know you aren't alone.

Take with You: Do you ever feel alone? How does the truth from Zephaniah 3:17 change your experience of feeling alone?

APRIL 30

Be not far from me,
for trouble is near,
and there is none to help. —Psalm 22:11

You may know that as a child of God, you are not alone. But you often feel alone. So much of human life can feel lonely or overwhelming. You may feel alone because of particular sins or different forms of suffering. You can let other people into your struggles, but they can only come halfway at best.

God has designed his universe so that only he can go all the way into your experience. Only God can know you fully and actually know what you're experiencing. That's what it means that you aren't alone.

How do you find your way from feeling alone to not alone? Psalm 22 shows us Jesus's experience of being alone as he was dying. As we read this psalm, we are watching someone else deal with that aloneness. We are watching Christ deal with it. He has been there. He is one of us.

It's so encouraging to see that this psalm is Jesus's honest process of wrestling between what he knows of God's faithfulness and the suffering he is experiencing. The turn of the psalm comes in verse 21, when he knows God is helping him. The psalm then moves to worship as the cry for help has been answered with God's care. *Jesus shows us how to move from alone to not alone—holding onto the promises of a loving and faithful God and waiting to see how he will meet you.*

Take with You: Read Psalm 22, telling God what you're experiencing. Then read it again and imagine Jesus praying these same words. Are you encouraged that Jesus knows what you are experiencing?

MAY 1

Remember your mercy, O Lord, and your steadfast love,
for they have been from of old.
Remember not the sins of my youth or my transgressions;
according to your steadfast love remember me
for the sake of your goodness, O Lord! —Psalm 25:6–7

It's so important to know what to expect of the change process known as sanctification. Until our last day, we will struggle. It won't be completely gone until we see Jesus face-to-face, when tears are wiped away and we are made like him.

How do you think about failure? You can expect to see both growth in your life, as well as moments of battling sin. You can be both extremely encouraged about your growth, while still always being aware of the fight with darkness.

The nature of the growth process is that over time you see your repentance more quickly. You have more self-awareness, and you grow in appreciating God's grace and your need for his power and promises. You learn to copy the psalmist when you cry out to God, "You are a God of steadfast love. When you remember my sin, remember your mercy."

You can have joy, even in the midst of continuing imperfection, not just by fighting sin well, but by growing in doing good. Everyone who makes any progress with persistent sin starts to care for other people. They discover that they have something to give away. With the mercy you have received in your troubles, you are able to comfort those in any trouble (2 Corinthians 1:4).

Take with You: What is one way you want God to change you—whether it's stopping a bad behavior, growing in loving others, or repenting more quickly? Ask him to help you grow today.

MAY 2

For the word of God is living and active, sharper than any two-edged sword, piercing to the division of soul and of spirit, of joints and of marrow, and discerning the thoughts and intentions of the heart. —Hebrews 4:12

Why do people do what they do? The Lord God has a lot to say about this. He denies other explanations we have by showing us that our motivation has to do with him. Scripture searches out the "thoughts and intentions of the heart," and the Searcher of hearts is the judge of what he sees in us (Hebrews 4:12).

Good questions help us see the patterns of a person's motivation. They help people identify the ungodly masters in their hearts. Good questions reveal "functional gods"—what or who actually controls our actions, thoughts, emotions, and attitudes. Think about when you become anxious, distracted, and filled with fear. As worry tightens its hold on your soul, perhaps you try to escape to some quick fix: eat food, watch TV, go shopping, play a game. Or perhaps you try to do something to take control: do homework all night, get mad, text your friends to support your anger. Why is all this going on?

You say God is your rock and refuge, a very present help in whatever troubles you face. You say you worship, trust, love, and obey him. *But in that moment—hour, day, or season—of anxiety, escape, or seeking to control, you live as if you need to control all things. But grace opens our eyes, cleanses us, and turns us back to our Lord.*

Take with You: What do you usually do when you get anxious? How could you turn to the Lord instead?

MAY 3

If your law had not been my delight,
I would have perished in my affliction. —Psalm 119:92

Psalm 119 has it all. It helps readers connect love and need to truth, and it helps our prayers connect truth to our need. This psalm is spoken to the God who speaks and acts. Listen to these statements and consider how they impact your life:

- You answered me (v. 26).
- The earth is full of your steadfast love (v. 64).
- You are good and do good (v. 68).
- Your rules are righteous and in faithfulness you have afflicted me (v. 75).
- I am yours (v. 94).
- You are my hiding place and my shield (v. 114).

This psalm tells you how the Lord sees suffering, what it means, and how he sees you. It shows that life has hardship, pain, difficulty, and suffering. As the psalmist talks to God, you see an example of thinking, feeling, reacting, and responding to suffering. He gets specific with God about what he's going through and where he's tempted. He asks God for what he needs. There's a constant desire for God to do things. He's asking for God to teach him, open his eyes, reawaken him. He knows he needs someone outside of himself to help him. *He tells God again that he is committed to him, and you see the joy that comes as a result: "I am your servant" (v. 125). This is the direction he will keep going toward, even if he gets overwhelmed by sin and suffering.*

Take with You: What would it look like to be specific with God about what you are facing today and to know his mercy toward you?

MAY 4

He does not deal with us according to our sins,
nor repay us according to our iniquities. —Psalm 103:10

Mercy has something in common with anger. Mercy says that what is wrong matters. Evil is horrible, and it matters.

Mercy does something about what's wrong. It's not passive, nor is it happy about what's going on. However, the biggest theme of mercy is love, not hatred. Mercy sees what's wrong and does something about it.

Mercy shows love in the midst of something that's wrong. Here are four different aspects of what mercy looks like:

1. *It's slow to anger.* Patience is willing to do something about wrong over time. When you are truly patient, you often see the wrong more clearly, because you do not immediately react with your own wrong. It's an act of courage, a choice to be in it for the long haul with something that needs to be fixed.
2. *It's forgiving.* It's a holy "unfairness" that sees the wrong for what it is but doesn't give back what it deserves. Forgiveness sees the wrong and then lets it go.
3. *It's generous.* Doing good to someone who has done wrong. Loving your enemies. Not returning evil for evil.
4. *It confronts evil.* It attacks the problem with constructive conflict, rescues victims, and calls wrongdoers out. It's an act of love to bring about what's good and beautiful.

How do you learn to do this? You learn because Jesus has already treated you this way, with patience, forgiveness, generosity, and a willingness to engage with what is wrong in your life.

Take with You: Think about the four aspects of mercy above. Who is one person you can show mercy toward today, demonstrating God's love?

MAY 5

So teach us to number our days
that we may get a heart of wisdom. —Psalm 90:12

Psalm 90 is an invitation for us to think about the fact that we are going to die. The last six verses are a request to God for his love and kindness to lead to something permanent: "Establish the work of our hands" (v. 17). Make what we do last, not just fly away like the mist.

What lasts? What holds up? The call to die to our sinfulness each day is really the same as asking yourself this question. One of the ways you learn to both die well and live well is that you fight your sin. This battle does not end until you see Jesus face-to-face and are made like him.

At the end of our lives, there are things that last. *Ask any Christ follower who has a near-death experience and they will tell you that nothing is as important in those moments of clarity as these two unfading purposes: love for God and love for people.* All the clutter and all the distraction goes away, and what's left is a God to know, love, adore, seek, and trust—and people to love well.

For we who are in Christ, what we do is not useless (1 Corinthians 15:58). Everything we do for the Lord will last. As you learn this perspective, you can then start to treat other people in ways that help them understand what really lasts.

Take with You: What do you think about the fact that everything good you do matters and will last into eternity?

MAY 6

Now may the God of peace . . . equip you with everything good that you may do his will, working in us that which is pleasing in his sight, through Jesus Christ, to whom be glory forever and ever. Amen.
—Hebrews 13:20–21

Think about the good things God works to create in us. His plans are extreme, radical, and beyond all you can ask or even imagine!

But then again, the Holy Spirit seems to create a life beyond what we expect with simple, ordinary things. His view of what's important makes "awesome" seem more ordinary (while being the furthest thing from boring). He's forming in you things that are good for the long haul. Good for times when you're lonely or in pain. Good for days, months, or years of perplexity and struggle. Good for the small deaths of old age and dying. Good for helping others going through the same troubles. He's forming what is good for living life well, wisely, and on purpose.

We long for drama and action, but right now, we need grace to carry us through all that happens in life until the Day when the dramatic finally happens once and for all.

Consider this list of "ordinary" graces that are given meaning with the unexpectant way of God. Ponder mercy, patience, gratitude, loyalty, honesty, helping others, relying on others, making peace, endurance, humility, love.

None of these sets off fireworks amid the routines and ordinary moments of life. But these are worth more than anything else you could desire. Jesus lived out these graces. He's making you into his image.

Take with You: What is one way God is growing you that seems ordinary or slow? How can you see it differently?

MAY 7

To you, O Lord, I call;
my rock, be not deaf to me,
lest, if you be silent to me,
I become like those who go down to the pit. —Psalm 28:1

In prayer, we connect our need with the promises of God. Prayer happens when our need and God's promises meet. We need wisdom, strength in hardship, and understanding every day. We need courage, humility, hope, faith, and love. We need forgiveness daily. We need the presence of God himself in our lives. We need him to provide for us, both physically and spiritually. We need hope to know the King will come. We need friendship that won't end.

These needs are met in who God is—his character and his nature. Deuteronomy 31:8 says, "It is the Lord who . . . will be with you; he will not leave you or forsake you. Do not fear or be dismayed." Your need for courage, for God's presence, and for hope are answered by who God is.

Faith has two sides. One side of faith is need. The other side of faith is gratitude. You have reason for both joy and heartache in life. So be honest about both in your prayers.

Be specific and talk straight to God. I often use the Psalms to guide my prayers. The Psalms are general so you can put your life experience into them. *You want to have an honest, real conversation about where you really are and who God really is. When this conversation happens, redemption explodes into our lives.*

Take with You: Practice praying through a psalm. Tell God about your need, and then remember one promise God has made that speaks to that need.

MAY 8

Because he inclined his ear to me,
therefore I will call on him as long as I live. —Psalm 116:2

Prayers in Scripture are honest, relatable, and grace filled. As we listen, we learn to talk honestly about what's good or bad about us. We learn to speak of hard and happy things in our lives. We learn to cry out where we need help and sing about how we're grateful. Our prayers can tell of our care and concern for others—"I pray that your love will abound more and more with knowledge and all discernment" (Philippians 1:9, author's paraphrase).

God teaches us to have meaningful conversations with each other. The way we talk with him directly relates to how we talk with each other. Ephesians 4:15 says we grow up in Christ by lovingly speaking truth with each other. How do we encourage each other in the face of hardship and sin's lies? How do we talk about what matters in a way that makes a difference?

Listen in to how Scripture shows us what it's like to talk with God. Then talk about the same kinds of things with other people.

Our Father teaches us to live in reality, and you can't do that without seeing the good and hard things, remembering your Lord in the midst of it. When you face the hard things, you can be honest about your need. When you receive the good things, you can tell God your joy and thanks. As you learn to pray about what matters, you also learn to talk with other people about what matters.

Take with You: Choose a psalm and read it out loud. This is God's gift to you, helping you start a conversation with him!

MAY 9

Blessed be the LORD,
for he has wondrously shown his steadfast love to me
when I was in a besieged city.

Be strong, and let your heart take courage,
all you who wait for the LORD! —Psalm 31:21, 24

We tend to think suffering is brief and not a condition. We think of it as seasonal, where life is miserable for a few weeks and then we're fine. But the reality is that human life includes long-lasting suffering. It's a gift from God that some of our suffering is seasonal and momentary, but in the bigger picture, we live in a broken world with broken bodies that are dying.

This reality should be fundamental to our understanding of suffering. Jesus did not just come to relieve the little aches and pains of life; he came to deal with our broken condition and give us hope. Those who deal with long-lasting suffering can live with an honesty about what life is and who they are and who Jesus is—broken humans can shine with the simplicity of faith.

When hard things happen, what do you live for? Hardship can be used by God to strengthen faith, or it can break people. *You can be strong and let your heart take courage by hoping in the Lord. This is where the peace of God begins to weigh more than the suffering.* Jesus Christ, the Holy Spirit, the promise of peace, and the presence of our Father aren't just religious ideas. If we seek him, we find him, and he brings comfort and joy.

Take with You: Jesus is our hope in suffering because he knows what it's like. He experienced it too. We are never alone!

MAY 10

"But I say to you who hear, Love your enemies,
do good to those who hate you, bless those who curse you,
pray for those who abuse you." —Luke 6:27–28

Godly anger does not need to "win." It does not have to successfully bring the wrong to justice. Godly anger's purpose is for the glory of God and the well-being of God's people. Godly anger is good for everyone. So when you see evil that's unrepented of, when your best efforts seem to have had no good or lasting effect, you don't have to become angrier. You can instead become more honest.

On the inside, mercy works to soften your heart. Jesus wants you to pray for the other person's well-being, including their repentance. On the outside, you are called to keep showing acts of undeserved kindness: "If your enemy is hungry, feed him; if he is thirsty, give him something to drink" (Romans 12:20). Also, on the outside, you may be called to join with others to give consequences to wrong behavior: telling a teacher or parent that someone bullied, tricked, lied, or hurt you or another person. Taking part in such things is serious and necessary. They set limits on our own personal efforts to help people. When others can help, they are a great comfort and good. It's often a great relief for a person who's facing persistent evil to know that others are also taking responsibility for making it right. It reduces the temptation to take matters into your own hand.

> **Take with You:** The next time you feel angry with someone, remember how you can follow Jesus in showing godly anger instead of sinful anger.

MAY 11

For we walk by faith, not by sight. —2 Corinthians 5:7

Now faith is the assurance of things hoped for, the conviction of things not seen. —Hebrews 11:1

Many people view faith as a feeling of trust, confidence, peacefulness, contentment, or happiness. Many people view prayer as an experience of certain religious emotions like excitement or familiar comfort. The Psalms illustrate how faith talks to God and can express itself in many different feelings, some pleasant, some unpleasant. And we should never forget that we could feel peaceful or excited or confident about false things too. *The state of your emotions does not accurately show whether you are actually depending on God.*

Faith means you live as though what God says is true. God does give more grace to the humble. Humble yourself. God does oppose the proud. Hold up your hands and surrender. He truly forgives those who open their eyes to their sins. Stop, open your eyes, and confess. He sealed his promise in the blood of Jesus. Count on it. He actually gives the Holy Spirit to his children who ask. Ask. "If any of you lacks wisdom, let him ask God, who gives generously to all without reproach, and it will be given him" (James 1:5). Ask unafraid, knowing your need. "You do not have, because you do not ask. You ask and do not receive, because you ask . . . to spend it on your passions" (James 4:2–3). Ask, repenting of your wrong desires. God himself is the One who grows fruit in you.

Take with You: He gives wisdom to follow in the way of Jesus Christ. What is one way you can walk by faith today, trusting in God and not in what you are feeling?

MAY 12

I therefore, a prisoner for the Lord, urge you to walk in a manner worthy of the calling to which you have been called, with all humility and gentleness, with patience, bearing with one another in love, eager to maintain the unity of the Spirit in the bond of peace.
—Ephesians 4:1–3

The Lord calls you to please him by humility, patience, honesty, generosity, and kindness to others. This calling is for all of us, and it doesn't matter what your role is. It creates an attitude of thinking about others that impacts every single relationship. *We are one with each other and we are equals before God, whether we've been Christians for years or days, are wealthy or poor, are competent adults or helpless infants. We live on level ground before God who doesn't prefer any person over another.* Differences of ability, power, wealth, intelligence, popularity, sex, age, and ethnicity vanish.

All of Ephesians 1:1–5:20 and 6:10–24 applies always, to every Christian, in every relationship. You have been given God's grace and are commanded by your Lord Jesus to give grace to others. Whether you are male or female, child or parent, student or teacher, you live in a community: one church, members of one body, fellow citizens, neighbors, God's household, brothers and sisters to one another. You are a *we*. So you are called to be patient and work for the good of every relationship and every interaction with others. No superiority, no double standard, no favoritism.

Take with You: Where are you tempted to treat others as less valuable, or where have they treated you this way? Isn't it amazing that God views all of us the same, as his beloved children?

MAY 13

For you did not receive the spirit of slavery to fall back into fear, but you have received the Spirit of adoption as sons, by whom we cry, "Abba! Father!" —Romans 8:15

If your father is demanding, harsh, absent, or selfish, you may have struggled to see God as a loving Father. Do you need to first experience a good human relationship for "God is my Father" to be an encouraging reality? No, this isn't true. It denies the power and truth of God's Word and the Holy Spirit. It's true that people with poor human parents often think the same is true for God.

But think about this: None of the words God uses to describe himself have wonderful parallels in our experiences. Sinful human fathers are not the only ones who misrepresent God. Does your experience of politicians, leaders, or teachers keep you from knowing God as King and Judge? It doesn't need to. Think about pastors you've known, God's shepherds. Some people can point with joy to a godly pastor in their lives. But others grew up under false teachers, men who were greedy, willful, arrogant, and selfish. Does this mean you can't be comforted knowing the Lord is a shepherd until you have a positive experience of knowing a godly pastor? Ezekiel 34 (and then John 10) argues the opposite. *God comforts us with truth about who he is even when people have harmed us. The Holy Spirit is more powerful than broken experiences.*

Take with You: Can you think of one person in your life who has misrepresented God to you? Ask God to show you how he is not like that person. He is full of love for you.

MAY 14

"For the Lord disciplines the one he loves, and chastises every son whom he receives." —Hebrews 12:6

God's love is active. He decided to love you when he could have justly condemned you. He's close to you. He's merciful, not simply putting up with your sins. He who hates sin goes after sinners and calls them by name. God is so committed to forgiving and changing you that he sent Jesus to die for you. He welcomes those who know they need him, the poor in spirit, with a shout and a feast. God is infinitely patient and doesn't stop working as he comes into your life.

God's love actively works for your good. God's love is full of blood, sweat, tears, and cries. He suffered for you. He fights for you, defending the suffering. He challenges you. He pursues you in power and gentleness so that he can change you. He's jealous, which means he cares deeply about who or what you love, even though your heart is prone to wander. He's not detached or indifferent. His empathy speaks words of truth to set you free from sin. He will discipline you as proof that he loves you. He himself comes to live in you, pouring out his Holy Spirit in your heart, so that you know him. His love includes power and energy. *God's love has hate in it: hate for evil, whether done to you or by you. God's love demands that you respond: believe, trust, obey, give thanks with a joyful heart, work out your salvation with fear, delight in the Lord.*

Take with You: God's discipline is full of love. What is one way you have recently seen God's love working for your good?

MAY 15

"Man does not live by bread alone, but man lives by every word that comes from the mouth of the LORD." —Deuteronomy 8:3

As you study God's Word, look for promises, ideas, or templates for experience. These passages are often invitations to apply the Bible to your own life.

Core promises and self-revelations of God. Exodus 34:6–7, Numbers 6:24–26, and Deuteronomy 31:6 tell us about God's foundational promises that appear in different ways throughout the rest of the Bible. Pay attention to what God says about who he is, what he's like, his purposes, and his promises. See how all these words are seen most clearly in Jesus Christ.

The joys and sorrows of many psalms. Think about how the Psalms speak broadly to all of us. They don't mention specific details so we can relate to them. We are given a template that can apply to any one of us.

The call of commands. In matters of obedience, the Bible often proclaims a general truth and doesn't mention any of the ways it could play out. In these places, the Bible speaks in large categories, speaking to countless different experiences, situations, and actions. Figuring out what it means in your specific situation isn't always clear, but the application process follows a straight line.

Stories explained. A story shows different aspects of relationship and experience that are hard to explain in other ways. Often a sentence or story speaks repeatedly and deeply to a person. *You are changed when you know that it matters when you take the time to listen, to think, to take to heart.*

Take with You: God is at work with bigger plans. Isn't it amazing that Scripture is applicable to our lives, because it tells us something about God?

MAY 16

This is my comfort in my affliction,
that your promise gives me life. —Psalm 119:50

What do you need to hear when life is hard and you're hurting? This truth: Jesus is a sympathetic friend, Savior, and someone who knows suffering. He has walked a hard road. He has felt his own sorrow and crushing pain (Isaiah 53). He understands. He is compassionate toward you. By the comfort of his presence and sympathy, he intends to draw you out and draw you to himself.

I encourage you to go to him and speak to him. There is something about our ability to find words to describe what we're experiencing that makes a true difference. *A wise Christian of many centuries ago said, "To open one's heart to one's friend—it doubles our joys and cuts our griefs in half."* I have found this to be true. There's something about speaking to someone who truly cares about you that soothes your wounds.

May you cry out to our God. He calls you his friend. He deeply cares for you. He is your Savior. Trust him. He has walked down this road before you. He promises to walk with you in this.

And I might say one more thing. Suffering must be walked through one step at a time. Be honest. Don't take any shortcuts. Let each day's trouble be sufficient for that day; don't go looking ahead for tomorrow's troubles. Look for your Father. If you look for him, you will find him.

Take with You: Take some time to tell God what you are experiencing today. He cares for you and promises to always be with you.

MAY 17

"And if anyone gives even a cup of cold water to one of these little ones who is my disciple, truly I tell you, that person will certainly not lose their reward." —Matthew 10:42 NIV

Do you ever just go through the motions with your faith? Let me share something I've found that has woken up my own sleepiness in faith. I often look at myself in light of the seven deadly sins. The one that always gets me is sloth or laziness. Laziness doesn't just mean you're just sitting around watching TV all day. It also means indifference. You don't care. It comes up a lot in our modern culture; we question whether or not anything really matters.

Everything actually does matter. The tiniest things we do, the most careless words we say, the smallest act of kindness toward another person—all these things actually count. From God's perspective, there's nothing we do that's outside his concern or gaze.

Think of how Jesus chose to focus on giving a glass of cold water to somebody who's thirsty. He thought that spotting someone else and serving them in some small way really, really mattered. Someone else's need matters to the point that you put your own desires aside.

Every choice, thought, word, action, and attitude really, truly matters. As you awaken to that, you awaken to the fact that you really need help. You're able to say, *"God, I really need you. I need your strength. I need your forgiveness. Give me the grace to care about things that really matter."*

Take with You: What is one way you can hold out a cup of cold water to someone today? Know that Jesus sees your selfless love and values even the smallest step of kindness.

MAY 18

Now may the God of peace himself sanctify you completely, and may your whole spirit and soul and body be kept blameless at the coming of our Lord Jesus Christ. —1 Thessalonians 5:23

God's anger at sin was shown—but for your good. Once and for all, God set you free from ever having to experience his anger against your sins. In steadfast love, he freely offered his innocent Son to receive the anger that guilty sinners deserve. God's anger punishes and destroys, giving our sin what it deserves—but it was taken by Jesus, the Beloved Lamb, the Savior of sinners. Because he loves us, he offers himself; the way of our salvation is his glory and our joy. God's loving anger, shown in a way that gives us blessing, is the foundation of new life from death: it assures us of true forgiveness. We are made right with God by faith and adopted as his children. *What we deserve, another took because he chose to love us. In this ultimate act of self-giving love, we experience God's anger acting for us instead of against us. In response, we can confidently repent and believe.*

In love, God's anger works to destroy the power of your sin. In steadfast love, he remakes us, not by just letting us sin, but by hating our sin. It's not always pleasant to be called out, feel guilt, and own up. It doesn't feel good. But mercy, encouragement, and a clear conscience feels good. God remakes us over time into love, joy, peace, and wisdom—his own image.

Take with You: Do you ever fear that God can't forgive you? Tell him about the sin that's weighing on your heart. He forgives you and will never stop loving you.

MAY 19

For where jealousy and selfish ambition exist, there will be disorder and every vile practice. But the wisdom from above is first pure, then peaceable, gentle, open to reason, full of mercy and good fruits, impartial and sincere. —James 3:16–17

Anger problems are only one part of the larger problem of fighting with others. To understand and solve anger problems, we must deal with fighting in all its forms. People fight with each other and with God. Sinful anger is just one of the weapons. As sinners, we fight for our own sakes.

Peacemaking is about Christ and how we're renewed in his image. He is the ultimate Peacemaker. *Christ made peace once for all between us and God; he continues to make peace, teaching us to do the same with each other; and he will make peace, finally and forever.*

We could look at many verses, but James 3–4 is the well-known passage that shows us what God thinks about this issue. In James 3:13–4:12, the Holy Spirit tells us the problem and solution: (1) The demanding, self-centered heart will bear the fruit of fighting and argument; (2) God commands our loyalty and destroys his enemies, but he is gracious and generous to people who repent; (3) The wise, humble heart will bear fruit of a life of peacemaking. This is the most accurate, deep explanation of why we fight. It's the most powerful promise of God's help that we've ever been given. James 3–4 shows us that God is always watching us, and he promises to give us grace upon grace.

Take with You: Next time you're fighting with someone, remember God's promise. He doesn't just forgive you for your sin. He wants to help you make peace with others.

MAY 20

What causes quarrels and what causes fights among you? Is it not this, that your passions are at war within you? —James 4:1

Why do you fight? The biblical answer is clear and gets right to the point. You fight for one reason: because you don't get what you want.

Our desires lead to conflict, which reveals something important not just about how we fight with each other but also about how we view God. What we desire can rule our lives and compete with God for total control of your life. This is our biggest problem. James 4:1 says our desires "battle" within us. This doesn't mean our desires battle against us or with each other. They're our desires, and they show who we are.

What's wrong with what I want? The Holy Spirit uses Scripture to show us our hearts, and Scripture makes clear that when our desires rule, they produce sin, not love. God sees what's behind our conflict; he sees the desires that rule us.

What is it that you want that makes you warlike, when Christ's rule in your heart would make you at peace? Answer honestly, and then you will see why you take part in sinful conflict.

James 4:6 makes an incredible promise: God gives grace to the humble. Grace is more and greater than sin. When we admit the truth about where we try to play God, we find amazing grace in Jesus: forgiveness, grace, cleansing, power, and freedom. Every aspect of God's grace is meant to cleanse and transform angry, judgmental, fearful, proud people.

Take with You: Think about a recent fight you had. What did you desire that led you to fight with them? Tell God about this. He forgives you and wants to help you.

MAY 21

Do not be anxious about anything, but in everything by prayer and supplication with thanksgiving let your requests be made known to God. And the peace of God, which surpasses all understanding, will guard your hearts and your minds in Christ Jesus. —Philippians 4:6–7

We have good reasons to be afraid, but we have better reasons to not be afraid. Here are six practical tips for dealing with fear.

1. *Identify your form of fear.* Learn what triggers your fears and how you respond to stress. Does worry make you nervous, frustrated, or want to escape?
2. *Consider your reasons for trusting the Lord.* The Lord is on your side (Romans 8:31). He will remain faithful (1 Corinthians 1:9). He will provide (Philippians 4:19). These are examples of promises that can help you rest in him.
3. *Name your real fears.* What do you worry about? What do you spend a lot of time thinking about?
4. *Identify what keeps you from trusting.* What makes you forget these promises?
5. *Have an honest conversation with God.* Tell him about your worries. Be honest about why you struggle to trust him and ask him for help.
6. *Do what you need to do today.* Each day has enough trouble of its own (Matthew 6:34). Trusting God includes doing what he has called us to do today.

Living your life in this way produces a kind of rest that's both simple and complex. It's not a magic answer, but it's a way to live and manage your fears.

Take with You: Working through the questions above, identify one promise of God's in Scripture that comforts your fears. Take that promise with you today as you do the things God's given you to do.

MAY 22

Be not wise in your own eyes;
fear the LORD, and turn away from evil.
It will be healing to your flesh
and refreshment to your bones. —Proverbs 3:7–8

There's something wrong about our knowledge of ourselves. It's like keys out of tune on a beautiful piano. We may have eagle eyes for the faults of others but be blind to our faults. When our ability to see is clouded, we are wise in our own eyes and don't listen to God. One of the biggest ways Christ changes his people is through lifelong retuning and repairing of the piano, to restore our sight so we can see the world the way it actually is. God is in the business of renewing our consciences.

When you struggle with low self-esteem, the biggest question is, *Whose eyes matter? Who judges me or gets last say in my life? Whose opinion does my life revolve around?* What you think about yourself and what others think about you is a half-truth. There's Someone else whose opinion matters more—God. His opinion matters because when his comes first, the other opinions are put into second place and don't have the most important place in your life. When this priority order is put in place, then you can actually learn from others' opinions or your own opinions of yourself. *An appropriate understanding of yourself only comes from knowing what God thinks of you, the One whose opinion really matters.*

Take with You: Do you ever worry what others think of you, or get discouraged by what you think of yourself? How does knowing what God thinks about you change that?

MAY 23

By this we shall know that we are of the truth and reassure our heart before him; for whenever our heart condemns us, God is greater than our heart, and he knows everything. —1 John 3:19–20

What calms your guilt and keeps you from sinning? Sometimes we try to make up for our own sin and guilt. We try to find friends to say good things about us. We try to go live a good life so we have something to be proud of. We affirm ourselves and tell ourselves we are okay. One of the biggest messages in our culture about how our failures are made better is that we are made right because of our faith in our own goodness.

The message of Christian faith is utterly different from this message. You are made right by faith in the Savior of the world who has loved you and accepted you, has washed you, and will be with you your whole life and finish the good work he started in you. He will have compassion on you as a father has compassion on his children.

Those who are truly free from sin and guilt understand the fear of the Lord—when we rearrange our lives to his opinion and standards. This is the beginning of wisdom. This is where all true peace and self-understanding begins. *You don't find self-esteem by following the wrong standard, but the Lord gives you self-worth when you depend on his standard.*

Take with You: Are you ever tempted to find your worth in what you do? Thank God that he gives us an identity more lasting and trustworthy!

MAY 24

Great is Thy faithfulness
Morning by morning new mercies I see
All I have needed Thy hand hath provided
Great is Thy faithfulness, Lord, unto me
—Thomas Chisholm, "Great Is Thy Faithfulness"

When you're afraid, you can trust your God—he has promised to be gracious, and he showed us this grace at extreme personal cost. God is for you. I know this because he says so, and he does what he says. Your story is still being written, and you can trust him and not be afraid.

Jesus is both patient and urgent with you. Patient means he's committed to you for the long haul. This is good news because you will struggle with sin your whole life. Urgent means there's always something to do today: someone to love, some way to think or seek him, something to repent of, or something to ask others for help with. His patience always has a purpose. His urgency is always full of mercy.

Sin can make you turn inward. *Change makes you look outward. As we change, we listen to God, seek him, grow in love toward him and others.* Every obedience makes us more like him and part of the victory of light over darkness.

Our Father, thank you that you're not ashamed to call us brothers and sisters. We can walk before you in the light of life. It's the story of what Jesus has done, is doing, and will do. Each of our stories is unique and beautiful. Thank you for changing us into beautiful people.

Take with You: What is something you are afraid of? How does the fact that God is with you transform how you view that fear and help you to look outward?

MAY 25

The aim of our charge is love that issues from a pure heart and a good conscience and a sincere faith. —1 Timothy 1:5

Christ's transformational work in our lives moves in two directions at the same time: the vertical (relationship with God) and horizontal (relationship with others). God is always reorienting both our worship of him and our walk with others, our heart motives and the way we live. Paul summarizes the purpose of his ministry in 1 Timothy 1:5. Love describes the transformation of our relationships with others. A pure heart, good conscience, and sincere faith describe the transformation of our relationship with God. An impure heart serves multiple gods. A bad conscience fails to think about life God's way. A hypocritical faith professes, sings, and prays one way, but trusts something else at the end of the day. When our heart, conscience, and faith are restored, it leads us to obey God.

Who or what is your functional god? What do you love, trust, fear, hope, seek, obey, and take refuge in? The Bible—the light-giving Word of the God who sees our hearts—looks beyond behaviors and emotions to show us our true motives, to open our hearts before the One who made us. When we're convicted of the ways we live contrary to the truth, the grace of the gospel can change our motives. *Honest repentance will make the love of Jesus your joy and hope. The grace and power of Jesus Christ changes both motive and fruit.*

Take with You: Where have you failed to follow God's ways? Thank him for his mercy. He convicts us because he loves us and wants to lead us in the way of life!

MAY 26

"You shall love the Lord your God with all your heart and with all your soul and with all your mind." —Matthew 22:37

Human life is relational. This means we will either love God or love something else. We take refuge in God or in something else. We hope in God or in something else. We fear and honor God or something else. Scripture will come to life in new ways as you start to see how we all live before the sight of God. These questions can help you think about how all of life is lived in relation to God:

What do you love? What do you hate? There's no better question for finding out why you do what you do.

What do you pursue? What are your goals and expectations? Where do you put your hopes?

What do you fear? What do you tend to worry about? Where do you find safety, comfort, escape, and pleasure? This is the Psalms' question, digging out your false trusts, the things you run to for comfort instead of the Lord.

What or whom do you trust? Trust describes our relationship with God—or to false gods and lies. Where do you place life-directing, life-anchoring trust instead of in the Lord?

By seeing how our motivation is always related to God, we see that what's wrong with us must have a solution that's also related to God: the grace, peace, power, and presence of Jesus Christ. Living faith in Jesus Christ is the only reasonable motivation, the radical alternative to a thousand forms of false gods.

Take with You: Where are you tempted to turn to value other things more than God? How does his great mercy for you change how you pursue them?

MAY 27

"Beware of practicing your righteousness before other people in order to be seen by them, for then you will have no reward from your Father who is in heaven." —Matthew 6:1

What do you think about God? What does your relationship with him look like, and how do you treat him? How do you treat other people? What do you do when you experience pain and hurt? How do you deal with your failures and sin?

Do you ever pray so other people notice you (Matthew 6:5–13)? Do you think your behavior is really important but you feel prideful toward other people who struggle (Luke 18:9–14)? False religion is about pretending and worrying about how others view you. It's not about relationship with God but all about how you act.

When we act this way, it's like we're saying God is a puppet, and we let selfish desires and fears take over. There's no real love, honesty, or humility in this. We forget about the grace of the Christian life.

So if you struggle in this way, how do you change? *You can tell the Lord where you need his grace. Be honest about your struggle and know that the Lord loves you. Know that he is with you (Psalm 23:4). He is your shelter and your shade (Isaiah 25:4). His grace can meet you with whatever you're dealing with.*

Take with You: Do you ever worry what other people think about you, or try to appear godly so they think better of you? Tell the Lord about this. Know he loves you and gives you more grace.

MAY 28

The commandments of the LORD are right, bringing joy to the heart.
The commands of the LORD are clear, giving insight for living.
—Psalm 19:8 NLT

The Bible is alive with the love of God in Christ Jesus. He invades our darkness with words of light. He understands our struggles. The wisdom of God speaks right into our lives. In the Bible, God shows himself working in every circumstance. Scripture speaks at just the right time in just the right way, to many different experiences, because that is how God is.

So how do you bring truth to life? How do you apply the Word of God? *Always ask two questions: What is your current struggle? What truth about God connects to this?* You might be facing sufferings and troubles of various kinds (James 1:2). You might be sinning—doing and thinking many wrong things (James 3:16). Usually it's a mix of both. God talks exactly about these things. How does the Savior enter these struggles? How does he help? How will he change you?

Apply one truth about our Redeemer to your heart's need or longing. For example, fight perfectionism with the truth that God is perfect, so we don't have to be. When he sees you, he sees the perfection of Jesus, and he will finish the work in you. When we remember this truth, it changes how we see ourselves in light of our perfect elder brother.

Jesus knows, more intimately than we can grasp, what we are going through. You can move toward him with full confidence that he cares *and* he knows.

Take with You: Think about one truth from Scripture, then think about one struggle in your life. Do this first in your life, then you can share these truths with others.

MAY 29

The precepts of the LORD are right, giving joy to the heart.
The commands of the LORD are radiant, giving light to the eyes.
—Psalm 19:8 NIV

In life, it helps to keep one simple goal in mind: *Connect one bit of Scripture to one bit of life.* What is your current struggle? And then what does God say about this? When you're learning kindness from your Savior, you will be able to be kind to unkind people. When you're learning to endure hard things, you will be able to relate to others who are hurting. It's the same with any other gift of the Spirit: courage, humility, patience, joy, wisdom, gratitude, mercy, generosity, and honesty.

Knowing truths about yourself—your natural tendencies, typical patterns, themes that replay throughout your life—doesn't change you. You must be able to see where you currently struggle, what it says about how you think about God, and what you must learn to grow. Today, what is your particular battlefield? You need to know the difference between truth and lies, clarity and confusion, hope and false hope, right and wrong, wisdom and foolishness, true need and selfish desires, love and selfishness, living faith and unbelief.

Where do you need God's forgiveness and help? When you are confused in your current struggle, you don't even know what to do. When the path to change is deep darkness, you don't know what makes you trip. The right bit of Scripture—six words, two verses, one story—reorients you. You need help, and the Lord is a very present help in trouble.

Take with You: What is one current struggle you need help with? Consider a place in Scripture where God speaks to that struggle or ask a trusted mentor to help.

MAY 30

Therefore, since we have been made right in God's sight by faith, we have peace with God because of what Jesus Christ our Lord has done for us. —Romans 5:1 NLT

It makes a big difference in your Christian life when you remember and believe that you're made right in God's sight because of what Jesus has done for you. This truth means you're forgiven, and you can have the courage to be honest about your sins. When we believe this truth, it doesn't only change us right when we begin to believe. It changes us each day for the rest of our lives. The New Testament letters are written to Christians who have already heard the truth, and so the letters often remind us of what Christ did for us. I have known many Christians who began to understand the importance of what Christ did on the cross, not all at once but little by little over many years. Growing in this knowledge is part of our growth as Christians, our assurance and confidence, our understanding of our sin, and our thankfulness.

Being made right with God by faith often powerfully changes people who think they have to earn God's love by what they do. It comforts people who are discouraged by their failures. It challenges those who are comfortable and confident in their own successes. *So whether you think you're too bad or think you're good enough, being right with God only happens by faith in Christ and what he has done.*

Take with You: Where are you tempted to think that your relationship with God depends on what you do? Thank God that we're made right with him because of what Jesus has done for us!

MAY 31

But truly God has listened;
he has attended to the voice of my prayer.
Blessed be God,
because he has not rejected my prayer
or removed his steadfast love from me! —Psalm 66:19–20

God has given us the Psalms so we have many ways of talking honestly with God. Some psalms speak to God about what we've done wrong (Psalms 32 and 51). Others speak about the ways other people hurt us (Psalms 10 and 31). Many psalms speak about both (Psalms 25 and 119). All the Psalms tell us about God, what he's like, what we need from him, and how we express love for him. The Psalms are not just songs. They are examples of how to talk honestly with God about things that matter. Psalms do not teach a technique, but they help us have *a relationship*. The way the Bible talks about things like anger is different from self-help books or medication.

Yet the Psalms are still very practical. If you're willing to have Jesus be your master and make following him your first priority, then you can even honestly express emotions like anger without being destructive. It can even be redemptive. Your conflicts won't end with slammed doors, hurt silences, and bad-mouthing. Instead, there will be a helpful back-and-forth of communication. This way of talking with people is merciful. It shows God working to change you into his image. *Your real relationship with God will allow you to grow in having real human relationships. The conflicts you have will become an opportunity to growing the fruits of the Spirit.*

Take with You: Practice using words from one of the Psalms listed above to help you talk to God about what you are feeling.

JUNE 1

"Would that we had died in the land of Egypt! Or would that we had died in this wilderness! . . . Would it not be better for us to go back to Egypt?" —Numbers 14:2–3

In the book of Numbers, we read about a typical human response to the hard things of life. Things are not going well for the people of Israel, so they grumble and forget God is good. They forget he's in control and that he will give what he promised. To forget God is a common human response.

Like the Israelites in the wilderness, my grumbling and complaining always includes a false view of myself—I believe I'm right and have the right interpretation of what's going on. I'm justified in complaining against God. That's often accompanied by a false view of the past, just as Israel started missing Egypt and thinking of it as the promised land.

There's also a false view of the future. God promised his people a land flowing with milk and honey, fruit trees, fields, and houses. But the best blessing was that it would be the dwelling place of God with his people. Israel forgot that. The journey from Egypt was intended to be a two-week trip, but by miscalculating God, themselves, their past, and their future, they brought on forty years of wandering in the wilderness instead.

Take with You: How are you responding to the hard things in your life? Are there any areas where you have allowed false beliefs to develop into false views of God, yourself, and your situation? You can always turn to the Lord for healing and rest (Isaiah 30:15).

JUNE 2

And it is God who establishes us with you in Christ, and has anointed us, and who has also put his seal on us and given us his Spirit in our hearts as a guarantee. —2 Corinthians 1:21–22

We are in Christ because of God's work. He has put his seal on us, and he has given his Spirit in our hearts as a guarantee of what is to come, a down payment of glory. *The Holy Spirit writes the promises of life on the human heart. The Holy Spirit counsels us—God himself comes on the scene to transform our lives.*

The Holy Spirit transforms us right in the middle of our sufferings. God uses times of suffering to make us little "Christs" in this world. They conform us to his image. We start to look and act like Jesus.

The word for comfort in 2 Corinthians is *parakaleo*. It's the word for the Holy Spirit in John 14–16. He is the one who comes beside a person to provide the immediate help we need, just right for the situation. This help includes words that bring light into our world. This light reveals our sinfulness, shows us the mercies of God, and invites us to him. God is up to something good for those who are his beloved children. He is always working to transform us into his image.

Take with You: What is difficult for you in life right now? Ask God to comfort and change you through even this. His Spirit offers you present grace. You can trust that he is with you.

JUNE 3

"Blessed is the man who trusts in the LORD,
whose trust is the LORD.
He is like a tree planted by water,
that sends out its roots by the stream,
and does not fear when heat comes,
for its leaves remain green,
and is not anxious in the year of drought,
for it does not cease to bear fruit." —Jeremiah 17:7–8

God tells us in his Word that in each moment of our lives we can either be what we are like naturally: full of thorns (like a thornbush in a desert) or transformed into those full of fruit (like a tree planted by water). What makes the difference? Who we are trusting.

When you trust in the Lord, a time of drought and heat or suffering does not terrorize you. The hard time reveals what's in your heart and what rules you, and God invites you to change. The big change is that you turn to Jesus in the hard times and trust him. This is what it means to bear good fruit instead of bad fruit. By relating to God and trusting him, you start to respond to people differently. When people are big in your minds and you fear them, you risk turning away from God and centering your life on another person. But to turn away from fear of man is to turn back to God. *This is the heart of the gospel—the good news of the Messiah who comes to transform who we are and what we live for and how we live.*

Take with You: What is your heat (the hard times)? Turn to God and entrust yourself to him, inviting him to change you in this season.

JUNE 4

Put off your old self, which belongs to your former manner of life and is corrupt through deceitful desires, and . . . be renewed in the spirit of your minds, and . . . put on the new self, created after the likeness of God in true righteousness and holiness.
—Ephesians 4:22–24

Sanctification is the word that describes God making us more like Jesus: more holy, loving, humble, true, joyous, self-sacrificing. This transformation process happens over time, not all at once. It's not done until we see him face-to-face. Sins like fear of man, pride, or the desire to control your world come naturally to everyone in a fallen world. Change isn't going to be a machete stroke that suddenly cuts off all the wrong in you. But there will be progress—the Spirit will make you more like Jesus.

There is a famous World War II metaphor for this. Jesus coming into the world is like the Allies landing at Normandy, a victory that turned the tide of the war. The defeat of Germany had begun. But there would be thousands of men killed and much heartache until Germany had fully been defeated. In Jesus's life and death on the cross, the spiritual victory has been won, but there will be battles until the victory is fully experienced at the end. *The Christian life is an up-and-down experience. Christ has pledged by his blood to complete the work he's begun. He will do it!*

Take with You: Do you ever feel like when you sin it means you're not "doing it right" with your Christian life? Remember that Jesus is working in your life over time. He invites you to fight the battle with confidence because the war is won.

JUNE 5

And I am sure of this, that he who began a good work in you will bring it to completion at the day of Jesus Christ. —Philippians 1:6

A Prayer for the Lord to Meet Us

Our Father, we thank you that in your tender mercies, we have been caught up into a wonderful kingdom, into the purposes of a Savior and King who will complete what he has begun. There will be a day when every one of us is no longer a person prone to fears, confusion, irritation, and little selfish acts. There will be a day that we'll be unafraid to live an open life. There will be a day that we will live in the light as children of light. Would you make it so. Lord, we are coming from many different places. Some of us feel like we haven't really suffered in very significant ways. Some of us have been shattered by things that have happened. We pray, Lord, that you would meet us, one and all. And we ask for growth in wisdom. I pray for this to be a good week—a week of careful thought, close reading, helpful meditation, and self-awareness. And most of all, I ask for a living faith that takes other people to heart. We ask this in Jesus's name. Amen.

Take with You: As you pray, consider whether there are areas of your life where you feel discouraged or grieved that you aren't where you hope to be spiritually. Remember that Jesus will continue his work in you. Invite him to meet with you and encourage you now.

JUNE 6

But he gives more grace. Therefore it says, "God opposes the proud but gives grace to the humble." Submit yourselves therefore to God. Resist the devil, and he will flee from you. Draw near to God, and he will draw near to you. —James 4:6–8a

You can read stacks of books on conflict resolution and never hear that at the heart of conflict is a heart that's far from God. Because they never get to the core of the problem, they never get to the core of the solution, which is repentance.

James 4 shows us the root of righteousness, faith, love for God, and need for God: humbling yourself, submitting yourself to God, resisting the devil, drawing near to God, cleansing your hands, purifying your hearts, mourning, weeping, and humbling yourself before the Lord. This is how to come close to the God who is gracious.

James does not content himself with just a list of abstract resolutions for conflict like, "Well, I should have faith," or "I should spend more time with God," or "I should trust him," or "Next time, instead of getting irritated at my parents, I'll just trust God more." Instead of that, James comes right into the moment and asks, "What do you do now?" Right now you can humble yourself before the living God. *Right now you can turn from your own way and go God's way. Right now you can bring your cares to the living God.*

Take with You: God wants you to bring your questions about evil, sin, and sufferings to the God who is merciful and powerful. You will find grace!

JUNE 7

Bless the LORD, O my soul,
and forget not all his benefits,
who forgives all your iniquity,
who heals all your diseases,
who redeems your life from the pit,
who crowns you with steadfast love and mercy. —Psalm 103:2–4

Extrospection means looking outside of ourselves. This is at the heart of everything that God is doing in your life. Faith awakens and seeks a God of mercy and power. We can break this into three pieces. Part one in our transformation is the wake-up.

The second piece is to see life as a moral drama. This is crucial. What I mean is that every day we have to answer basic questions about which direction we will take and what part we will play in the drama: *Will I be a fool or will I be wise? Will I be hateful or loving? Will I be proud or humble? Will I worship myself or God?* These are the daily choices that shape your life. You either turn toward God or away from him.

The third piece of the change process is to see God as truly gracious, that his grace is your only hope. If you're awakened to God, if you realize life is a moral drama on a big stage, then you know you need help, right? Sin puts us in this little cramped world. But mercy puts us in a big, spacious world. *God's grace gives us the power to turn toward him—the one who crowns you with steadfast love and mercy.*

Take with You: Do you tend toward unhelpful introspection (looking within)? Practice extrospection today, looking outside yourself and to the Lord. Ask for grace to play the right part in the drama of life.

JUNE 8

Consequently, he is able to save to the uttermost those who draw near to God through him, since he always lives to make intercession for them. —Hebrews 7:25

We often think first of what Jesus has done for us in the past, but there's a present ministry of Jesus. Right now he intercedes for you. The Bible often talks about Jesus being the mediator, the one who goes between God and us, on our behalf. Hebrews reminds us that Jesus is able to save us when we draw near because "he always lives to make intercession." Paul reminds us that Jesus is at the right hand of God interceding for us (Romans 8:34). He's doing this for you still. He's continuing to work out a living salvation for all who call on him by faith.

The High Priest is now *mediating. It's an ongoing ministry to us as his children. He's with us to the end.*

It's my prayer that these truths would sparkle in your life and form the way you think about other people, the way you process your own life and your deepest struggles. Jesus intercedes and prays for you, even for the places where you are weak, vulnerable, struggling with sin, feeling overwhelmed, and feeling like life is out of control. God's grace is tailored to these things.

Take with You: As you remember that Jesus is your mediator right now, ask him for what you need: *Strengthen me, shield me, help me, forgive me. Let me find all these things in you.*

JUNE 9

For we do not have a high priest who is unable to sympathize with our weaknesses, but one who in every respect has been tempted as we are, yet without sin. Let us then with confidence draw near to the throne of grace, that we may receive mercy and find grace to help in time of need. —Hebrews 4:15–16

God will use your difficulties and suffering as the door into a deeper knowledge of his love. You will come to know yourself better too. As you read the Psalms, you see that those who know God well know themselves to be afflicted, weak, oppressed, broken, humble, and needy. Psalm 31:5—"Into your hands I commit my spirit"—was on Jesus's lips as he hung on the cross, powerless and in great pain. He faced all this for us.

Jesus lived in weakness. He knows what it's like to depend on the mercies of God for every breath. *Jesus's experience of weakness is the door to one of the most marvelous promises of God in our passage above: "Let us then approach God's throne of grace with confidence, so that we may receive mercy and find grace to help us in our time of need" (Hebrews 4:16 NIV).*

You are struggling. Life is hard. Your Lord sympathizes with your need. He promises you grace and mercy—immediate help in your need.

Take with You: What is your need? Do you feel weak and afflicted? Ask Jesus to come close to you and give you a deep sense that he understands what's hard and loves you through it.

JUNE 10

The LORD is my shepherd; I shall not want.
He makes me lie down in green pastures.
He leads me beside still waters. He restores my soul.
He leads me in paths of righteousness for his name's sake.
Even though I walk through the valley of the shadow of death,
I will fear no evil, for you are with me; your rod and your staff,
they comfort me. —Psalm 23:1–4

Knowing your weakness and God's power changes how you live. You start to depend on Jesus one day at a time. Jesus says, "Therefore do not worry about tomorrow, for tomorrow will worry about itself. Each day has enough trouble of its own" (Matthew 6:34 NIV). Jesus wants you to depend on him daily. Learn to not worry about tomorrow. Whatever your future, you are called to live by faith today.

To do this you must meditate on who Jesus is. More than any other passage, Psalm 23 brought Jesus to life for me in my struggles with weakness. The psalm is full of promises—he provides, he restores my soul, he is with me, his goodness and mercy pursue me all of my days. Make this psalm your own. It's a promise: Jesus, your Good Shepherd, will fill you with confidence. God doesn't always meet us the way we want, but he does restore us. *No matter what you're facing, you have a Shepherd who's with you, restoring you, and bringing good things—himself—into your life.* Learn to trust him and you truly have something worth living and dying for.

Take with You: Do you depend on other things besides God? Ask God for what he promises in Psalm 23. He will bring you comfort and confidence.

JUNE 11

You have kept count of my tossings; put my tears in your bottle.
Are they not in your book?

This I know, that God is for me. In God, whose word I praise,
in the LORD, whose word I praise,
in God I trust; I shall not be afraid. —Psalm 56:8, 9b–11a

Have you ever been told if you just get the right answers during your hard times, you can solve all your problems? That's not God's way. God is a gardener who prunes his vines over years.

So look for slow, steady change. What can you expect? When your pain is raw and overwhelming, you can expect that your pain will lessen as you start to bring it to God by using Psalms 55, 56, and 57.

Healing and peace grow not in an instant but over time. Some difficulties may not leave you until Christ returns. Only when Christ returns, when he makes all things new, will every tear be wiped away (Revelation 21:4). You may be scarred by suffering, but you've learned to take small steps of obedience, wise love, and hope. Most amazingly, you will be able to help others who suffer. God has a purpose for you that flows out of your life experience. *As you learn about how Jesus Christ meets, enters, and transforms your times of affliction, you can help others who are facing all kinds of affliction.* Your compassion, wisdom, and hope for redemption will bring the light of God to a world suffering in darkness.

Take with You: Have you noticed going through hard times opens doors to help others who are going through hard times? Is there anyone in your life now who could use your help?

JUNE 12

"Blessed is the man who trusts in the LORD, whose trust is the LORD.
He is like a tree planted by water,
that sends out its roots by the stream,
and does not fear when heat comes,
for its leaves remain green,
and is not anxious in the year of drought,
for it does not cease to bear fruit." —Jeremiah 17:7–8

It's right in the middle of hard realities that your trust in God grows. In Jeremiah 17:7–8, Jeremiah is talking about living in a desert where life is hard and brutal. The desert in the Bible is the place of death. There's no water, no food. It's hot. There are predators and snakes. It's the place where your faith is tested. Do you feel that grief and confusion have brought you into a spiritual desert? As you deepen your trust in God, your desert will become the place where you find God's living water of hope, mercy, and blessing.

God's living water is his presence. He says, "I am with you." He is the only person who can profoundly reassure your heart. Though you may be feeling alone, he is with you. His presence means that even in the darkest of circumstances you can be unafraid. Let me say it again: He is with you. He is with you.

Because God is with you, you will be fruitful, even in the aftermath of heartache and confusion. He promises that one day all sorrow, pain, and tears will be wiped away (Revelation 21:4).

Take with You: What about your life feels like a desert right now? Ask God to give you what you need to grow and even thrive in the desert.

JUNE 13

What then shall we say to these things? If God is for us, who can be against us? —Romans 8:31

Beloved, never avenge yourselves, but leave it to the wrath of God, for it is written, "Vengeance is mine, I will repay, says the Lord." —Romans 12:19

Many of us struggle with the idea that God is all-powerful and yet evil exists. Understanding God's loving anger helps to resolve these questions. God's anger brings him glory and brings us blessing. He justly condemns evil, he cuts off the power of evil, and brings relief to those suffering. Many psalms connect the steadfast love and mercies of the Lord to this loving wrath. By acting against evil, God delivers his children from their sins and from those who harm them.

God's wrath brings hope to his children, but it brings despair to his enemies. But those enemies do not have to stay enemies. If they are willing to believe in Jesus Christ, enemies will be changed into friends. The truth is that you can't understand God's love if you don't understand his anger. This is the message of the book of Psalms.

God's loving anger is for our good. It nourishes and encourages our faith. *God's beloved children hope and trust that at the return of Christ, his anger will make things right. In anticipation, we groan and eagerly wait.*

Take with You: Have you thought of God's love in this way before? Think about the evil that tempts you and the evil that others do against you for a moment and ask God to work against it and redeem.

JUNE 14

"My sheep hear my voice, and I know them, and they follow me."
—John 10:27

God is with you, immediately and personally at work. He is at work in you and in those whom you seek to help by speaking the truth in love. John 10:27 and John 15:1–5 give you confidence: Christ's sheep hear his voice; the Vinedresser prunes those who are in Christ. God works within his people; therefore, we can reach out to others. He promises to continue to work until the day when glory and joy are revealed, until the day when the intimacy of faith becomes the intimacy of sight.

The highest hope and happiness can be said in four words: God is with us. This is one of Jesus's names: Emmanuel. *This is the greatest promise: I will be with you. This will sustain you while you live and when you die. When you are elated, your happiness will be filled with thankfulness. When you agonize, your suffering will be filled with hope because of "Christ in you, the hope of glory" (Colossians 1:27).*

The Bible is about closeness with God. He can meet with you and will meet you. God has not left us grasping to understand his ways. He has not left us to be tossed around by the highs and lows of life. He has revealed his ways to us. He has revealed himself. The living faith that listens to the living Word of the living God will experience the sort of living closeness with God that gives us a glimpse of heaven.

Take with You: Have you felt this kind of closeness with God? Ask him to fill your good times with gratitude and your hard times with hope.

JUNE 15

"Fear not, little flock, for it is your Father's good pleasure to give you the kingdom." —Luke 12:32

Your heavenly Father cares tenderly for you, like a parent for a beloved child. The One who touches base with you and connects with you is your Shepherd. He plans to walk with you today. So he can keep an eye on you? That's part of it. He will protect you and nourish you. But he is also your Counselor whose voice speaks wisdom to your heart. That is the God we serve, the One we want to love, the One who wants us to walk with him every day and tells us not to fear.

> *Our Father, will you hear us? Will you help us? Will you meet us? Give to us your Holy Spirit, your very self. Shepherd us, master us, protect us, and encourage us.* Where we are weak, strengthen us. Where we are anxious, calm us. Where we get frustrated, will you soothe what troubles us? Will you in every way meet us one and all? Each of us, Lord, that we'd be encouraged, that we would live our lives with more light and tenderness for others and more genuine joy, gratitude, and need toward you. Please help us and meet us. And we pray in the name of Jesus Christ our Savior. Amen.
>
> **Take with You:** Pray aloud the second paragraph above, making it your own. What is your anxiety and your trouble? Who do you find it difficult to be tender toward? Ask for this specific help. God loves to answer these prayers.

JUNE 16

And hope does not put us to shame, because God's love has been poured into our hearts through the Holy Spirit who has been given to us. —Romans 5:5

The grace of the Lord Jesus Christ and the love of God and the fellowship of the Holy Spirit be with you all. —2 Corinthians 13:14

Bear one another's burdens, and so fulfill the law of Christ. —Galatians 6:2

A Prayer for a Tender Heart

Lord, I thank you that you have called me to bring my need to the one who loves me. Thank you that, like a father, you have compassion on me. I thank you that you care for me like a good father who cares, feels tenderly, supports, and even carries his child. I ask for a heart to receive the love of God in Christ Jesus, to rejoice in you and love you, to be lifted up to you, to have greater confidence and steadiness and hope and love for you and a tender heart that holds others in our hearts. *Help me increasingly see beyond my own small frame of reference and see the needs of the kingdom—the needs of brothers and sisters who suffer and struggle, the needs of the poor. Help me have the same kind of heart that you have.*

Lord, speak to me through your Word, and make those words alive in me and make me alive to you. I ask this in the name of Jesus Christ who embodied all this and more. Amen.

Take with You: Think of a specific prayer request you have for someone else. Carry this with you today and ask God to answer your prayer.

JUNE 17

In him we have obtained an inheritance, having been predestined according to the purpose of him who works all things according to the counsel of his will. —Ephesians 1:11

The letter of Ephesians reminds us that God is in control. Things happen by his will (Ephesians 1:1, 3, 5, 8, 11). The universe works according to God's plan to glorify himself in Christ and in all believers.

Life isn't a sloppy, confusing mess. Life is like a tapestry or rug. A tapestry has two sides—one looks good, and the other looks like a big mess. From our perspective, we look at life from the tangled, knotty side of the tapestry. But one day, we'll see the beautiful pattern on the top side. That's a useful metaphor, but Ephesians lets us see the top side of the tapestry too. God says, "It's all working out according to a definite plan. A hand is on the controls of history and of your life, with the power to perform what he chooses."

Paul says you were "predestined according to the purpose of him who works all things according to the counsel of his will" (1:11). He's not stirring up debate about how much free will humans have. The big point is this: God is in control. Any other view would be absurd—God spins galaxies and holds atoms together, after all. *Because his purposes will not be thwarted, you can be courageous, optimistic, persevering in love through troubles. His purposes sustain you through it all.*

Take with You: What feels confusing about life right now? Ask God to show you his purposes for you, and to give you trust despite what doesn't make sense today.

JUNE 18

Be at peace among yourselves. And we urge you, brothers, admonish the idle, encourage the fainthearted, help the weak, be patient with them all. See that no one repays anyone evil for evil, but always seek to do good to one another and to everyone.
—1 Thessalonians 5:13b–15

You and I have been given a gift of life in Christ. The purpose of the gift is that we show God's love in the world. A phrase to describe this is *the constructive displeasure of mercy*. Rather than using destructive anger, we want to be constructive and build up even when we have to express displeasure. And we are merciful. We don't demand vengeance. It means treating people the way Jesus treats you. When we do wrong, he demonstrates his constructive displeasure and mercy to us. *He is patient with us. He forgives us and doesn't turn against us. He is generous to us, giving us grace upon grace. He talks straight to us, bringing what's wrong to light in order to set us free of what blinds us.*

You and I learn to do what's modeled for us. You may have experienced this from a good parent, a wise boss, an excellent coach, a thoughtful teacher, a mature friend, a genuine pastor. Have you noticed that when you are treated this way, it tends to bring out the same in you? You get a glimpse from someone else of a higher purpose for your life. You get a bigger perspective on troubles and troublesome people.

Take with You: Can you think of someone who's kind even when giving or receiving criticism? Ask God for grace to help you love others in this way.

JUNE 19

He has told you, O man, what is good;
and what does the LORD require of you but to do justice,
and to love kindness, and to walk humbly with your God? —Micah 6:8

Because Jesus hates suffering and loves sufferers, sufferers find help and joy in him. Because Jesus hates sin and loves sinners, sinners find forgiveness and joy in him.

Jesus's response involves a mix of justified anger combined with mercy and active efforts to make true peace where there's trouble. The constructive displeasure of mercy is similar to anger, but it's also very different. It's not harshness or hostility. Like anger, it says, "That matters. It's wrong and offensive. I want to do something about it." But unlike just getting mad, it says, "That's wrong—and I will be constructively merciful in pursuing whatever is just, whatever makes things right, whatever does good."

Mercy is an entirely different way of reacting to offenses, to things we think are wrong. Think about this: When you're merciful toward someone, it doesn't mean you don't care about what the person did wrong. And it's the furthest thing from approval—because what's happening *is* wrong. Mercy includes a component of forceful anger. But the tone isn't like anger's hostility, vindictiveness, and destructiveness.

True mercy proceeds hand in hand with true justice. It brings mercy to victims by bringing justice. While working hand in hand with justice, it offers mercy to violators. Mercy contains a combination of attitudes and actions that proceed in a constructive, not destructive, way.

Take with You: What particular evils in the world make you angry? Who do you struggle to have patience with? Ask God to grow this constructive displeasure of mercy in your heart.

JUNE 20

The Lord is not slow to fulfill his promise as some count slowness, but is patient toward you, not wishing that any should perish, but that all should reach repentance. —2 Peter 3:9

Patience is an odd response to something that's wrong. Think of it this way: When you're patient, it's a time when you have a good reason to be angry. You feel this: "That's wrong. What you're doing does not please me. It offends me. It hurts people." Patience isn't passivity, indifference, or tolerance of evils. You do not just put up with bad things. It's not an easygoing tolerance and neutrality. It doesn't accept anything and affirm everything. *Patience hates what's happening. Then it rolls up its sleeves to fix what's wrong.*

Patience sees what's wrong, but it's "slow to anger." This is a prime characteristic of God. He's gracious, compassionate, and slow to anger (Exodus 34:6). It's the first characteristic of love. "Love is patient" (1 Corinthians 13:4). God is love, and God is slow to anger. He will make us like himself in this way. To be slow to anger means you are willing to work on something that's wrong over time—like God is. "The Lord is not slow to fulfill his promise as some count slowness, but is patient" (2 Peter 3:9). God chooses to work over a scale of moments, days, years, decades, centuries, millennia. And he will accomplish what he's set out to do.

Take with You: What problems in your life do you wish could be resolved more quickly? Ask God to fulfill his promise to continue his work in you, giving you his patience.

JUNE 21

"Pay attention to yourselves! If your brother sins, rebuke him, and if he repents, forgive him, and if he sins against you seven times in the day, and turns to you seven times, saying, 'I repent,' you must forgive him."
—Luke 17:3–4

Forgiveness comes in two forms. First, you forgive another person before God, whether or not that person admits any wrongdoing. This is *attitudinal* forgiveness.

Jesus speaks of how forgiveness is connected to our relationship with God (the vertical dimension): "Forgive, if you have anything against anyone, so that your Father also who is in heaven may forgive you your trespasses" (Mark 11:25).

You stand alone before God dealing with your attitudes. Forgiveness changes you, not to deal with the other person (the horizontal dimension). It prepares you so you will go to the other person already willing to be merciful. You're no longer holding the grudge, bitter, defensive, or vengeful.

The second aspect of forgiveness is *transacted* forgiveness. Jesus says if your brother sins, bring it up with him directly, and if he repents, forgive him, and if he sins against you seven times in the day, and turns to you seven times, saying, "I repent," you must forgive him (Luke 17:3–4, author's paraphrase). Jesus envisions a conversation with the other person. You bring it up constructively; the other person asks to be forgiven. The interaction is honest and full of mercy (a rare combination!) because the attitudinal forgiveness has already happened.

This combination of attitudinal and transacted forgiveness helps make sense of many common and extremely tangled situations.

Take with You: Are there people in your life who are difficult to forgive? Ask God to carry the hurts too great for you to carry.

JUNE 22

For all the promises of God find their Yes in him. That is why it is through him that we utter our Amen to God for his glory.
—2 Corinthians 1:20

God is not an idea, an energy, or an experience you work up within yourself. We so easily forget he's a person. That's why he so often reminds us: Remember! He takes the initiative. He willingly comes to you. We hear his words to us in the Bible, revealing how Jesus fulfills God's promises and purposes—Jesus is the Yes! To God's promises. But he's not bound within the pages of the book. His book reveals a God who really speaks. He's active. He tells us his names so we can talk with him. He's your hands-on Father. He's the Vinedresser at work pruning you to make you fruitful. He's your Good Shepherd who gave his life for his sheep. He walks with you and watches over you. He is the Holy Spirit who makes his home in you so you become a person of faith and love. This most wondrous Person is the game changer.

God's Word tells us who God actually is. *It's important to me to have God as my true friend, because so many hard things in life become a true enemy, like cancer and dying. It's one of the many shadows of death, one of the many evils. But Christ willingly walks with me through every valley shadowed by death. He's your Shepherd too.* Remember. It requires looking to him in the neediness and dependency of faith.

Take with You: Ask and you will receive. Ask for mercy for all the ways you do not follow him. Trust his death in your place, the price for all your wrongs.

JUNE 23

Do not be anxious about anything, but in everything by prayer and supplication with thanksgiving let your requests be made known to God. —Philippians 4:6

The Lord is listening. Paul tells us in this passage to make our request known to God. Think about that for a minute. If the Lord is near, if he is someone who knows what's on your heart, who knows what weighs heavily on you and preoccupies you, then he listens to you as his beloved child.

Many psalms start out by pleading with God—*Lord, listen to me, bend your ear, you must hear me, I need you to listen and act on my behalf.* These are not calm psalms; they are intense and pointed. In Psalm 28, David tells God that if God doesn't hear him, he will die. This is the voice of a desperate faith, and David talks this way because God is listening.

God's listening does not guarantee that what's making you anxious will go away—that your family problems will be solved, that you will be cured of cancer, or that whatever else is worrying you will disappear. You may not be healed, people you love may die, and you may struggle with family troubles. But God comforts, strengthens, and gives hope in the midst of the most difficult circumstances. Jesus didn't want to drink the cup of God's wrath. But God strengthened him, and he was fully willing. There's help from him for whatever worries you.

Take with You: When you are anxious, pour your heart out to God. He is listening, and he knows what your heart needs most.

JUNE 24

I know how to be brought low, and I know how to abound. In any and every circumstance, I have learned the secret of facing plenty and hunger, abundance and need. I can do all things through him who strengthens me. —Philippians 4:12–13

God taught Paul a secret we all need to know: the secret of contentment. Contentment, unlike indifference, is the opposite of worrying and obsessing. When you worry, you're trying to hold onto what you might lose, or you're grabbing for what you don't have. Indifference means you are trying not to care about what you don't have or might lose. But that's not contentment. *Contentment offers a fundamental stability that comes from knowing that the all-powerful Lord of the universe is near. He's listening to your cries and guarding you day and night. No matter what this life brings, he will never leave you.*

Paul learned contentment by depending on his Lord. He said, "I can do everything through Christ, who gives me the strength" (Philippians 4:13 NLT). Paul knew that, no matter how the circumstances of his life changed, God would be his constant, faithful, loving protector.

You are his child, and he wants a relationship with you. God's peace comes to us as our relationship with him becomes deeper, more honest, and more intimate.

Take with You: Think of a worry or an area of life where you lack contentment. Ask God to help you release the urge to grab onto what you don't have. Ask him to be your protector and to help you face what feels scary.

JUNE 25

Having the eyes of your hearts enlightened, that you may know what is the hope to which he has called you, what are the riches of his glorious inheritance in the saints, and what is the immeasurable greatness of his power toward us who believe, according to the working of his great might that he worked in Christ when he raised him from the dead and seated him at his right hand in the heavenly places. —Ephesians 1:18–20

God's grace to sinners demonstrates that he is with us and in us. He has shown past grace, and there is future grace. But this is present grace, here with you right now. How do you know he is with you? The love of God has been poured into our hearts through the Holy Spirit given to us, by whom we cry out, "Abba, Father" (Romans 5:5; 8:15). The good news is not simply what happened long ago on the cross. Jesus is present with us and works powerfully in us. Our Father gives wisdom and invites us to ask for it. The Holy Spirit comes to us and responds when we ask. God invites us to ask for good things from him. The Bible repeatedly invites us to ask for present grace. Do you want to you die to yourself and live a new life? Present grace gives you confidence to seek help, to question those old felt needs, desires, opinions, and lifestyles, to put to death what's not beautiful.

Take with You: Present grace nourishes faith. Ask God for where you need grace and the power of the Spirit to make changes and do good in the world.

JUNE 26

He also told them a parable: "Can a blind man lead a blind man? Will they not both fall into a pit?" —Luke 6:39

Do you ever talk with people about their problems or about your own? You might not be a "counselor," but we all need counsel sometimes, and we all provide it sometimes. That's true even if you are "just" a neighbor, friend, sibling, or child. How do you help a person you love get their thoughts sorted out?

We have to remember that human selfishness makes it hard to see clearly. We need an outside perspective and grace. God's grace changes us and opens our eyes. Sin blinds us, but grace helps us see God.

Our souls resist this sort of change. Something in us doesn't want to release the illusion that we are in control of our lives. It takes humility to receive the Word of God. We don't naturally want to see the truth about ourselves. Yet to resist submission to God means we have a harder time seeing God and a harder time seeing ourselves accurately.

God doesn't give up on us. The Spirit patiently goes about the business of remaking us. *God persistently teaches us to fear him, trust him, love him, and so, when we have ears to hear, we begin to serve him.*

Take with You: Ask God to show you places in your life where self-centeredness makes you see yourself less accurately. He is a good Father who wants to help us grow.

JUNE 27

Then Jesus told his disciples, "If anyone would come after me, let him deny himself and take up his cross and follow me."
—Matthew 16:24

It's vital to face up to your sin and your resistance to God. This leads to big changes. You can see clearly and act gently, helping others to face up to themselves as well. The Bible has several names for this change. Jesus says, "Become a disciple." In other words, sign on for life learning. A learner is committed to becoming different. Are you overconfident about your opinions, feelings, choices, and habits? Do you find yourself saying, "That's just how I am," and is that something you insist on? As soon as I'm willing to say, "Not necessarily," I step off the death spiral and onto the learning curve.

Jesus says, "Follow me." To follow somebody else runs completely opposite to the self-will that characterizes what I do instinctively. Listening to him runs directly opposite to our opinionated and proud ways. This change will make you out of step with the world around you. To follow somebody else runs directly opposite to the entitled self-assertiveness that Western culture reinforces in us every day. This change will make you radically countercultural. Yet it is a path of wisdom and life. Every alternative to "Follow me" is just another way of going with the flow.

Take with You: When Jesus says, "Follow me," do you feel relieved at the idea of not feeling lost or straying, but knowing where to walk? Where do you see in yourself places of rebellion remaining, or places of resistance to the kind and good leadership of Jesus?

JUNE 28

Your testimonies are righteous forever;
give me understanding that I may live. —Psalm 119:144

You should ask the same things of the Bible that you ask of people. Why not? The Bible is about people, troubles, mercies, choices, struggles, and hope. So ask of Scripture, *What were those people facing back then? What did God choose to reveal to them?* Today's specific situations and choices are never exactly the same, but there are always common themes. And though our God never works in exactly the same way twice, he is the same yesterday, today, and forever.

The Word of God reveals God's person, promises, will, and ways in the story of real human lives. The Word of God shows people facing challenges and choices. They are tempted to believe lies, choose wrongs, and live in ways that are ugly, perverse, and complicated. Scripture also shows us the Lord of life who enters the human condition redemptively, making wrongs right, speaking wisdom that we need.

Scripture shows some people believing what's true, choosing what's good, and living in simply beautiful ways—people after God's own heart. They turn to the Lord. Most of all, we witness the true Man after God's own heart, the Lord Jesus, Word made flesh, living with us, touched by our weakness, full of grace, truth and glory, loving God and neighbor. This is the goal of our discipleship: following Jesus in this way of life.

Take with You: Who have you known who lived beautifully, like the best examples of love and goodness in the Bible? In what ways were they like Jesus? Ask God for grace to follow their example, and to give you glimpses of this beautiful life with Jesus.

JUNE 29

For from his fullness we have all received, grace upon grace. —John 1:16

Each aspect of grace is what you and I need to walk more steadily in the light and to run from darkness.

Past grace means Jesus's life and death for us on the cross. He left his Father's throne above, came down, and emptied himself of all but love. He died for us, made us right with God by faith, brought us into his family as sons and daughters, and gave us new life by the power of the Spirit. If you're dealing with guilt and anxiety about yourself and feeling like you're a failure, you need this grace. Grace reconciles us, bringing us to God even when we've been far from him.

Second is *present grace*. Present grace means God is with you now. He's on the scene, ready, willing, and a present help. He is working in you. We experience present grace when we pray for God's power and presence, when we call on God to reveal himself to us and through us, to shield and strengthen us for whatever we face.

And then there is *future grace*. God will come for you. Everything that's wrong right now is going to be made right. Experiencing the promise of future grace means having confidence that one day all tears will be wiped away, and the difficult things will be filled with joy.

The medicine for what ails you is grace—God's great working of past, present, and future grace.

Take with You: Grace means unearned favor, God's free gift of love and kindness. Where do you see God's grace in your past and present? What future grace are you looking toward?

JUNE 30

And I am sure of this, that he who began a good work in you will bring it to completion at the day of Jesus Christ. —Philippians 1:6

A Prayer of Thanksgiving for Christ at Work in Us

Our God and Father, thank you that you have given us Jesus, your Son, and that the Lamb of God—the Lion of Judah, the King of kings, the long-awaited Messiah has come for us. Thank you that Jesus is a very present help, guide, friend, shield, and Savior. He guards us and holds us.

And we thank you that we cry out to one who is a living Shepherd, one who does not leave the universe and the church to wander along, does not leave us to our own devices. We are so grateful that you persevere with us. We are so grateful that there's evidence in our lives that there is someone else who's at work, someone who will bring us into daylight. Someone who has begun good work and will finish it.

We ask you to continue to work in us even right to the finish line, that you will bless us and keep us and watch over us and make us alive to you, make your words bright and shining with life, and rich with meaning and deep with hope, powerful to transform us. We ask these things in your name, Lord Jesus, and we ask it, thanking you that you are faithful to do all that you have promised. Amen.

Take with You: Pray this prayer, making it your own, adding in specific things you would like to give thanks for.

JULY 1

And, as shoes for your feet, having put on the readiness given by the gospel of peace. —Ephesians 6:15

The gospel of peace—reconciling Jews and Gentiles to God and to each other—is a central theme in Ephesians 2–3. In the gospel of peace, relationships are reconciled, forgiveness triumphs over anger, and a community of mutual kindness is established. This comes through powerfully in Ephesians 4:25–5:2. The gospel brings peacemaking power.

Where did Paul find this picture? It comes from Isaiah 52:7:

How beautiful upon the mountains
  are the feet of him who brings good news,
who publishes peace, who brings good news of happiness,
  who publishes salvation,
  who says to Zion, "Your God reigns."

Whose feet are beautiful with the good news of peace? In Isaiah 52:6–10, the shoes belong to the Lord who is coming in person. Every eye sees the Lord returning to Zion, bringing comfort and redemption. A few sentences later, Isaiah 53 will tell us how he will do it. The Lamb of God will bear the iniquity of us all.

Jesus Christ is the good news of peace to the ends of the earth. The man wearing those shoes is on the march. Stand up and join him.

Take with You: The gospel is good news of peace. Where do you see conflict around you? Ask the Lord to help you become someone who helps bring peace.

JULY 2

In all circumstances take up the shield of faith, with which you can extinguish all the flaming darts of the evil one. —Ephesians 6:16

The Bible sometimes compares God's people to soldiers in a spiritual battle against a spiritual enemy—the devil. We are on the march, but the enemy fights back—hard. He lies, schemes, accuses, hurts, divides. He would enslave you and kill you if he could. The devil is behind lies and hostility in relationships (4:25–27). We must stand against the devil's purposes and plans (6:11).

The shield is the only piece of weaponry with a protective role. Our shield repels "the flaming darts of the evil one." *Where does this shield image come from? The Lord himself is a shield to those who take refuge in him.* In numerous psalms, our enemies are called liars and murderers. They hate the Lord and his people.

Psalm 18 is an example of faith seeking protection and strength in the Lord. David piles up every safe-place metaphor he can think of. This is what it looks like when a person takes up the shield of faith:

> I love you, O Lord, my strength.
> The Lord is my rock and my fortress and my deliverer,
> my God, my rock in whom I take refuge,
> my shield and the horn of my salvation, my stronghold.
> I call upon the Lord, who is worthy to be praised,
> and I am saved from my enemies. (vv. 1–3)

Faith looks with confidence to the Shield who protects and strengthens.

Take with You: Where do you see spiritual darkness or attacks around you? Ask the Lord to be your shield. Take comfort in your rock and refuge.

JULY 3

And take the helmet of salvation . . . —Ephesians 6:17a

Christ is our salvation from death and sin. Think of these words: *Salvation! A Savior!* He comes in person for people who have lost their way and are dying. He saves. He rescues. He came for us, and we go forth to bring this help to others. We are living the message, wearing this helmet of salvation. Paul has spoken about this Gift of gifts throughout his letter.

What was that first truth we anchored ourselves to as we sought the Lord's strength? Ephesians 1:13 tells us, "When you heard the word of truth, the gospel of your salvation, and believed in him, you were sealed with the promised Holy Spirit."

And what was that breastplate, footgear, and shield? It is the reality that Jesus Christ saves us from death, depravity, and the devil. We were dead, and the Spirit made us alive (Ephesians 2:5). He awakened faith by his power. The Lord freely gifts all good, and we gratefully receive. *The gift of the new covenant in the coming of Christ our Savior, and the gift of the life-giving Spirit, and the gift of words of salvation—this is what we learn in Ephesians. This is the light that we bring against the darkness.*

Take with You: Ask God for the awareness that you walk through life wearing this "armor"—that you are covered in his saving help and that you are sent to offer this help to others.

JULY 4

And take . . . the sword of the Spirit, which is the word of God.
—Ephesians 6:17

The Bible often provides rich metaphors and illustrations to help us understand spiritual things. As we stop and reflect on the imagery, we get the point in deeper ways. Paul's doing this in Ephesians 6 as he piles up pictures of Christ's strong weapons of lifesaving war. What we see in Ephesians 6 are different ways of saying the same thing—how to strengthen yourself in the Lord, how you walk in the light, how you respond to the. He Word of Truth wants us to get the point: God gives you what you will need, he equips you for everything he calls you to do.

This final piece of weaponry in this list of the armor of God comes from Isaiah 49:2, which tells us about the weapon of divine words. These are the words of the servant of the Lord, the Messiah, who says, "He made my mouth like a sharp sword." This sword expresses the wisdom of the Spirit, destroying evil and bringing in the peaceable kingdom.

We are invited to take up this sword of the Spirit and proclaim the one who was made "a light for the nations, that my salvation may reach to the end of the earth" (49:6). *Strengthen yourself in this Lord, and go where the darkness reigns.*

Take with You: We are often fearful to share God's Word with others. Ask God to give you his words and confidence to take it out to the world so that it will do good and accomplish God's purposes. Ask him to make you someone who brings light into dark places.

JULY 5

Praying at all times in the Spirit, with all prayer and supplication. To that end, keep alert with all perseverance, making supplication for all the saints, and also for me, that words may be given to me in opening my mouth boldly to proclaim the mystery of the gospel, for which I am an ambassador in chains, that I may declare it boldly, as I ought to speak. —Ephesians 6:18–20

Faith responds to God's truth by interceding for the real needs of others. Paul had prayed for us to know the Lord's strength, love, and presence (1:16–23; 3:14–21). He called each of us to find strength in the Lord (6:10) and to take refuge in the Lord (6:16). Now, personal need moves to concern for the needs of others. Faith in God moves us into love for others. We pray for our fellow saints who have the same need for the Lord's truth, strength, love, presence, and protection. Others need your prayers for strength in the Lord. And the people they love need the same care from them.

What Paul says next is astonishing. He has called us to pray for one another. Now he puts himself first in line as one of the needy ones in verses 18–20. He needed our Lord's help as much as you do. He, too, needed the full armor of God to enable him to engage in Christ's mission—this belt, breastplate, shoes, shield, helmet, and sword of life that invades darkness with truth, faith, and love.

Take with You: Do you sometimes think of other Christians as needing less help from God than you? Remember that we all stand in need of the same grace to follow Jesus and love others.

JULY 6

The heart of the wise makes his speech judicious
and adds persuasiveness to his lips.
Gracious words are like a honeycomb,
sweetness to the soul and health to the body. —Proverbs 16:23–24

As you get older, you'll have more opportunities to mentor others or encourage peers, maybe in a small group or Bible study. Here are a few tips to help someone struggling. First, the encouragement that's helpful to somebody else is usually short and sweet. I can rarely take in more than a line or two of Scripture in a way that makes a difference.

Second, you can invite people to slow down to make Scripture personal. For instance, in James 1:2, we read "count it all joy . . . when you meet trials of various kinds." Think together about why it's so hard to find joy in this situation. Look at how tender God is about our faith. He says if we lack wisdom, to ask for it, and he'll help us (v. 5). Help people put their lives into passages like these.

Our tendency when someone is struggling is to just look up passages directly related to their struggle, such as anger, bitterness, or something else. And it's valid that you would do that, but *it's also important to connect their struggle to God's grace and promises.* We can model God's love in times like this, showing patience and support. When we show love like God's love, it's like shining a little night-light in the darkness, helping the person long for God who is the Sun.

Take with You: Pray that your light will shine for someone who needs it and that they will come to God as the great light.

JULY 7

But immediately Jesus spoke to them, saying, "Take heart; it is I. Do not be afraid." —Matthew 14:27

What's the most frequent commandment in the Bible? *Fear not. Don't be afraid. Don't be anxious.* This is a very different kind of command—it's not just "stop it." It's more of a voice of reassurance to you.

We have very good reasons to be afraid, because everything we value is fragile and vulnerable and out of our control. God's "command of reassurance" is honest about all that's fragile and scary. Fear and anxiety are responses to something that seems overwhelming and out of control.

In saying, "Don't be afraid," God is concerned to give us reasons to trust. The book of Philippians gives you reasons to not be anxious: "He who began a good work in you will bring it to completion at the day of Jesus Christ" (1:6). This helps you see your life as a journey, giving you hope that one day the struggle is going to be over. "Christ Jesus . . . did not count equality with God a thing to be grasped, but emptied himself, by taking the form of a servant . . . by becoming obedient to the point of death" (2:5–8). Jesus walked into our chaos. He faced what we face. He died in our place and is alive. "My God will supply every need of yours according to his riches in glory" (4:19).

You have very good reasons to be afraid, tense, anxious, and stressed, but you have better reasons not to be afraid.

Take with You: Make this prayer your own: *Lord, I have good reasons to be afraid, but better reasons to trust you. Remind me of these reasons today.*

JULY 8

Then the LORD said to Moses, "Behold, I am about to rain bread from heaven for you, and the people shall go out and gather a day's portion every day, that I may test them, whether they will walk in my law or not." —Exodus 16:4

Imagine this: You've left Egypt. Your food is gone and you're in the desert. There are good reasons for anxiety, because you don't know where food is going to come from. You, your family, and your people could die.

In the middle of this trouble, God hears and gives you manna. You open your tent the next morning, and there is manna. It's exhilarating. You know you're not supposed to take too much, but you're afraid about tomorrow, so you take more, and it rots.

That night you go to bed a little less anxious. You wake up and, sure enough, there it is again. This time you gather just enough for the day, and you do the same the next. Could you imagine by around day 1,000 that you're finally waking up confident because you know the manna is going to be there?

The New Testament version of manna is grace. God will give you all the grace you need today, but not for tomorrow, because if you had manna for the next week, you would trust in your storehouses and forget about God.

There are good reasons why the Lord's strategy is to give you all you need for today but not for tomorrow. That's this principle of manna. The grace you need to face tomorrow will be yours just when you need it.

Take with You: Remember that God wants to stay in relationship with you and to bless you in your dependence on him.

JULY 9

But you, O Lord, know me;
you see me, and test my heart toward you. —Jeremiah 12:3a

A Prayer to the God Who Knows Us

Almighty God, to whom all hearts are open and all desires known, and from whom no secrets are hidden.

You have searched us, and you know us (Psalm 139:1). You know our thoughts; you know our fears. You know things about us we don't even know about ourselves. You know our sorrows and our joys. You know the places where we have been given wisdom; you know the places where we are still foolish. You know what breaks our hearts and what delights us.

This day we are open before you and we ask you that you would cleanse the thoughts of our hearts by your Holy Spirit. Breathe upon us, meet us, and give to us your very self. Our Father, wash, strengthen, and shelter us. Protect, lead, and guide us throughout this day, that we would trust you and would know you. Make your Word alive in our hearts.

Teach us to love you and to magnify your holy name. Teach us to treat others with the kindness and clarity of purpose that expresses your love. Make us come alive to you and your Word. We commit ourselves to you through Jesus Christ, our Savior and our Lord. Amen.

Take with You: Make this prayer your own. Ask yourself, *What do I need protection from? In what areas of life am I asking God to lead me?* Fill in the blanks and ask for these things.

JULY 10

Let your speech always be gracious, seasoned with salt, so that you may know how you ought to answer each person. —Colossians 4:6

Let no corrupting talk come out of your mouths, but only such as is good for building up, as fits the occasion, that it may give grace to those who hear. —Ephesians 4:29

Every one of us has been helped by hearing someone else talk personally. Hearing from others about their struggles, goals, and experiences builds us up. We are encouraged by hearing Christians give testimonies.

How do we best talk about our testimonies? How do we also listen well? *We need to become wise in how to approach others so we can help connect them to Jesus, who best understands people and their suffering and sin. We want every word out of our mouths to meet the need of the moment.*

We were made to know others and to be known by them. When we are isolated, we cannot thrive. Others need to hear God's words from us. We need to hear God's words from others. The Christian life includes the call to imitate God, who loves us with a purposeful patience that's willing to keep pursuing good ends all the way to the finish. It's not that we have to figure out a quick fix to our or others' problems today. The change process takes a lifetime, and this gives you hope as you seek to take the next step, say the next helpful word, in each moment.

Take with You: Be quick to listen to other believers. You need their encouragement! Also, share what God has taught you. They need your encouragement!

JULY 11

No temptation has overtaken you that is not common to man. God is faithful, and he will not let you be tempted beyond your ability, but with the temptation he will also provide the way of escape, that you may be able to endure it. Therefore, my beloved, flee from idolatry. —1 Corinthians 10:13–14

I'm going to speak to you as one who is beloved, as one who is tempted, and as one who has a way of escape. This is important for times when you are struggling with a persistent sin. What does change look like?

First, there is always a wake-up call. You wake up to who you really are. You realize you have been in a dream and that you have been lying to yourself. You take personal responsibility for your sin, and you realize that your life purpose is to be in a transformative process going from darkness and foolishness to light and wisdom.

Second, you wake up to what's really going on in your world. You have been misunderstanding the nature of the world in which you live. It's full of temptation, trial, lying voices, and false pleasures.

Last, you wake up to your need of God. *You need exactly the things that God promises to give, to be, and to do. You reach out for his mercy, you flee sin and temptation, and you run for daylight. You cry out to God in your need, and you ask for help.* This leads to opening yourself up to other people, because we were never made to change alone.

Take with You: Think of an area of temptation in your life. What escape has God provided? How will you take hold of it?

JULY 12

"And forgive us our debts,
as we also have forgiven our debtors." —Matthew 6:12

Be kind to one another, tenderhearted, forgiving one another,
as God in Christ forgave you. —Ephesians 4:32

Change happens in relationships. We need one another. You do not change on your own. Talk to people about your troubles. Confess your sins to one another. Where you've hurt others, ask for forgiveness. You must also forgive others when you've been sinned against.

Jesus is unrelenting here. You must forgive, even if they are dead, even if they are still your enemy, even if they never come and ask. There must first be forgiveness in your heart to God, whether there's ever the transaction of forgiveness within a real relationship. Every alternative to forgiveness is evil—anger, bitterness, clamor, slander, and malice.

You've got to grapple with what people have done, just as you've got to grapple with what you have done. As you do this, *where will you turn amid your pain and trouble? You must take refuge in the living God. God as your refuge stands against every alternative refuge.* Hard times will come, but there's a fountain of living waters—the Lord, who can be trusted. And you will not fear when the heat comes. Your leaves will remain green, you won't be anxious in the year of drought, and you won't cease to bear fruit (Jeremiah 17:7–8). Alternately, taking refuge in yourself and other refuges will always fail you.

> **Take with You:** Do you find yourself gravitating toward anger rather than forgiveness? Do you feel let down by anger—burdened by and ready to release it? Forgiveness is difficult, but the alternatives are worse.

JULY 13

This is my comfort in my affliction,
that your promise gives me life. —Psalm 119:50

What is the usual effect suffering has on you or the people you know? You turn in on yourself. You become preoccupied with your pain, being betrayed, your physical pain or disability. It just hurts. It's just hard.

What's the intrinsic effect of sinning, forgetting God, straying and wandering? I turn in on myself. My whole world consists of me. Sin curves into itself. I am the only one speaking in the theater of my mind.

Psalm 119 also starts with only one person speaking, but it goes in a different direction. It becomes a conversation. *The psalmist is getting outside of himself by declaring to God who God is and what God says. He then tells God what he's facing, both internally and externally. Then he asks God for help.* This is an out-loud relationship. You see honest cries of need coming from this person to God.

As you experience suffering, learn from this psalmist. You need fresh strength as you face this suffering. Ask God to revive you, to give you life (vv. 25, 107, 156). You are afflicted, prone to wander, and you need the Lord near to help you. Ask God to give you understanding (vv. 34, 73, 125, 144). Then recommit your way to God, in trust of him and his character (vv. 57–62). Cling to his promises in hope (vv. 49–50). He himself will be your "comfort in affliction." What better comforter could you have?

Take with You: Have you noticed your suffering and struggles tend to turn you inward? Practice turning to God in these moments, inviting him into your troubles.

JULY 14

Beloved, do not be surprised at the fiery trial when it comes upon you to test you, as though something strange were happening to you. But rejoice insofar as you share Christ's sufferings, that you may also rejoice and be glad when his glory is revealed.
—1 Peter 4:12–13

Each day will bring you "its own trouble" (Matthew 6:34). Some difficulties are in your face today and forgotten tomorrow. Other hardships last for a season. Some troubles are cyclical. Other afflictions become chronic. Some worsen, progressively bringing pain and disability into your life. And other sufferings arrive with finality—the death of a dream, the death of a loved one, your own death. But even these deaths are not stronger than Jesus. *Whatever losses you face will change in light of the resurrection of Jesus Christ and the promise that you, too, will live. He is stronger than death.* You can learn to say with all the saints: "We do not lose heart. Though our outer self is wasting away, our inner self is being renewed day by day. For this light momentary affliction is preparing for us an eternal weight of glory beyond all comparison" (2 Corinthians 4:16–17). We can learn to say it and mean it because it's true.

If you take the book of Psalms to heart, if you ponder the second half of Romans 8, if you read Job, if you let 1 Peter sink in, then you see how God's grace works in hardships. He is working, even when new challenges come.

Take with You: The wisdom to suffer well is like manna—you can't store it up, but you must receive nourishment every day.

JULY 15

Your words were found, and I ate them, and your words became to me a joy and the delight of my heart, for I am called by your name, O LORD, God of hosts. —Jeremiah 15:16

What chunk of Scripture has made the biggest difference in your life? What makes these words frequently and immediately relevant? Your answer will likely include one of the truths about reading and applying the Bible.

First, this passage became your own because you listened. He is saying this to you, and you need these words. When you forget, you drift, stray, and flounder. When you remember, and put it to work, God's truth rearranges your life.

Second, the passage and your life come together. A specific word from God connects to your struggle. Something God says invades your darkness with his light. He meets your need with his mercies. To apply the Bible to your life, start by being honest about where you need help.

Third, God meets you before you meet him. The passage caught your attention. God arranged your struggle with sin and suffering so you would need this exact help. Without God's initiative, you would never make the connection. The Spirit chose to rewrite your inner script, pouring God's love into your heart. He awakens your sense of need, gives you ears to hear, and freely gives wisdom.

Fourth, the application of beloved passages is usually straightforward. *A passage becomes personal when you add your own details into what's said. God is a very present help in trouble—this trouble.*

Take with You: Pray to God who is near with present grace in your time of trouble. Name the specific trouble you're facing today.

JULY 16

Speaking the truth in love, we are to grow up in every way into him who is the head, into Christ, from whom the whole body, joined and held together by every joint with which it is equipped, when each part is working properly, makes the body grow so that it builds itself up in love. —Ephesians 4:15–16

The Lord's people are called to help each other grow up spiritually. We are called to speak helpful words, to "counsel" each other. We are called to speak the truth in love as brothers and sisters. This is true for us at all ages. God really wants us to help one another with encouraging words.

Jesus is a wonderful counselor. He's generous and merciful. He's approachable. He asks great questions. He's firm in the ways he needs to be. And he turns lives upside down. In comparison, we might be bumbling, misguided, ignorant, ineffectual, harsh, or timid. We might not even want to think of ourselves as "counselors"—though from Jesus's point of view, all of us always offer counsel, whether foolish or wise. *Sure, we've got a long way to go. But it is into that image of Jesus that we are all being transformed. It's our joy that such a transformation turns churches into communities of wise love.*

We rightly see that preaching and teaching the Bible is important, but ministering to people in conversations is equally important. In fact, good preaching and teaching directly lead to us all having more encouraging conversations with one another.

Take with You: Who has God put in your life to speak truth in love? Care for people the way God does, ask good questions, listen well, and encourage others.

JULY 17

"Truly, truly, I say to you, whoever hears my word and believes him who sent me has eternal life. He does not come into judgment, but has passed from death to life." —John 5:24

Because of Jesus, you don't have to fear that when you die you will experience God's judgment. Jesus already experienced that for you. What waits for you after death is real life—eternal life. You don't have to earn this life. It's God's gift to those who put their trust in Jesus. This is how the apostle Paul explains it: "For the wages of sin is death, but the free gift of God is eternal life in Christ Jesus our Lord" (Romans 6:23). *We all deserve death, but Jesus died in our place. When you trust in him, you no longer have to fear death, because now you share in Jesus's life.*

The eternal life Jesus gives is life the way it was meant to be—free from evil, sorrow, and sadness, and rich in joy, peace, and purity. In a fallen world, the natural payment or wages of human life bring death and grief, but God's mercy and grace bring us his joy forever.

Sharing in Jesus's life is how you face all the shadows of death in this unhappy, fallen world and how you face the final darkness of death itself. Because he's alive, you know he will be with you when you die. Because he's alive, you know he will be waiting for you after you die. Because he lives, so do you.

Take with You: Do you sometimes fear death or avoid thinking about it? Ask God to give you hope of a joyful life in him.

JULY 18

How precious is your steadfast love, O God!
The children of mankind take refuge in the shadow of your wings.
They feast on the abundance of your house,
and you give them drink from the river of your delights.
For with you is the fountain of life;
in your light do we see light. —Psalm 36:7–9

You cannot face death with courage unless you look forward to meeting Jesus—the one who faced death and lives for you. Are you looking forward to meeting the Lamb of God who took away your sin? Do you long to hear your Good Shepherd call you by name? Are you looking forward to going to your heavenly Father's home? *In God's home all wrongs are made right, all darkness becomes bright, all losses are restored, and all tears are wiped away.*

When you pass through death, and faith becomes sight, you see the one you love. To die in the hope that God is with you is to lose everything and gain everything, into the gain of Christ.

If you look to God, the Lord of life and the giver of all mercies, you can look death straight in the eye. You're able to look past death toward something that's good, lasting, and wonderful. When you look past death with the eyes of faith, you will see a river of delight in the presence of the Lord himself; you will see yourself feasting at his table and drinking from the fountain of life (Psalm 36:7–9).

Take with You: Have you had moments of enjoying spending time with God? When you feel close to God, you start to anticipate the homecoming of being with him someday forever.

JULY 19

The Lord is my shepherd; I shall not want.
He makes me lie down in green pastures.
He leads me beside still waters. He restores my soul.
He leads me in paths of righteousness for his name's sake.

Even though I walk through the valley of
the shadow of death, I will fear no evil,
for you are with me; your rod and your staff, they comfort me.

You prepare a table before me in the presence of my enemies;
you anoint my head with oil; my cup overflows.
Surely goodness and mercy shall follow me
all the days of my life,
and I shall dwell in the house of the Lord forever. —Psalm 23

Take a moment to see your own life in this psalm. How has Jesus been your Good Shepherd? What places of beauty, peace, and safety has he led you to? Thank him for the ways he has guided you. What hard times has he walked with you through? Can you say with faith that "goodness and love will follow me all the days of my life" (v. 6 NIV)? When it's hard to pray this, ask Jesus to teach you about himself. Go to John 10 and see the Good Shepherd. Ask him to give you the joy of hearing him call you by name, of knowing that he walks with you. These are prayers God delights to answer. *He promises that when you seek him, you will find him (Jeremiah 29:13). When you find God, you find the greatest pleasure there is.*

Take with You: Pray through the psalm, filling in the blanks: *You are my Shepherd. You have led me in good ways, like_____. You protect me, as you did when_____. You bring me good things like_____.*

JULY 20

The LORD is my shepherd; I shall not want.
He makes me lie down in green pastures.
He leads me beside still waters.
He restores my soul. —Psalm 23:1–3a

When I say Psalm 23 to myself, lingering over each phrase, every word applies to my life. My life depends on the watchful mercies of the one who willingly restores my soul—and he is bringing me home. David's life experience inhabited every word of Psalm 23. *The Holy Spirit inhabits every word. And when I inhabit every word, I live. Every Christian has a feel for this. We know God speaks to us powerfully through his Word, his counsel to us. The Bible's counsel—God's message about how reality actually works—is personal, relevant, and true.*

We are not reading just one more theory about human nature. We are encountering the person who intends that we need him and know him, trust him, and love him. God's counsel reveals himself. In the light of who he is, you discover who you truly are: a dependent creature, a stray and renegade, a beloved child, a much-afflicted human being. You learn that life is a stormy conflict between true and false, good and evil, right and wrong, faith and fear, love and hate, refuge and threat, life and death. You awaken to the everyday, cosmic drama in which you participate. You come to know the Giver of life even when you must walk through the valley of the shadow of death. The Bible's counsel awakens us, reorients us, and redirects us.

Take with You: What has knowing God taught you about yourself? What do you need from him now? Remember that God speaks to us through his Word.

JULY 21

Open my eyes, that I may behold wondrous things out of your law.
I am a sojourner on the earth; hide not your
commandments from me! —Psalm 119:18–19

We've all experienced times when Scripture seems irrelevant, when our relationship with God is distracted, indifferent, or filled with complaining. Let me offer two suggestions. One asks God to do something for you, and the other asks you to notice some things about yourself.

Ask God. What can you ask the Lord to do when he and his words seem distant? Psalm 119 teaches us to say: "Make me understand. Make me alive. Teach me. Open my eyes. Don't forsake me." The psalm writer was no super-saint. He knew the same struggle you and I have. You can take this to heart. "God, awaken me to what is written." We can talk to God about the experience of disconnection. This psalm sets an example of honesty with God.

Notice Your Own Life: When Scripture and God seem hazy to us, we're also hazy about ourselves. If God seems far away, where are you? When we're far off, we're also asleep to where we need specific help today. What are you facing? Where are you struggling? *Whenever you become vividly aware of where you actually need outside help—today—then the kingdom of God comes near and Scripture sparkles.* God's promises speak exactly the hope you need right now. God's commands give exactly the guidance that will set you free. God's perspective is exactly the perspective that will reframe what you're facing.

Take with You: Ask yourself, *Does God seem out of focus? Am I out of focus?* Pray with the psalm the requests offered to us.

JULY 22

Who is the man who fears the Lord?
Him will he instruct in the way that he should choose.
His soul shall abide in well-being,
and his offspring shall inherit the land.
The friendship of the Lord is for those who fear him,
and he makes known to them his covenant.
My eyes are ever toward the Lord,
for he will pluck my feet out of the net. —Psalm 25:12–15

Consider how the Psalms are written. Unlike the stories in the Bible, the personal details are stripped away. Instead, a psalm speaks in general categories about human experience, inviting you to fill in details of what you're facing and how you're either struggling or being blessed. Psalm 25, for example, grapples with feeling the assaults of a godless world. It breathes an awareness of personal failures, and thus a need for the Lord's forgiveness and instruction. It voices honest distress at life's pressures and afflictions. It moves naturally to care for brothers and sisters who face these similar problems and need similar help. I guarantee, some or all of Psalm 25's realities are relevant to you today. *The promises of God in the Psalms—steadfast love, faithfulness, mercy, blessing, watchful care, refuge, and the like—speak directly. And they can also be filled out with New Testament details that show how every promise is "Yes" in Jesus.* Steadfast love and watchful care come in person. It matters that he's near. It matters that he's listening.

Take with You: Continue to practice filling in your specifics where the Bible is general. In this psalm, ask God to keep your eyes on him and protect you from "the net," and name the things that threaten to ensnare you.

JULY 23

The troubles of my heart are enlarged;
bring me out of my distresses.
Consider my affliction and my trouble,
and forgive all my sins. —Psalm 25:17–18

Self-analysis cannot save us. It can become simply one more form of self-fascination. Others-analysis cannot save others. It can become simply one more form of judgmentalism.

True self-knowledge is a fine gift. *And true self-knowledge always leads us out of ourselves and to our Father who, knowing us thoroughly, loves us utterly.* True self-knowledge does not wallow around inside. God intends to draw us out of self-preoccupation. Seeing how the vertical dimension (our relationship with God) relates to our struggle with sin and death, we reach out more boldly to the One who is life and light.

It is helpful to name the lust, fear, felt need, or expectation that hijacks God's place. When you can name these specifics, repentance goes deeper. There's more to share, and more to ask God to change. I can bring to the Father of mercies both my visible behavior and my inner motives. His love is magnified because I see my need for mercy more clearly. "For your name's sake, O Lord, pardon my guilt, for it is great" (Psalm 25:11). And he freely, willingly forgives his beloved children. When he thinks about me and about you, he remembers his own lovingkindness, and he answers our plea.

Take with You: Do you find yourself discouraged and thinking about your own sins? Hold fast to Jesus, and pray boldly for him to grow and change you.

JULY 24

"For where your treasure is, there your heart will be also." —Matthew 6:21

Trust in him at all times, O people;
pour out your heart before him;
God is a refuge for us. —Psalm 62:8

Our motives are all active verbs: What are you seeking? What are you loving? What are you fearing? What are you trusting? Where are you taking refuge? What voices are you listening to? Where are you setting your hopes?

The answers to these questions describe characteristics of the whole person. Every part of who we are orients toward either God or something else. Our motives drive us to treat people wisely or foolishly—so they're closely linked to behavior, emotions, and attitudes. When we take the Bible's verbs and turn them into questions, we're exposed for what we are. For example, the Bible calls me to seek God, but what am I actually seeking? Such questions help you see how and why you're straying. Our answers to these questions tell us where our sins start growing, how we curve in on ourselves and lose sight of God and his will.

But such questions never intend to send you on an inward journey. They don't make you intrusively probe others for hidden dirt. They invite us to come out of the dark and into the light of Christ. Seek him who is worthy. Trust him who gives freely. Love him who is lovely. Fear him before whom we stand. Take refuge in the One who truly is our shelter.

Take with You: Answer the questions, *What am I seeking? What do I love? What do I fear?* Name the things that sometimes take God's place in your heart and ask him to replace these things with himself.

JULY 25

Do nothing from selfish ambition or conceit, but in humility count others more significant than yourselves. Let each of you look not only to his own interests, but also to the interests of others.
—Philippians 2:3–4

Self-sacrifice brought Christ into the world and self-sacrifice will lead his followers into the midst of people. Wherever people suffer, we will be there to comfort. Wherever people strive, we will be there to help. Wherever people fail, we will be there to uplift. Wherever they succeed, we will be there to rejoice. Self-sacrifice means caring about these seasons of joy or sorrow and caring about our fellow human beings. It means entering into people's hopes and fears, longings and despairs. It means cultivating rich relationships that are others-focused.

We don't ever atone for anybody's sins, yet we're called to live out in our relationships what Christ did in atoning for our sins. This is the summary of Paul's discussion in Ephesians 5:1–2: "Therefore be imitators of God, as beloved children. And walk in love, as Christ loved us and gave himself up for us, a fragrant offering and sacrifice to God." That means we are called to essentially lay down our lives for others in a secondary way. *We imitate Christ as we lay down our lives for the happiness of others, to alleviate the sufferings of others, to grieve their failures and heartaches, and to rejoice in their successes and blessings.* That is the kind of fundamental sympathy we are called to.

Take with You: When you think of the people closest to you, what are their joys and sorrows right now? How can you join them by rejoicing with those who rejoice and weeping with those who weep?

JULY 26

Trust in the LORD with all your heart,
and do not lean on your own understanding.
In all your ways acknowledge him,
and he will make straight your paths. —Proverbs 3:5–6

There's so much going on in our lives. How do we sort it all so we have clarity on what we're hearing and seeing? We get disoriented. We're confused, baffled, and overwhelmed when things are going on in life, either sufferings, sins, chaos, or ignorance. We stumble in the dark—sometimes (often) feeling extremely confused.

One of the goals of biblical change is reorientation. It's like knowing what direction is east, south, west, north. It's knowing where you are, not being lost in the woods. You need to have a sense of where you are and where you're heading. *Where am I in all this chaos, and where is it that I need to get to?*

So as in all change, as in every psalm, there's a connection between our struggles and our reactions. Our sins and sorrows are connected to the things that erupt out of us. We have this God who comes to help us change. He enters the stage of human need and invades mercifully and powerfully to shield us, strengthen us, forgive us, help us, lead us, care for us, and be a refuge for us. When we trust him with our whole hearts, when we lean on him, he will make our paths straight. He will reorient us, not once, not twice, but every day, every time we ask.

Take with You: Do you feel lost in your efforts to change? Ask God to reorient you and show you the way forward.

JULY 27

"You shall love the LORD your God with all your heart and with all your soul and with all your might." —Deuteronomy 6:5

A Prayer for Transformation

Our Father in heaven, thank you for inviting your people of all generations to be listeners from the heart. Speak to us and reveal:

> what it means to know you, how it is that we seek you,
>
> what it means to love you, to need you, to fall on our faces before you, trembling, to delight in you.
>
> And we pray that as we think about the way in which you meet us, and transform us,
>
> we ask that you would give to us your Holy Spirit himself, the one who enlivens us, awakens us, gives us ears to hear, who writes words of life upon our hearts and reveals who you are.

Show us our need, reveal your promises of mercy, and remind us that you do what you say and that your actions back up your words. *We pray that we would be men and women who enter into the good things that you offer and pray for you to help us be those men and women who give to others freely, humbly, caring for them, because of all the good things you give to us.* Amen.

Take with You: What request most resonates with you from this prayer? Write it down and pray it throughout the day.

JULY 28

If then you have been raised with Christ, seek the things that are above, where Christ is, seated at the right hand of God. Set your minds on things that are above, not on things that are on earth. For you have died, and your life is hidden with Christ in God.
—Colossians 3:1–3

Every day we hear voices and messages from the world's value system. We're told to judge our value based on physical appearance, wealth, education, and more. We're told we're worth more if we're thin, rich, and smart. We hear other messages predicting all kinds of disasters right around the corner. The world tells us what we should aspire to, what we should be anxious about, and what should make us feel superior or inferior to others. It's hard to see that these messages are lies if our minds are set on earthly things.

But Paul calls us to a different way of thinking: to see life through the lens of Christ on the throne. Your life is hidden in him. You can view all the pressures and problems from a heavenly perspective. Human beings live with an unfolding story, and we can see our life story with this heavenly perspective. We all have a significant past, a backstory. *Our life story is still unfolding. There is a future. The story has hope. We will be raised with Christ—that's the heavenly way of thinking that quiets all earthly voices.*

Take with You: What messages trouble you the most? Ask God to shape your values more and more to fit with the life story he is writing.

JULY 29

For you are my rock and my fortress;
and for your name's sake you lead me and guide me;
you take me out of the net they have hidden for me,
for you are my refuge.
Into your hand I commit my spirit;
you have redeemed me, O LORD, faithful God. . . .

my strength fails because of my iniquity,
and my bones waste away. . . .

Be strong, and let your heart take courage,
all you who wait for the LORD! —Psalm 31:3–5, 10b, 24

It's essential to rely on God's goodness and mercy to grow as a believer. When you want to change, sometimes it's easy to think about yourself a lot. But it's important to have something you're focusing on outside of yourself. Consider God's promises. Consider how he shows himself to you in his graciousness, in his goodness. Notice how in Psalm 31's description of coming from danger into the safety of God's presence, there's a clear reliance and trust in God. *We can't change without continually going to the Redeemer, the merciful God. The result of repentance is gladness and thankfulness for real mercies.* Although we see ourselves differently as we are growing and changing, the result is not that we get stuck looking at ourselves too much. We look outside ourselves in two ways: faith and love. When you move from darkness to the light of faith, God's love moves you out into your world courageously, constructively, and mercifully to help others.

Take with You: Ask God to lift your eyes to him and to others. Pray for his love to flow through you. Turn to God in faith, and reach out to other people in love.

JULY 30

Let all that you do be done in love. —1 Corinthians 16:14

Everyone has a map for how to navigate life. A map tells you where you are in relation to other things. A reality map is a belief system, a way that you understand how the world works. It tells you how to travel through your relationships, avoid what you want to avoid, and get where you want to go.

For example, perhaps you struggle with talking to a particular relative about anything significant. Why would that be true for you? Or anyone? It's likely that your reality map tells you that it's because this person is cranky, feisty, or "difficult." *But in God's reality map, the reason we fail to reach out may be that we do not love them. Perhaps we do not trust God in such a way that we're able to act in love toward them.* That's just one example where a change in the reality map means a change in how we understand one another's sinfulness and self-centeredness. We will only have a reason to move toward this person when our motivation changes.

Our reality map is what guides us as we move into relationships. Our reality map tells us what the world looks like and then describes how we intend to proceed into the world. But what would it be like if we gave up our reality map and lived in God's world? When we live in God's world, love is the overriding motivation for all we do.

Take with You: What does your reality map tell you about how to navigate life? Ask God to give you his map to navigate life.

JULY 31

"I the LORD search the heart
and test the mind." —Jeremiah 17:10a

All of life is connected to our relationship with God. For example, the world might notice that someone is very concerned about what other people think about him or her. But they don't see it for what it is: what the Bible calls "fear of man." Fear of man is actually an alternative to the fear of God.

Similarly, pride is an alternative to seeing Jesus as King. We can all notice people who are proud. But we can't always see that pride is a way of exalting ourselves in the universe as if we were king—an alternative to the real King Jesus.

Our struggles, like fear and pride, can motivate us to do all kinds of bad things. The Bible helps us see that these struggles and the heart motives they come from are connected to our relationship with God. It's not possible to fully know our own heart motives. We know that we don't see ourselves in the way that God sees us. There are layers of ignorance in us that will only be revealed on the last day. And we certainly can't see into other people's hearts. *From a Christian point of view, our hearts and motives actually have to do with how we're relating to God. It's the Lord who searches the heart and tests our minds and our motives. Only in our relationship to him will we find clarity about our own hearts.*

Take with You: Do you struggle with fearing people when you feel far from God? Ask God to show his greatness and strength so that even when people are scary, you experience his refuge.

AUGUST 1

Therefore, as you received Christ Jesus the Lord, so walk in him, rooted and built up in him and established in the faith, just as you were taught, abounding in thanksgiving. —Colossians 2:6–7

The Bible teaches that we grow and change through relationships, and especially your relationship with God. Let me draw a couple of contrasts. One of the pieces of advice that you'll often hear about how to change is that you need to "look to Christ" or "look to the cross." But the idea of looking is kind of passive, right? Most people don't understand what that means or how to do it. But it means more than just seeing—it means seeking.

Seeking God changes us.

The Bible also talks about the language of "remembering," like remember your identity in Christ. Remember you're a child of the King, that you've been justified by faith. Remember that God works all things for good. Now, again, similar to "look," there's nothing wrong with remembering. But the Bible doesn't teach that changing depends on your ability to remember something. Instead, change happens in relationship. When you're struggling, you need to reach out of yourself and seek the One who is merciful and not try to think your way out of the problem. *When you're overwhelmed by all the forces of evil and face-plant into sin, you need to experience God for who he is. He's there for you right in the hard time, coming close, and merciful. This is how we change.*

Take with You: Ask God to show you how your relationship with him is. Invite him to come close and help you take the next step of change.

AUGUST 2

Therefore be imitators of God, as beloved children. And walk in love, as Christ loved us and gave himself up for us, a fragrant offering and sacrifice to God. —Ephesians 5:1–2

As we learned yesterday, change happens in relationships. The Spirit changes how we relate to people (the horizontal dimension) and how we relate to God (the vertical dimension). If you stay horizontal, you will drift toward moralism. This means changing just to feel like a good person for others or compared to others. And if you stay vertical, you will drift toward a spiritual-sounding faith that doesn't work its way out in real life. You love God in some sense, but it doesn't lead you to love others. But there really is a connection between the vertical and horizontal—both in the negative and the positive sense.

In the negative sense, your behavior toward others and what's in your heart before God are linked. What you think, feel, and do always expresses what's going on in your relationship with God. If you're worshipping anything more than God—like money, control, or being liked by others–this will affect how you live. Your actual functional god, where you find your refuge and comfort, is always coming out in every reaction.

On the good side—to the degree that you are seeking and finding and trusting the God who is Lord—you are able then to love people. You're able to move toward people constructively, with love for others and living faith in God.

Take with You: Have you noticed this connection between your relationship with God and your relationship with others? Ask God for faith that moves upward and outward.

AUGUST 3

Therefore, if anyone is in Christ, he is a new creation. The old has passed away; behold, the new has come. —2 Corinthians 5:17

For many people, there's a huge disconnect between "God talk" and where their life is actually lived. That can be discouraging when you're trying to encourage someone spiritually. So where do you start as you talk with others, and as you think about your own relationship with God? Begin by looking for good things. Start with the places you see God's grace already working in a person's life. List the ways that person has grown.

There's this tension in redemption. On the one hand, you're new; you're part of the new creation. You have been awakened to Christ. There are actual good works that God has prepared for you to walk in. And on the other hand, you've still got parts of the old life hanging around—that's the problem of indwelling sin, and that all our works are imperfect. That's one of those many places where there's a continual need to move from the old to the new by the mercy of Christ. We're always moving on from old to new. It's always because of the goodness of Christ to you and to me. That is always the bridge to change. It's always the hope that we have.

Every day there's a place where the battle happens. We'll be tempted to be asleep, deaf, and blind. And we need to wake up, see, and hear. And we need to turn toward the Lord and his mercies.

Take with You: If God feels far away, take a moment to look for where God is already changing you and working in you, and give thanks.

AUGUST 4

Put on then, as God's chosen ones, holy and beloved, compassionate hearts, kindness, humility, meekness, and patience, bearing with one another and, if one has a complaint against another, forgiving each other; as the Lord has forgiven you, so you also must forgive. —Colossians 3:12–13

Part of "putting on" a new life is learning, bit by bit, to ask forgiveness when you've hurt people. Did you know most angry people don't ask for forgiveness? But you can put on humility, not just saying, "I'm sorry if you feel hurt," but instead, "It's wrong for me to speak to you that way. I'm sorry for hurting you. Please forgive me." This is a huge step of growth.

Another step is learning to put on patience—for your buttons to not be pushed as easily. Things may still push your buttons. Is it good that ten things push your buttons? No. Is it good that now it's only ten instead of fifty? Yes.

Putting on a new way of life, little by little, is how the Christian growth process works. That's how our Lord works with us. There's a growing quickness to repent, appreciation for the grace of Christ, willingness to repair relationships. Outbursts are less frequent and intense. You can even move into some really hard things—like someone who used to struggle with a temper actually becoming a peacemaker. That's huge. And that, too, is another one of these little steps forward.

Take with You: We are in the hands of the Peacemaker. And he's committed to walk all the way through with us and make us in his image. Rejoice today that he will complete the work in you.

AUGUST 5

Let all bitterness and wrath and anger and clamor and slander be put away from you, along with all malice. Be kind to one another, tenderhearted, forgiving one another, as God in Christ forgave you.
—Ephesians 4:31–32

Forgiveness is a conscious choice you make when you understand God's mercy to you. It recognizes that what happened was wrong. It makes no excuses for what happened. And then it lets it go.

Patience and forgiveness are the first two key aspects of the constructive displeasure of mercy for a reason. As we respond with patience and forgiveness to wrongs we have experienced, we have gone a long way toward redeeming anger. But there's more—we also need to respond to true wrongs with charity and constructive conflict.

Charity moves toward the person who has done wrong with kindness, even when the person doesn't deserve the kindness. But there's also a place for entering into constructive conflict when wrongs have been done. *Mercy doesn't stand by while others go in the wrong direction or when someone—oneself or another—is being mistreated. Mercy wades into difficult situations and is willing to get involved. It's willing to raise difficult issues, apply justice or allow consequences when needed, and persevere to see good come out of evil.* Constructive conflict continues the work that patience, forgiveness, and charity have begun.

Take with You: How do you respond to and engage with conflict? Do you avoid it, or do you have destructive conflict? Ask God for help in engaging conflict in a way that builds up the relationship and makes things better.

AUGUST 6

"You have heard that it was said, 'You shall love your neighbor and hate your enemy.' But I say to you, Love your enemies and pray for those who persecute you, so that you may be sons of your Father who is in heaven. . . . For if you love those who love you, what reward do you have? Do not even the tax collectors do the same?"
—Matthew 5:43–46

Philosophy of Life 101 for most people is: You scratch my back, I'll scratch yours. You do me wrong, I hold a grudge or get even. That's the easy way—and it's the recipe for disaster, estrangement, and war. Our Father doesn't operate by that philosophy. *He teaches his children to love in a way that's hard, but good. It's the path to reconciliation and peace.* He gives us three pictures.

First, notice the weather. "Your Father . . . makes his sun rise on the evil and on the good" (Matthew 5:45). We need sun and rain to have food, and God doesn't discriminate in doing basic good. Can you do that too?

Second, notice how even bad people treat their friends right: "If you love those who love you, what reward do you have?" (Matthew 5:46). Can you take it a step up from bad people?

Third, notice how people everywhere recognize a special bond between family members. "If you greet only your brothers, what more are you doing than others?" (Matthew 5:47). Can you take it a step up from the us-them loyalty that comes naturally to everyone and love even those difficult to love?

Take with You: Who do you find difficult to treat with kindness? Ask God to give you his love for them.

AUGUST 7

Whoever walks with the wise becomes wise,
but the companion of fools will suffer harm. —Proverbs 13:20

Somehow it seems like sickness is more contagious than good health, and a bad attitude travels faster than a good attitude. It's also hard to "catch" patience or righteous anger from others. But it can happen. Did you ever know a parent or close friend, a teacher or coach, who was patient and generous with others, not easily set off, even when mistreated? Did this person save their anger for when there was a wrong that really mattered? Was anger expressed cleanly and constructively, as part of love for others that tackled wrongs? Wonderfully, some people express anger in ways that tackle the problem to solve it.

"He who walks with the wise grows wise" (Proverbs 13:20, author translation). There's nothing like a good role model to give you a vision for how it's possible to do life well. This is the type of person you can become, by God's grace. You can learn to walk with Jesus—the wisest person in the world—and become more like him in how you respond when life goes wrong.

Blessed are the peacemakers. To respond constructively to trouble is like mastering a fine art, gained through long practice. Jesus is our perfect example, and he's always near. We can ask God to make us more like him in wisdom, patience, and kindness.

Take with You: Can you think of someone who shows patience and also firmness when needed? Ask God to provide you with good examples and mentors so you can learn from them.

AUGUST 8

But you are a chosen people, a royal priesthood, a holy nation, God's special possession, that you may declare the praises of him who called you out of darkness into his wonderful light. —1 Peter 2:9 NIV

Christ is Lord and Master. He bought us with a price. Part of what it means to have faith is to know and embrace that we belong to him and make it a core part of our identity. We say, "I am a servant of Christ for life."

We're connected to God for life, like a marriage vow. The Bible speaks of the Lord as married to his people. He patiently nourishes and cherishes his wife, the body of Christ. We need husbanding from someone faithful, kind, protective, and generous. Having faith means we know and embrace this core identity. We say, "I submit to Jesus."

God searches every heart. We live before his eyes. Having faith means we know and embrace this core identity. We say, "I am a God-fearing person." Our God is good, mighty, and glorious. He is worthy of our trust, praise, gladness, and gratitude. Having faith means we know and embrace this core identity: "I am a worshipper."

We could go on! The pattern is obvious. Every core aspect of our identity expresses some form of humility, need, submission, and dependency before the Lord. Here is the pattern of Jesus: Weakness leads to strength. Serving leads to mastery. Deaths lead to resurrections. *When your core identity is meek and lowly—like Jesus—then your calling develops into his image of purposeful, wise, courageous love.* You become like God.

Take with You: Which of these core identity statements will you take with you today? Write it down, remember it, and ask God to make it yours.

AUGUST 9

"Blessed are the poor in spirit, for theirs is the kingdom of heaven.
Blessed are those who mourn, for they shall be comforted.
Blessed are the meek, for they shall inherit the earth.
Blessed are those who hunger and thirst for righteousness,
for they shall be satisfied." —Matthew 5:3–6

In the Beatitudes, the right kind of strength comes from the right kind of weakness:

- *"The poor in spirit are blessed."* Jesus is described as one who, though he was rich, became poor—for you. He became dependent and needy. He died as a human in weakness and vulnerability.
- *"Those who mourn are blessed."* Jesus is portrayed as one who mourns (Isaiah 53:3). He mourns for your sake, he mourns the suffering that he must face, he mourns all the things that are wrong in this world, and he comes on a mission to make wrongs right.
- *"The meek are blessed."* Jesus describes himself as meek and lowly in heart. Meekness is not weakness in the negative sense. It's weakness in the positive sense. Jesus lived under God's calling, following the voice of his Father, fully trusting God's promises, fully obeying God's will.

Jesus is blessed because he hungers and thirsts for righteousness. He makes right what's wrong. He makes true what's false. And he remakes what's evil for the good of his people.

Jesus was weak and needy, and yet strong to save. He warmly welcomes the weak and needy to the throne of his grace, that we might receive the mercy we need and the grace specific to our troubles (Hebrews 4:16).

Take with You: When you feel weak and needy, ask God to show his strength to you, help you rest in his strength, and strengthen you.

AUGUST 10

"Blessed are the merciful, for they shall receive mercy. Blessed are the pure in heart, for they shall see God. Blessed are the peacemakers, for they shall be called sons of God. Blessed are those who are persecuted for righteousness' sake, for theirs is the kingdom of heaven." —Matthew 5:7–10

Jesus was not afraid to be weak in public. Jesus personally embodied and modeled what he tells us in the Beatitudes. We want to see the image of Christ in our lives and look like Jesus in these ways. *The Beatitudes show us how the right kind of weakness leads directly to the right kind of strength, a strength grounded and founded in need.* Think about the qualities of strength that the last four beatitudes portray.

Jesus says, "Blessed are the merciful," describing a life of deep concern for the welfare of others—to be generous, openhearted, and openhanded.

Jesus says, "The pure in heart are blessed," describing the ability to treat people unselfishly, not looking for what we can get from them.

Jesus says, "Peacemakers are blessed. They're nothing less than the children of God." Peacemaking is the ability to be candid, constructive, and caring—to pursue peace in a world that is full of war, dissension, conflicts, arguments, and avoiders.

Jesus says, "Those who are persecuted are blessed." He calls us to joyful purposefulness, finding courage in affliction, finding perseverance in opposition. These are wonderful traits. These are the traits of leadership and loving fruitfulness in Jesus's life—and in ours as well.

Take with You: Pick one of the qualities of Jesus we see in the Beatitudes and ask God to make it more and more true of you.

AUGUST 11

If you turn at my reproof,
behold, I will pour out my spirit to you;
I will make my words known to you. —Proverbs 1:23

The Proverbs are written to go straight to the heart. They make you face some basic questions: What are you pursuing in life? What voices are you listening to? How are you relating to friendships, money, food, drink, rest, school? These topics relate to everyone, across time! I flipped open Proverbs today and was struck by the first line of chapter 17: "Better is a dry morsel with quiet than a house full of feasting with strife." I realized I'd been irritable that morning. I had created strife. So I asked for forgiveness. We gained a house full of quiet. Try reading in Proverbs until something strikes home and take that one bit of wisdom into the rest of your day.

When you wake up to what is really happening in your life—for me it was being irritable—it's impossible for your devotional life to be stale. God, in his Word, intersects, speaks into, and touches what's going on. But you must stop to notice. And then you must ask. The Beatitudes (Matthew 5:3–12) lie at the heart of Jesus's greatest sermon. Jesus places his first blessing on the "poor in spirit" for a reason. When you know your need for outside help, for gifts that only the Lord can give, then the kingdom of God is yours. The King will show up in your day today.

Take with You: Stop, take some time, and really notice what is happening in your life. Then ask God to make his Word come alive for you today.

AUGUST 12

And everyone who thus hopes in him purifies himself as he is pure.
—1 John 3:3

Everyone knows that Christianity has a lot to say about sex. We are right to think that Christianity stands against sexual immorality. The Bible says that it leads to death and judgment: "On account of these the wrath of God is coming" (Colossians 3:6). But we are wrong to think that this is *all* that the Bible says. The Bible makes at least three other major points about sex.

First the Bible is not shy: Scripture speaks openly, sometimes even graphically, of rape, homosexuality, pornographic fantasies, voyeurism, seduction, bestiality, incest, prostitution, and the like. Not only does God speak freely of sexual sin, but God speaks freely of how alluring it can be (see Proverbs 7). He does this not to tempt us but to help guard us against temptation.

Second, the Bible celebrates sex in the context of faithfulness—faithfulness first to God and second to one's husband or wife. God made sex. God made it to be good. Sexual intimacy is intended to give great pleasure, to express love, to be given generously and gladly.

Third, *Christianity is about forgiveness.* Christianity teaches us that transformation is possible. We are neither stuck in our sinfulness nor told to fix ourselves on our own. Instead, *Christ bridges the divide between the shameful and the glorious and invites us to cross over. In Christ, the immoral are transformed into the faithful.*

Take with You: Whatever your sexual history, whatever your temptations, whatever shame you carry around with you, entrust all of it to your heavenly Father. Tell him everything. He will not be surprised. Trust in his forgiveness and his power to transform.

AUGUST 13

Make me understand the way of your precepts,
and I will meditate on your wondrous works. —Psalm 119:27

What makes Scripture relevant in your life? One, God does it. He makes it relevant. He awakens you. Two, name your troubles. You know yourself, and you know where you need help. Three, think about what God says. *Meditate throughout your day. It's the Scripture I think about later in the day, that revisits me a second time, that actually makes a difference in my life.* It's not when I read something in the morning once—it's the second time it has a go-round in my life that it ends up changing how I live.

Our Father, will you make these things so? We are dependents; we are like birds (Luke 12:22–31). We cannot store up your Spirit. We need you to help us to do the hard thinking about your Word. We need you to help us be honest about where we struggle, where our troubles are.

We need you to make us see that it's in the love of Christ that we have life. It's in your tenderness for us as a Father. It's in your life—giving to us yourself, the Spirit of life—that we have life.

We pray these things in confidence that Jesus Christ will lead us through thorny ways to the joyful end we're heading to. We pray this in the name of that Christ. Amen.

Take with You: Take one piece of God's Word into your day. Write it down. Post it somewhere you can see. Let it return to you and speak into the different moments of your day.

AUGUST 14

"It is the LORD who goes before you. He will be with you; he will not leave you or forsake you. Do not fear or be dismayed."
—Deuteronomy 31:8

What are the big questions that trouble you? At some level, all of us carry around the same questions: *What will happen to me? How will my life turn out? Will I be abandoned? Am I all alone? Is God really for me?*

Scripture speaks straight to these questions. Psalm 1 is about how your life will turn out. Will you end up as chaff that is nothing, or are you a tree planted by streams of water, yielding its fruit in its season? Deuteronomy 31 speaks to the question of abandonment. God promises, "I'm with you, I'm for you, I won't abandon you." Romans 5 speaks straight to the heart of our deepest, most anguished question: Are we loved, even in our failure? The answer: There is nothing that can separate us from the love of God in Christ Jesus our Lord (Romans 8:38–39).

The love of God pours straight into these deepest questions. *Scripture reaches us when our faith reaches out. It's when we feel most homeless and unlovable that Scripture gives us a home.* When you cut below the surface, what are you asking? What are your friends asking? When you ask the right questions—your truest questions—you will always find that the Word of the living God, the grace of the living God, the mercies of Jesus Christ will answer.

Take with You: What's your biggest, rawest, most haunting question about life? Admit it openly and honestly, then look for the answer in God's Word.

AUGUST 15

Seek the LORD and his strength;
seek his presence continually! —Psalm 105:4

No one wants to suffer. Most people do all they can to avoid it. Yet Martin Luther said suffering is necessary to faith. It's the touchstone that teaches us how right, true, sweet, mighty, and comforting God's Word is. *It's in life experience that the Word actually comes to life and gains reality. There's something about facing hardship that makes real the things of the Bible. Suffering works to transform us into the image of Jesus.* Jesus entered into our world of difficulty to love people who also face struggle and difficulty.

Our suffering comes from both the things that happen to us and the things inside us. We are often very aware of the ways our circumstances cause us to suffer, but we must not forget that, at our core, we are weak, sinful, and mortal. One of the best ways to describe the big picture of our human weakness is the word "temptation." We are led astray by what looks good to us from the outside and what we want from within. When we recognize this, we can find the door to help. Our weakness drives us to look to the Lord for his strength, power, and presence.

"Draw near to the throne of his grace that [you] may receive mercy and find grace to help in time of need" (Hebrews 4:16).

Take with You: What is your biggest struggle right now? How might God be using it make his promises more real in your life? Draw near to God. Ask for his grace and mercy in your situation.

AUGUST 16

He put a new song in my mouth,
a song of praise to our God.
Many will see and fear,
and put their trust in the LORD. —Psalm 40:3

God's Word doesn't stop with us. It always goes out and connects to other people. It has this built-in dynamic. God's purposes are not just to make you better or to give you a sense of self-satisfaction and joy. His purpose is to create people who get out of themselves. As you see and experience for yourself how God and his words connect, it leads you out of yourself to offer faith and love to others. We go outward to people in love, patience, kindness, and generosity.

When the Bible comes to life in your life, it doesn't end with you.

Psalm 40 is a great example of this. David looks back at the Lord's deliverance in the past (vv. 1–3a). Then he immediately moves to other people (v. 3b). David's testimony is your testimony too. This is what happened to you. You were in great trouble, and God met you. You've got a story to tell, and it's going to have an effect on other people because the gospel is not just a theory—the gospel is lived out in and through your life. It's a story of deliverance that you get to tell as you live within it.

Take with You: Have you ever shared the story of how God rescued you? Think of one person in your life—a friend, a classmate, a neighbor, a family member—who needs to hear your story, who needs to see the gospel alive in you. Then, go start a conversation!

AUGUST 17

Search me, God, and know my heart;
test me and know my anxious thoughts.
See if there is any offensive way in me,
and lead me in the way everlasting. —Psalm 139:23–24 NIV

How can you find help in dealing with anxiety? First, identify what's going on within you. Is anxiety hiding under anger or a desire to control everything? Are you squandering your life in aimless fun? Anxiety can show up in many ways. Second, remember that you aren't alone and the Lord is with you. You may have good reasons to feel afraid and anxious right now, but you have better reasons not to be afraid. Third, name your troubles, whether it's loneliness or academic pressure or relational conflict.

Once you have thought deeply about your struggle, have an honest conversation with God. Bring your troubles to the one who can actually help. After you've poured out your heart to God, the next step of faith is to faithfully do whatever needs doing today. Give yourself today's task. *Of all the things you worry about, very few of them are in your control, and of those things that are in your control, not all of them are your responsibility today. What are you called to do today? Giving yourself to the small acts of obedience is extremely liberating.*

Anxiety opens the door to faith and a door to loving God and others more deeply. But this can only happen if you face your anxiety honestly and bring it, again and again, to God.

Take with You: What's your small obedience for the day? Find freedom in pursuing only the calling God has given you for today and trusting the rest to his control.

AUGUST 18

I have calmed and quieted my soul,
like a weaned child with its mother;
like a weaned child is my soul within me.

O Israel, hope in the LORD
from this time forth and forevermore. —Psalm 131:2–3

Psalm 131 is a show-and-tell for how to become peaceful inside. The psalmist has learned the only true and lasting way to calm, and he shares the details of what peace is like.

Amazingly, this man isn't noisy inside. Not obsessed or on edge. The to-do list and pressures to achieve don't consume him. Failure and despair don't haunt him. Anxiety isn't spinning him into freefall. He's quiet.

But Psalm 131 does not portray blissful, unruffled detachment. It isn't a Zen-like state of higher consciousness. It's not about becoming unfeeling and philosophical about life. It's not about having an easygoing personality or having low expectations so you're easy to please. It's not a retreat from the troubles of life.

The composure of Psalm 131 is learned—in relationship. This kind of quiet is purposeful. It's awake and aware. It's chosen. It's a form of self-mastery by the grace of God. You are "discipled" into such composure. You learn it from Someone. When you truly understand yourself to be a chosen, anointed, loved, and blessed child, the words of Psalm 131 will be yours.

Take with You: Are you quiet inside? Is Psalm 131 your experience too? If your answer is no, ask yourself some follow-up questions: *What is the "noise" going on inside me? When do I get worried, irritable, wearied, or hopeless?*

AUGUST 19

O LORD, my heart is not lifted up;
my eyes are not raised too high;
I do not occupy myself with things
too great and too marvelous for me. —Psalm 131:1

Do you remember *Alice in Wonderland*, how Alice was either too big or too small? Because she was never quite the right size, she was continually disoriented. We all have that problem. Because of our proud self-will, we're the wrong size. We imagine ourselves to be independent and autonomous. We become obsessed by tiny, insignificant things. We pursue our self-image, our self-importance, and even our selfies. We become afraid of our own shadows. We become noisy inside.

If you aren't proud, then quietness and calmness make sense. When you pursue what you're called to pursue, it makes sense you'd have peace. You've discovered what you're made for. When you go after the right things, you'll find what you're looking for. Quiet your noisy self to know the peace that passes understanding.

How does a proud heart become a humble heart? You do not wrestle yourself down by pain and punishment. You do not destroy the noise of self-will by sheer will. You only wrestle yourself down by the promises of God's lovingkindness. You need the invasion of the Redeemer, the hand of the Shepherd. *We escape ourselves by being loved by Jesus Christ through the powerful presence of the Holy Spirit himself. We escape ourselves by learning a lifestyle of repentance, faith, and obedience.*

Take with You: What are you pursuing? What are the things in your life that make you feel too big or too small, that create noise and chaos in your heart? Could it be your relationships, your grades, your social media? How might you repent and turn toward Jesus?

AUGUST 20

"Therefore I tell you, do not be anxious about your life, what you will eat or what you will drink, nor about your body, what you will put on. Is not life more than food, and the body more than clothing? Look at the birds of the air: they neither sow nor reap nor gather into barns, and yet your heavenly Father feeds them. Are you not of more value than they?" —Matthew 6:25–26

Why did Jesus say to not be anxious? He focused on really simple things: God cares for mere birds, and he feeds them. How much more for you? God clothes the lilies of the field. And you—God knows what you need. He gave you Jesus to rescue you from yourself.

The troubles of life can be magnified by our all-consuming fears. It feels very threatening when things happen that we cannot control. We feel fragile and vulnerable.

The experience of extreme fear is isolating. You are all alone and you've got chaotic thoughts and feelings. In this struggle, you need to know there's another voice speaking into your situation: God's voice. He sympathizes with your weaknesses. He's willing to enter your struggle. You can approach the throne of grace with confidence that you will find mercy and help in time of need (Hebrews 4:15–16).

You may have good reasons for fear, but you have even better reasons for courage, faith, and love. We have hope, and that hope is Christ.

Take with You: When your head and heart get noisy with anxiety, take a moment to zero in on Jesus's voice—the voice of your Rescuer—saying, "Do not be anxious about your life. I love you."

AUGUST 21

"And do not seek what you are to eat and what you are to drink, nor be worried. For all the nations of the world seek after these things, and your Father knows that you need them. Instead, seek his kingdom, and these things will be added to you." —Luke 12:29–31

Jesus lists all the reasons why you shouldn't be in the grip of fear and worry. He says to consider the ravens and how God feeds them—how we're even more valuable than the birds. "And which of you by being anxious can add a single hour to his span of life? If then you are not able to do as small a thing as that, why are you anxious about the rest?" (vv. 24–26).

Jesus addresses our driven, obsessed state of mind, the preoccupation with money and possessions. "Your Father knows that you need them. . . . seek his kingdom, and these things will be added to you."

There's so much more to who you are than what you have or don't have. His promise is far more than "God will take care of you." It's "God will clothe you in nothing less than his radiant glory!" *God's giving you a life that's radiant and indestructible and full of glory. Having given you so much, your Father calls you to the radical freedom of giving your life away.*

Take with You: Focus today on all that you have been given in Christ—the sure, certain, and wonderful reality of being saved, being changed, and being glorified.

AUGUST 22

Trust in him at all times, O people;
pour out your heart before him;
God is a refuge for us. —Psalm 62:8

Anxiety is a universal human experience, and you need to approach it with a plan. First, name the pressures. You always worry about *something*. What things tend to hook you? What "good reasons" do you have for anxiety? Second, identify how you express anxiety. For some people it's feelings of panic clutching their throat, or just a vague unease. For others, it's repetitive, obsessive thoughts, or even anger. Third, ask yourself, *Why am I anxious?* Worry always has its inner logic. If I've forgotten God, who or what has edged him out of my mind and started to rule in his place?

Fourth, go to your Father. Talk to him. He cares about the things you worry about: your friends, health, money, the future, etc. You can go to him with your concerns. You'll have to leave your worries with him. They're always outside of your control! You have good reasons to be concerned about such things, but you have better reasons to take them to Someone who loves you.

Finally, give. Do and say something constructive. In the darkest hole, when the world is most confused, there's always the next right thing to do. There's always some way to give yourself away. The problem might seem overwhelming. *You could worry, but instead you're called to do some small, itty-bitty thing. There's always some way to give. Be about the business of today. Leave tomorrow's uncertainties to your Father.*

Take with You: What is your small, itty-bitty thing today? What is one way you can give or serve others even in the middle of your worry?

AUGUST 23

Be still, my soul: the Lord is on thy side.
Bear patiently the cross of grief or pain.
Leave to thy God to order and provide;
In every change, He faithful will remain.
Be still, my soul: thy best, thy heav'nly Friend
Through thorny ways leads to a joyful end.
—Katharina von Schlegel, "Be Still, My Soul"

God works in and through suffering. How has God worked in my own suffering? First came the suffering itself. Amid cascading losses and troubles, everything I did and everything I thought I knew were thrown up in the air. My faith and love had to grow up—again.

A handful of wise, godly friends played a significant role. Some were going through similar experiences. They understood. Other friends poured their sympathy into helping me plan and to act within the limitations of my circumstances. I needed both the tenderness and the realism. Both embody Jesus Christ.

I was also sustained by the wisdom of saints whose race finished long ago. I had never realized how many hymns inhabit suffering. The hymns spoke to me: "The Lord is on your side, even in this. He is your best friend who will not disappoint you. He rules this storm too. He will restore to you love's purest joys."

God met me with his words and his Spirit—through preaching, the Lord's Supper, the informal counsel of friends, and my own reflection on Scripture. In my suffering, many words I had heard before took on new meanings. Obedience had to take new forms. My faith needed to find expression in new ways.

Take with You: How is your suffering prompting you to find newness—new insight, obedience, love toward others, faith?

AUGUST 24

In the way of your testimonies I delight
as much as in all riches.
I will meditate on your precepts
and fix my eyes on your ways. —Psalm 119:14–15

It takes thoughtful work to apply the Bible's stories, histories, and prophecies, even many of the commands, teachings, promises, and prayers to your life. If you take them straight—as if they speak directly to you, about you, with your issues in view—you will misunderstand and misapply Scripture. For example, the angel's command to Joseph, "Take the child and his mother, and flee to Egypt" (Matthew 2:13), is not a command to anyone today to buy a ticket for Cairo! Attempts to take the entire Bible as if it directly applies to you distort the Bible. It's like treating the Bible like a magic spell book teeming with private messages and meanings. God does not intend that his words function that way.

These passages do apply. But most of the Bible applies by extension and analogy, not directly. In one sense, such passages apply exactly because they are not about you. They draw you out of the temptation to see God through the lens of yourself and your own needs.

Understood rightly, all these other parts of Scripture give a changed perspective. They locate you on a bigger stage. They teach you to notice God and other people. They call you to understand yourself within a story—many stories—bigger than your personal history and immediate concerns.

Take with You: When you read a passage of Scripture today, try to take yourself out of the center ("How does this apply to me?") and put God at the center ("What does this show me about God's character and story?").

AUGUST 25

Hear my cry, O God, listen to my prayer;
from the end of the earth I call to you when my heart is faint.
Lead me to the rock that is higher than I. —Psalm 61:1–2

Why do you pray? I suspect you and I are probably alike.

When we're honest, we say the reason we pray is that we need to pray. It's the door of life. And if we don't, we perish. If we don't, we're insane.

To explore how prayer goes right, it helps to identify ways prayer goes wrong. Here are a few ways prayer drifts:

- Prayers can be vague and confusing.
- Prayers can function as a wish list.
- Prayers can be superstitious, a way to ensure bad things don't happen and good things do happen.
- Prayers can just be a religious practice, a habit that separates the "good" from the "bad."
- Prayer can be a mantra that seeks to create good feelings, treating prayer as a psychological experience.
- Prayer can be a reflex—something we simply do before we "get down to business" or after something is completed.
- Prayer can be something we simply tack onto life.

But prayer goes right when it's an honest conversation with the Lord we need, trust, and love. Prayer is a spiritually needy person's communication with the God who hears. When you pray, you live with a basic humility before God and others. This humility reflects reality—everyday needs can only be met by God himself.

Take with You: As you pray today, remember that you're speaking to a real God who really hears you and who really knows you. Let this truth help lead you to greater honesty in your prayer life.

AUGUST 26

I cry out to God Most High,
to God who fulfills his purpose for me. —Psalm 57:2

It's fair to say that having a "quiet time" is a misnomer. We should more properly have a "noisy time"! By talking out loud you live the reality that you're talking with another person, not simply talking to yourself inside your own head. Of course, silent prayers are not wrong (1 Samuel 1:13; Nehemiah 2:4), but they are the exception. Even in such silent prayers, the words could be spoken out loud if the situation warranted or the state of mind allowed.

In Jesus's teaching and example, a praying individual seeks privacy so he or she can talk out loud with God. "Go into your room and shut the door" (Matthew 6:6). That's so you can talk straight, rather than being tempted to perform. Jesus "would withdraw to desolate places and pray" (Luke 5:16). Why? He was talking out loud. And when Jesus walked off into the olive grove that Thursday night in order to pray, his disciples could overhear his fervent, pointed words (Matthew 26:36–44).

You can do the same sort of thing. Close the door, take a walk, get in the car—and speak up. Of course, in group contexts throughout the Bible, in public gatherings, God's people naturally pray and sing aloud, just as they hear the Bible aloud. We naturally do the same in corporate worship, whether in liturgy, in led prayers, or in small-group prayer.

Prayer is verbal because it's relational. It's a verbal connection with someone you know, need, and love.

Take with You: Find a quiet space today and get loud with your prayers. Try speaking your prayers aloud to the God who hears.

AUGUST 27

With my voice I cry out to the LORD;
with my voice I plead for mercy to the LORD. —Psalm 142:1

I've known many people whose relationship with God was significantly transformed as they started to speak up with their Father. Previously, "prayer" fizzled out in the internal buzz of self-talk and distractions or got swallowed in worries and fears. Previously, what they thought of as prayer involved certain religious feelings, a set of spiritual thoughts, or a vague sense of comfort. Prayer was basically indistinguishable from thoughts. But as a person begins to talk aloud to the God who's there, not silent, listening and acting, there's a person-to-person relationship. Speaking up is no gimmick, but out-loud prayer becomes living evidence of an increasingly honest and significant relationship.

Of course, God tells us to be quiet. Be still. Slow down. Stop. Reflect. But the purpose is not to learn a technique for accessing an inner realm of silence. *The true God quiets us so we notice him and notice what's going on around us and inside us. This true God is profoundly and essentially verbal, not silent (Genesis 1:9; John 1:1).* We take the time to hear his words of grace and truth. We consider Jesus.

Do be quiet, and for the right reasons—so you can notice and listen, so you can learn to think, feel, and talk the way the Psalms think, feel, and talk. This living God is highly verbal and listens attentively. He made us in his image, highly verbal, meant to listen attentively.

Take with You: As you pray today, work on listening. Cry out to the Lord verbally, but then be still so you can notice him better and hear him more clearly.

AUGUST 28

Let no corrupting talk come out of your mouths, but only such as is good for building up, as fits the occasion, that it may give grace to those who hear. —Ephesians 4:29

Jesus says God is actively listening to every word, even the most casual, unthinking things we say (Matthew 12:36). He takes note of what we are saying and weighs our words. Are your conversations empty, misleading, inappropriate, or judgmental? Or is the way you talk nourishing, constructive, timely, and grace-giving (Ephesians 4:29)?

Jesus never said a pointless word to other people. He always engages the important matters. His conversations always go somewhere helpful. Jesus speaks life-giving words: candid, constructive, relevant, and redemptive. And one of the constructive things Jesus talks about is helping us to assess the quality of what we talk about. "Out of the abundance of the heart the mouth speaks"—either good or evil (Matthew 12:34).

The Holy Spirit helps us generate wise conversations. Scripture demonstrates how every conversation can go somewhere good. It even captures how, in some important moments, what must next be said is to be silent. Sometimes there are no more words to say. Perhaps you are grieving. Perhaps you are thinking or praying. Perhaps your quietness communicates how much you care. When Jesus was silent before his accusers, his silence was the most eloquent thing that could be said. *A meaningful silence expresses what is true, constructive, most appropriate, and grace-giving. And then you will find the right words at the right time.*

Take with You: As you go about your day, think about how to use your words and silences to give grace and build others up.

AUGUST 29

"Fear not, little flock, for it is your Father's good pleasure to give you the kingdom. Sell your possessions, and give to the needy. Provide yourselves with moneybags that do not grow old, with a treasure in the heavens that does not fail, where no thief approaches and no moth destroys. For where your treasure is, there will your heart be also." —Luke 12:32–34

Having given you so much, your Father calls you to the radical freedom of giving your life away. It's both a reason and an alternative. Everything before was "get." We're anxious because we want to get. We don't want to lose what we've got. We become entitled and kick back into a life of leisure because we have "gotten." Everything is "get," "got," "gotten." But the end of Jesus's message in Luke 12 is all "give." Because you have been given a sure thing—because there's nothing to really worry about—then give. It's his pleasure to give to you, so you can give too. When that sinks in, a marvelous transformation takes place. You have good reasons to let your worries go. We tend to be obsessed and anxious about money. But we become able to open our hands.

That doesn't mean you have to live exactly like Francis of Assisi who famously embraced a life of poverty—but you have to have Francis of Assisi's attitude. That's the only true freedom and the only real happiness. *It's an attitude of trusting your Father and living a life that's worth something. You can give yourself away. You can use your gifts. Your life can be about giving.*

Take with You: What's one practical thing you can give to someone else today? Your time, money, stuff, food, kindness?

AUGUST 30

For all that is in the world—the desires of the flesh and the desires of the eyes and pride of life—is not from the Father but is from the world. —1 John 2:16

I think that "idols of the heart" is a great metaphor (if we don't overuse it!). People are always reaching out to worship something, anything—either God or the mini-gods, like popularity, status, comfort, and control. Sin causes us to operate as if we were self-governing and self-contained. But our souls are made to be accountable to and in relationship with the God who made us.

If I go on an "idol hunt" into myself, I become intensely introspective and self-analytical. Similarly, if I go on an "idol hunt" into you, I try to read your mind, as if I could peer into your heart, as if I had the right to judge you. Idol hunts of any kind forget that knowing ourselves and others is not an end in itself. Accurate knowledge of our neediness leads directly away from ourselves and into the mercies of God for us and for others.

Faith makes self-knowledge look to God and relate to him. Faith is not introspective. Love makes knowledge of others generous-hearted and merciful. Love is not judgmental.

Faith and love draw us out of sin's habit of self-obsession (including obsessive introspection). Our Savior gives us his own joy, which is an interpersonal emotion. He throws open the doors to the fresh air and bright light of a most kind grace.

Take with You: Are you more interested in knowing yourself than in knowing God? Self-knowledge is helpful, but it must always redirect us to God himself. Turn your eyes to the Lord.

AUGUST 31

Little children, keep yourselves from idols. —1 John 5:21

The last line of 1 John is a verse that has troubled me for a long time. It comforts, then commands us: "Beloved children, keep yourselves from idols" (v. 21). After 104 verses on living in vital fellowship with Jesus, the Son of God, how on earth does that unexpected command merit being the final word?

John's last line points us toward the importance of idolatry in Scripture. It leaves us with that most basic question that God continually poses to each human heart. *Has something or someone besides Jesus the Christ taken your heart's trust, preoccupation, loyalty, service, fear, and delight? It's a question that reveals the immediate motivation for one's behavior, thoughts, and feelings.* In the Bible's understanding, your motivation reveals your lordship. Who or what "rules" my behavior: the Lord or a substitute? Earlier in 1 John, the Bible shows us answers to this question that we are to avoid—see 1 John 2:15–17; 3:7–10; 4:1–6; and 5:19.

In contrast, to "keep yourself from idols" is to live with a whole heart of faith in Jesus. It's to be controlled by all that it means to be "Beloved children" (see 1 John 3:1–3; 4:7–5:12). The alternative to Jesus, the swarm of alternatives, is idolatry.

> **Take with You:** What are your go-to alternatives to Jesus? How do they motivate you? What do you pursue when you are not pursuing Jesus? Take time to examine what God says in 1 John to try to understand the dynamics of idolatry better.

SEPTEMBER 1

You have kept count of my tossings;
put my tears in your bottle.
Are they not in your book? —Psalm 56:8

Grief is not wrong. It's part of being made in the image of God to grieve hard things. When Jesus was facing the cross, he was grieving. He said, "Let this cup pass from me" as he cried and sweated blood (Matthew 26:39).

On the cross Jesus quoted two psalms of great suffering, grief, and heartbreak. He cried out, "My God, my God why have you forsaken me?" (Psalm 22:1) and, as he breathed his last, "Into your hand I commit my spirit" (Psalm 31:5). Yet the direction his grief went was not toward hopelessness and despair. Because he trusted God fully in the valley of death, hope and joy reverberates from his grief. Hebrews says that he went to the cross for "the joy that was set before him" (Hebrews 12:2). *Jesus knew God's Word, and he trusted in his heavenly Father. So, just as he withstood Satan's temptations in the wilderness, he was also able to stand against Satan's temptation to despair.* On the cross he is utterly powerless. He is utterly dependent. He can't raise himself. He must depend on his Father. He's dependent on the Spirit of life to rescue him from death. So he casts himself into God's care—and he died in faith. His death now opens the way for us to also face death by committing our spirits into our heavenly Father's hands.

Take with You: Meditate today on Jesus's dependence on the Father. How can you commit yourself into the Father's hands in a specific way today? He is with you in grief and heartbreak.

SEPTEMBER 2

We are afflicted in every way, but not crushed; perplexed, but not driven to despair; persecuted, but not forsaken; struck down, but not destroyed; always carrying in the body the death of Jesus, so that the life of Jesus may also be manifested in our bodies.
—2 Corinthians 4:8–10

So often the initial reaction to painful suffering is, "Why me? Why this? Why now?" The real God comes for you, in the flesh, in Christ, into suffering, on your behalf. He does not offer advice and perspective from far away; he steps into your suffering. He will see you through and work with you the whole way. He will carry you even in the most difficult situations. This reality changes the questions that rise up from your heart. That "Why me?" question quiets down.

You turn outward, and a new and wonderful question forms. "Why you? Why you, Lord of life? Why would you enter this world of evils? Why would you go through loss, weakness, hardship, sorrow, and death? Why would you do this for me, of all people? But you did this for the joy set before you. You did this for love. You did this showing the glory of God in the face of Jesus Christ."

As that deeper question sinks in, you become joyously sane. *The universe is no longer supremely about you. Yet you are not irrelevant. God's story makes you just the right size—neither too big nor too small. Everything counts and everything matters, but the scale changes to something that makes much more sense.*

Take with You: When you find yourself tempted to ask, "Why me?" today, turn toward Jesus and ask, "Why you?" Ask Jesus, "Why would you endure the cross for me?"

SEPTEMBER 3

"Ask, and it will be given to you; seek, and you will find; knock, and it will be opened to you. For everyone who asks receives, and the one who seeks finds, and to the one who knocks it will be opened."
—Matthew 7:7–8

How do you get the living hope that God offers you in Jesus? By asking. Ask God for help, and don't stop asking. You need him to fill you every day with the hope of the resurrection.

At the same time you are asking God for help, tell other people about your struggle with hopelessness. God uses his people to bring life, light, and hope. Getting in relationship with wise, caring people will protect you from despair and acting out of despair. Share your struggles with those who love you and ask them to pray for you. God will answer your cries and theirs.

Become part of a community of other Christians. Look for a church where Jesus is at the center of teaching and worship. Get in relationship with people who can help you, but don't stop with just getting help. Find people to love, serve, and give to. Even if your life has been stripped barren by lost relationships, God can and will fill your life with helpful and healing relationships.

Take with You: We are not meant to do life alone. Reach out and ask! First, ask the Lord to fill your life with Christian community, and then invite other people into your life—ask them to listen, ask them to help, ask them to pray, and offer the same in return.

SEPTEMBER 4

Through him we have also obtained access by faith into this grace in which we stand, and we rejoice in hope of the glory of God. Not only that, but we rejoice in our sufferings, knowing that suffering produces endurance, and endurance produces character, and character produces hope, and hope does not put us to shame, because God's love has been poured into our hearts through the Holy Spirit who has been given to us. —Romans 5:2–5

It's natural to want to pursue pleasure and avoid pain. But somehow, our willingness to enter into the experience of pain, disappointment, loneliness, and stress—facing it without bolting for some lesser pleasure—winds up being the door to the greatest pleasure of all. And with the best come the other true pleasures, felt deeply.

We see this dynamic all over Scripture. In 1 Peter 1, suffering is the context in which you experience "joy inexpressible and full of glory" (v. 8 NASB). In James 1, trial is the context of purpose, endurance, meaning, and joy. In Romans 5, we are told that we "rejoice in our sufferings" (v. 3). In sorrows, anguish, misery, and pain we come to know that "the love of God has been poured out within our hearts through the Holy Spirit who was given to us" (v. 5 NASB). *Walking into suffering with eyes wide open, and not running after escapist pleasures, opens the door to knowing the love of God.*

Take with You: What's your go-to escape hatch from pain and discomfort? Your phone? Your friends? Substances? Video games or bingeable shows? The next time you feel the urge to turn toward a lesser pleasure, remember that true pleasure comes from being rooted in God's love even in suffering.

SEPTEMBER 5

Such were some of you; but you were washed, but you were sanctified, but you were justified in the name of the Lord Jesus Christ and in the Spirit of our God. —1 Corinthians 6:11 NASB

What mental image comes to mind when you hear the word "sanctify"? I suspect your ideas, like mine, are easily confused. Let's define terms to orient ourselves.

Sanctification is a growing-up process, a learning curve, a development of particular life skills. God has given us a familiar illustration: Growth in Christ is similar to how a child's competence matures from helpless baby into capable adult. But growing in Christ is also different. Competence never means independence; it means growing dependence. And our maturing takes place in the broader context of time: Your sanctification occurs in the past, present, and future tenses.

- *You are already sanctified. It's past tense.* By a decisive and defining act of God, you're his saint, his child, and you're righteous. This identity is given to you as a gift. In the Bible, the word "sanctification" is most often used with this past tense meaning, describing something that has already happened.
- *Your sanctification is now being worked out. This is your life in the present tense.* God continues working with you—on a scale of days, years, and decades—to remake you into the likeness of Jesus.
- *Your sanctification will be perfected. It has a future tense.* Faith will become sight. You will be saved when Christ comes for you and imbues you with his glory. You will live.

Take with You: Meditate on the three tenses of sanctification. What does it mean that you've *already* been sanctified in the past, are being sanctified currently, and you will *surely* be perfected in the future?

SEPTEMBER 6

I lift up my eyes to the hills.
From where does my help come?
My help comes from the LORD,
who made heaven and earth. —Psalm 121:1–2

To be a *saint* and to become *sanctified* is simply to become more human and humane. Your faith becomes honest, simple, and purposeful—like the Psalms, like Jesus. You need God. You know God. You love God. You're thankful for all the good in your life, and even more thankful for the lifesaving realities of Christ's love. There's nothing more honest than needing outside help every day. You size up the Lord, yourself, and other people more accurately. You better understand people's limitations and strengths—including your own. You're more realistic about life's problems and blessings. Greater sanctification means learning to love more thoughtfully, specifically, and helpfully—like the Proverbs, like Jesus. You care. So you help practically, pray honestly, and speak constructively. You are more kind and more realistic, less cynical and less naïve.

In other words, to be holy and to grow in holiness means you are becoming a wiser, more engaged, more realistic human being. You deal better with your money, your sexuality, your emotions. You work hard; you stop and rest. You become a better friend and family member. You are a better listener. When you talk, your words bring more sense and wisdom, more joy, more reality. Your prayers bring together God's promises and human need. You worship from the heart.

Take with You: What does it look like for you to lift your eyes up to the hills? How does knowing that you need help, knowing where to find it, and knowing that you will receive it help you become more human and humane?

SEPTEMBER 7

May the Lord make you increase and abound in love for one another and for all, as we do for you, so that he may establish your hearts blameless in holiness before our God and Father, at the coming of our Lord Jesus with all his saints.
—1 Thessalonians 3:12–13

"Saint" and "holiness" seem like big, loaded words. But they describe the most desirable life a human being could ever hope to live. There's nothing more practical or honest. There's nothing more God-given. There's nothing you could want more.

True sanctification does not make you religiously obsessive, self-righteous, self-hating, paranoid, or detached from the storms of life. The Holy Spirit is wise in the ways of humankind. Jesus knows all about our sorrows and our sins, joys, and graces. Our Father loves us. So you live with clear-minded hope. You know the purpose of your life. You roll up your sleeves and get about doing what needs doing today. You do menial tasks willingly because they're important. You do things others think are important without becoming self-important. You're more patient and more firm, more gentle and more honest with others. You're truly thankful for good things. You candidly face disappointment and pain, illness and dying.

To be a saint, to be holy, means to be human. All these holiness and saintliness words simply describe becoming oriented to God and other people the way human beings are meant to be oriented.

Take with You: Roll up your sleeves today and do what needs to be done. Whether important or menial, do the work God has given you to do today with the purposefulness of holiness.

SEPTEMBER 8

Thus says the LORD:
"Cursed is the man who trusts in man
and makes flesh his strength,
whose heart turns away from the LORD." —Jeremiah 17:5

Scripture describes life concretely. The question, "Which way are you turning?" helps us understand that we're always making significant choices. We're never neutral, static, or directionless. *We are always in gear, always in motion, always heading somewhere. That somewhere will either turn out very good or very bad. If we're going bad, we can turn and reverse direction. The gospel of grace turns us around.*

But people also take a turn for the worse. The heart grows hard. The conscience becomes calloused. The lifestyle darkens. The Bible pays close attention to turning the wrong way. We have a built-in tendency to forsake God in favor of someone or something else. This passage in Jeremiah is one particularly vivid passage about taking a bad turn.

Trusting in yourself or other people—trusting in innate strength and ability—means you actively turn away from trusting the Lord. There are consequences. Forsake the Giver of life and you embrace the curse of death. You will be "written in the earth." You return to dust, rather than flourishing as a living tree planted beside streams of fresh water.

> **Take with You:** Who do you trust the most—yourself, your significant other, your friends, your parents, or the Lord? Is the motion of your heart turning you toward God or away from him? Ask him to help you turn toward him.

SEPTEMBER 9

"Sanctify them in the truth; your word is truth." —John 17:17

False messages invite us to turn toward darkness. Lies are anti-Scriptures. They powerfully affect how we think about who God is, who we are, the purpose of life, the meaning of suffering, the source of redemption. Lies directly shape how we handle interpersonal conflict, failure, success, money, and everything else. False views become collected and organized into words to live by: a worldview, a popular philosophy of life, a cultural value, a view of God, an explanation of why we do what we do, a bit of advice, a political agenda. The Bible is not the only persuasive voice in the marketplace of ideas! Other widespread cultural messages, whether informal or formal, are eager to shape our hearts.

Lord, deliver us from the Lie in its 10,000 disguises. Turn us to the truth.

False messages come humanly embodied. We're flooded by plausible, deceptive voices and, in a visual culture, flooded with compelling, deceptive images. People tell us lies, we believe lies, we become people of those lies, we become liars. False values, false explanations, and false beliefs are woven into everyday conversations. When friends, parents, therapists, pastors, or popular opinion assert things that aren't true and endorse wrong things, they express the voice of "the world."

Which way are you turning? Every one of us is a full participant in the epic action adventure between good and evil.

Take with You: Where are the messages you're receiving coming from—friends, family, ads, social media, etc.? What are the core beliefs of these messages, and do those beliefs resonate with truth or with lies? Ask God to help sanctify you in the truth.

SEPTEMBER 10

"Our Father in heaven, hallowed be your name.
Your kingdom come,
your will be done, on earth as it is in heaven.
Give us this day our daily bread,
and forgive us our debts, as we also have forgiven our debtors.
And lead us not into temptation,
but deliver us from evil." —Matthew 6:9–13

Notice how the Lord teaches us to pray. The Bible rarely focuses on health, money, travel mercies, doing well on a test, finding a job, or the salvation of unsaved relatives. These are legitimate things to pray for, because God cares for all of life. But he never intends that these topics dominate our prayer requests. They miss the real action of God's dealings with his beloved people. They skirt our real problems and God's front-and-center concerns.

Notice the central concerns in the Psalms, in the Lord's Prayer, in the letters of Paul. *Biblical prayers ask God to show himself so we will know him. They name our troubles and seek refuge in him. They name our sins and seek mercy from him. They ask for the clarity of mind and strength of purpose to love others. They name our holy desires and commitments. They name our God, remember his promises, seek his will.*

When people start to identify where they really need God's help, they're entering the realm where both prayer and change live. We step into reality.

Take with You: As you pray today, let the Psalms and the Lord's Prayer be your example. Focus on the Lord himself—his character, kingdom, heart, and his will—before you focus on your list of desires or outward circumstances.

SEPTEMBER 11

For God alone, O my soul, wait in silence,
for my hope is from him.
He only is my rock and my salvation,
my fortress; I shall not be shaken. —Psalm 62:5–6

Why do we listen to God? Because ours is a speaking God: "God said . . . and it was so. . . . In the beginning was the Word . . . and the Word was made flesh and dwelt among us." So we listen. We take the time to hear his words of grace and truth. We consider Jesus. And we pay attention to what's going on in our lives, seeing the world and ourselves in truer colors.

Becoming quiet to listen to God enables us to pray more intelligently and more honestly. We can think straight, feel authentically, and choose well. There's great benefit in turning off the noise machines, the chatter, the music, the crowd noise, the talk—whether it's playing inside your head, or all around you, or both. Turning off the distractions is not actually *prayer* to the living God. Instead, being quiet helps you notice and listen, so you can find your voice. Your God speaks *and* listens attentively to you.

We change as we begin to talk aloud to the God who is here. He isn't silent or inactive. He listens. He cares. He acts. We begin to deal with him person-to-person. God wants to catch your ear to awaken your voice. When you have your "quiet" time, may you trust that God listens to the sound of your voice!

Take with You: Turn the volume down on distracting noise today. In the silence take time both to listen and to speak to the God who made you.

SEPTEMBER 12

May all who seek you
rejoice and be glad in you!
May those who love your salvation
say evermore, "God is great!"
But I am poor and needy;
hasten to me, O God!
You are my help and my deliverer;
O LORD, do not delay! —Psalm 70:4–5

The book of Psalms essentially breaks down into what we could call the minor key and the major key. The first ninety psalms are largely minor key. They are psalms of need, guilt, trouble, affliction, anguish, feeling overwhelmed. Major key psalms are scattered in, like Psalm 23, which mentions the dark side in the context of the Lord as our Good Shepherd. And then the last sixty psalms are largely major key: the royal psalms, the Psalms of Ascent, the great hallelujahs, with just a few minor key psalms scattered in. *You could say that the flow of the entire Psalter expresses something of the essential nature of the Christian life—the sorrow and heartache and need and struggle and joy.*

The emotional modes—the voices of minor key and major key in the Psalms—also happened to be built into the sacrificial system. There are the sacrifices for sin and guilt. Then there are the sacrifices that are expressions of gratitude and joy and worship and confidence. Taken together, the sacrificial system and the book of Psalms show us how to go to God with everything that's on our hearts.

Take with You: Go to God with whatever is on your heart today! Whether you are in a major or minor key, the whole Bible shows you how to bring the whole of your experience to the Lord. Look for help in the Psalms.

SEPTEMBER 13

Count it all joy, my brothers, when you meet trials of various kinds, for you know that the testing of your faith produces steadfastness. And let steadfastness have its full effect, that you may be perfect and complete, lacking in nothing. —James 1:2–4

This passage contains a call that we would grow up into wisdom. We grow up into this wonderful grace that gets called endurance or steadfastness, which isn't the same as just grinning and bearing it when life gets hard. It's a purposeful going forward in the midst of everything we face in a broken, dying, hard, stressful world.

But how on earth can I count it all joy when I meet various trials? I can only do that if I understand there's a big circle around my entire life, there's a God who's actually purposefully working my good, joy, endurance of faith, steadfastness, and wisdom rather than chaos. There's a purpose, something that's being done behind the scenes. And the reason James (or any of us) can, "count it all joy" is because he knows there's a larger purposefulness in the hand of God.

We're going to find when the heat hits us that we struggle, and we show our foolishness. But when we turn to the book of James, we get this overwhelming sense throughout that we serve a God who gives. A God who's generous—the Giver who helps us and meets us in our need.

Take with You: O Lord, help me to see myself encircled by your love and care today. Let this awareness of your purposeful hand in my life help me to grow in steadfastness and joy, even in the middle of my struggles.

SEPTEMBER 14

O LORD, the hope of Israel,
all who forsake you shall be put to shame;
those who turn away from you shall be written in the earth,
for they have forsaken the LORD, the fountain of living water.

Heal me, O LORD, and I shall be healed;
save me, and I shall be saved,
for you are my praise. —Jeremiah 17:13–14

Jeremiah teaches us that sinful deeds lead to a parched life. "Like the partridge that gathers a brood she did not hatch, so is he who gets riches but not by justice" (Jeremiah 17:11). The simile is a little hard to follow, but the passage is talking about making money through manipulation: deceiving, angling, giving less than you promise. All those things that are so characteristic of life in a fallen, broken world. Here is the warning that follows: "In the midst of his days, they will leave him." The "they" here is the riches, the ill-gotten gain. His riches will leave him. They are not going to last.

While Jeremiah warns others of the dangers of sinfulness, he's not a hypocrite. Jeremiah is aware of his iniquity, of the depth of this darkness. He cries out to God and beseeches him for mercy. He is convinced that God alone can heal him. *God alone can make it right. God alone can save him, and he will be saved. And the conclusion is, again, to turn toward God: "You are my praise" (17:14).*

Take with You: When you find yourself surrounded by injustice, unfairness, and sin, is your instinct to turn toward others in accusation or to turn toward the Lord and confess your own sin? Are you, like Jeremiah, convinced that the Lord can heal you?

SEPTEMBER 15

"Blessed is the man who trusts in the LORD,
whose trust is the LORD.
He is like a tree planted by water,
that sends out its roots by the stream,
and does not fear when heat comes,
for its leaves remain green,
and is not anxious in the year of drought,
for it does not cease to bear fruit." —Jeremiah 17:7–8

We know from Jeremiah 17 that we're called to trust the living God, who is the fountain of living water. We are called to turn away from our idolatries and trust only him (v. 7). So, these are the most important questions to consider: Who is your god at this moment? Who do you love? Whose voice are you listening to? What do you want? Do you want the will of the Holy Spirit? Or do you want the will of the flesh, the devil, of sinful human beings?

At all times, at the most fundamental level, we are all doing something with God. Both good and bad thoughts and actions—thorns or sweet fruit—come out of the heart, what motivates you. *So your relationship to God gets expressed in how you deal in life—every emotional reaction you have, every thought pattern that hooks you, every choice you make. All of these things, at bottom, express the core of who or what you worship.* Change comes as what you worship shifts from your own desires to Christ, your Redeemer and Friend.

> **Take with You:** Are you living a dry, parched life or are you bearing fruit? Take a good look at your roots. Where is your heart planted? Who do you love? Jesus is the only true fountain of living water.

SEPTEMBER 16

May the LORD give strength to his people!
May the LORD bless his people with peace! —Psalm 29:11

A Prayer for Living Faith and Living Love

Our great Lord, we do thank you that you have poured upon us pure promise. And we ask you above all else to give us ears that we might hear the kind, powerful, merciful, hopeful things you say to us. Let us see the ways you are at work in this broken world. A world with rivers of sorrow, a world that has suffering, a world where every one of us, should we live so long, will end up aged and decrepit and dying. So we ask that you give us courage. Give us hope and strength. Give us wisdom and insight.

You will give us nothing less than a living faith and a living love that's willing, able, empowered, and grateful to serve you and serve the welfare of our brothers and sisters. And, Lord, you will enable us to serve the welfare of a world that's filled with woe, a world where sorrow seems infinite. We love you. Help us to rejoice in this day you've made. Remind us of your present help. You establish our steps, and you lead us gently. We pray for your particular wisdom to us even now, in the name of the Savior of the world, Jesus Christ. Amen.

Take with You: Find a quiet, private place and try praying this prayer out loud. Commit this day to the Lord, remembering that he alone can grant you living faith and living love.

SEPTEMBER 17

For we do not want you to be unaware, brothers, of the affliction we experienced in Asia. For we were so utterly burdened beyond our strength that we despaired of life itself. Indeed, we felt that we had received the sentence of death. But that was to make us rely not on ourselves but on God who raises the dead. —2 Corinthians 1:8–9

How does God redeem our suffering? I want you to pay very close attention here. Notice how precisely 2 Corinthians reveals particular things about God. The actual turning point is a simple little line in the middle of verse 9 where Paul in effect says, "I almost died in Asia suffering affliction, *in order that* something else good would happen." Paul is pointing directly to the sovereign, purposeful, intervening God, with whom there are no accidents. He doesn't just show up later. "In order that" captures Paul's sense that our sufferings are meaningful. They are purposeful.

We often struggle to find God's purpose in things that seem broken, destructive, and hopeless. How could there be anything constructive in this? And yet, there is. The situation is terrible, but God is up to something good in suffering.

In some fundamental way, every destructive behavior arises out of self-trust, self-reliance. But God is up to better things in Paul's life and in your life. *"In order that" shows us that God wants to change us at a deeper level: "to make us rely not on ourselves but on God" (v. 9).*

> **Take with You:** When we suffer, we cannot always understand what lies on the other side of "in order that." No matter your circumstances, trust that God is up to something good. Above all, trust that *he's* good.

SEPTEMBER 18

And he answered, "You shall love the Lord your God with all your heart and with all your soul and with all your strength and with all your mind, and your neighbor as yourself." —Luke 10:27

Every person who walks into a relationship with any other person, at some level, is asking, "Are you trustworthy?" and "Can I be honest with you?" With someone you trust, you're willing to be honest about things that matter—dark moments, happy things, hard times, struggles, guilts, sins, and joys. We can talk about the light and the deep, and we can talk about the happy and the sad. The most important questions we ask ourselves and others are about our relationships with God: "Will I embrace the change purposes of Christ? Will I get a biblical agenda for my life?" Will faith work through love or will lies and idolatry work through selfishness and fear?

Now think through these questions from the lens of your relationship with God. *Do you trust God? Is the quality of your conversation with God up to what it is with people? Our best human relationships can shine a mirror and say, "Now, the reason I trust that person is because he or she actually, in some tiny way, is like God. They're manifesting something of what the real God is like.* If I'm able to have this kind of head-on, genuine relationship with that person, how much more with the real God who stands behind the person?"

Take with You: Are you mirroring God's trustworthiness and love in your relationships with others? Ask him to show you how to love others through your conversations.

SEPTEMBER 19

Who can discern his errors?
Declare me innocent from hidden faults.
Keep back your servant also from presumptuous sins;
let them not have dominion over me!
Then I shall be blameless,
and innocent of great transgression. —Psalm 19:12–13

The average person believes that for something to count as sin, it must be consciously chosen. But our desires often deceive us, so we aren't even aware we're sinning. We're blind to ourselves. Think of some of the biblical metaphors: "drunken," "asleep," "like an unreasoning animal." Sin is like a madness in our hearts, something we aren't even aware of.

Circumstances do not cause us to sin. Circumstances do not create the lustfulness of our hearts. A situation might be the stimulus, but then our hearts generate their own, tailor-made cravings. *Only a Christian's worldview says that our desires are about our relationship with God—either because we want the things God wants, or we want, contrary to God, our will to be done. You can't actually understand desire without understanding the God-relatedness of it.*

When the Bible talks about the lusts of the flesh, it's giving us a way to understand ourselves at the most basic level as worshippers. When we worship something or someone besides the living God, that can be described as a "lust of the flesh," and it can result in a variety of sinful behavior. One particular act of wrong can come from many different possible desires. What rules you comes out and what comes out reveals what rules you.

Take with You: *O Lord, help me to submit my desires to you. Teach me to love what you love and desire what you desire. Help me to worship you above all things.*

SEPTEMBER 20

Peter, an apostle of Jesus Christ,

To those who are elect exiles of the Dispersion in Pontus, Galatia, Cappadocia, Asia, and Bithynia, according to the foreknowledge of God the Father, in the sanctification of the Spirit, for obedience to Jesus Christ and for sprinkling with his blood: May grace and peace be multiplied to you. —1 Peter 1:1–2

A Prayer of Thanksgiving to the Triune God

Our Father, how great and good this salvation is. *Jesus Christ*, how great and good, humble, merciful, powerful is your work of saving us from all that is dark, from sin and death, from the evils that surround us. Thank you that you have promised your protective care. *You are our Shepherd, Friend, and Shield. You are the King who has shed his own blood that we might live.*

Holy Spirit, thank you that you minister unto our hearts individually and together as your Church, nothing less than the presence, love, power, and truth of Jesus Christ and the Father. We thank you that you come to dwell within us. As we continue to talk, think, wrestle, and interact, will you, Holy Spirit, write the Word of Truth, the Word of Life upon our hearts? Help us to be people who live in the light, empowered by the God of power, shielded by the God who's good to his beloved children. We thank you. We love you. We ask that you help us grow before you by the grace of Jesus Christ. Amen.

Take with You: As you pray throughout the day, practice talking to all three persons of the Trinity: Father, Son, and Holy Spirit.

SEPTEMBER 21

Bear one another's burdens, and so fulfill the law of Christ.
—Galatians 6:2

Who of us can see ourselves perfectly? We all have a million flaws. We may be aware of some of them, but other people often see us better than we see ourselves. One of the characteristics of wisdom in the Proverbs is that the wise person listens and invites correction—wants correction. We need to develop a willingness to invite one another into the real, moral dramas of our lives. God created community for this reason—we need each other.

I can't think of how many good sermons I've heard on "one-anothering"—for you to forgive one another, for you to love one another, to do toward other people the things you want done toward you. And the main point of the exhortation is to encourage us to bear one another's burdens. But every one-anothering passage also implies a reciprocity. I'm to bear your burdens, and you need to let me know your burdens. I've got burdens too, but how can I seek help unless I share them?

One-anothering cuts both ways. And the giving of help replies on the asking for help. *Who can you reciprocally share burdens with today? Friendship and fellowship come alive when you open yourself up in that way. You start to create a community in which people are both asking and giving of aid, bearing one another's burdens, praying for one another about real stuff.*

Take with You: Are you always the helper? Are you always being helped? How can you nudge your Christian friendships toward the full reciprocity of one-anothering?

SEPTEMBER 22

Put on then, as God's chosen ones, holy and beloved, compassionate hearts, kindness, humility, meekness, and patience, bearing with one another and, if one has a complaint against another, forgiving each other; as the Lord has forgiven you, so you also must forgive. And above all these put on love, which binds everything together in perfect harmony. —Colossians 3:12–14

How do we create a truly Christian community? We move toward people. We create a climate of grace and relate to others with a large-hearted and generous spirit. We aren't suspicious, narrow, self-preoccupied, critical, guarded, quick to look for fault, opinionated, judgmental. Love is patient. Love is kind. These are essential practices for approaching others. We must have this attitude, this stance toward people

The qualities God desires in us are the ones that mirror his own attributes. They communicate how God deals with a broken world: with patience, endurance, compassion, perseverance, and faithfulness.

Father, give us a vision for a life that is fruitful and flourishing. By your grace, help us to shed some light in a dark world, do good to others, and live purposefully and with reconciliation, kindness, repentance, humility, faith, joy, and gratitude as grace plays more and more of a part in who we are. We confess, Lord, that we get really stuck. We get into some ruts; we get blind and stubborn. In your great, patient mercy, show us how to treat others the way you treat us. Keep working with us, contending with us. Teach us to contend with ourselves in the right way. Amen.

Take with You: Thank God that one day, all manner of things will be well. Let this truth encourage you when you feel stuck.

SEPTEMBER 23

If we are afflicted, it is for your comfort and salvation;
and if we are comforted, it is for your comfort,
which you experience when you patiently endure the same
sufferings that we suffer. —2 Corinthians 1:6

Ultimately everything we learn, even a small increment of wisdom or comfort, becomes something to give away. You know, as we look at 2 Corinthians 1, everything you learn becomes the content you can use to reach out to another person in love.

We need to understand that our fundamental call is to this redemptive engagement: bringing mercy and light into a world of darkness and sin. Why, if we've been given some excellent gift, would we not go outside the gates and try share it with others?

> Lord, I pray that each one of us, by the mercy of God, would become wiser, that we would live more fruitfully, more quickly repent of our sins, more quickly cast our burdens on you, and more quickly have a hand to reach out to another person. Would you also teach us to pray wisely, to rejoice more wholeheartedly, to suffer more honestly, to seek help more quickly from our brothers and sisters? And we beseech you to make that little part of the kingdom that we represent and have an impact on a brighter place, full of the evident sparkling goodness of the living God. Amen.
>
> **Take with You:** Do you think of your life experiences as gifts that you can offer to encourage others? What are some small ways you can move into other people's lives with constructive purposes?

SEPTEMBER 24

The night is far gone; the day is at hand. So then let us cast off the works of darkness and put on the armor of light. . . . But put on the Lord Jesus Christ, and make no provision for the flesh, to gratify its desires. —Romans 13:12, 14

For good, biblical, and practical reasons, Christians have always understood that we face a threefold moral enemy: the world, the flesh, and the devil. Over this unholy trinity hangs the specter of our last enemy—the shadow of death and death itself.

Even though the term "spiritual warfare" doesn't appear in Scripture, here are four ways to understand this idea biblically.

First, spiritual warfare is a metaphor for standing on the Lord's side in the epic struggle between the Lord and his enemies. Second, spiritual warfare is a moral struggle. It's a conflict over who you are, what you believe, and how you live. Third, spiritual warfare is a synonym for the struggles of the Christian life. Fourth, it's a battle for lordship. At its core, it's the battle for who you will serve.

In whose image are you being made? *Will you resemble the Good Shepherd who lays down his life for his sheep? Or will you grow more and more like Satan, the liar and destroyer? This is a battle that encompasses all of life.* Not just for a few odd or bizarre moments, but in every moment of every day we're in a battle for who we will serve.

Take with You: *Father, clothe me in your armor of light. Help me put on Jesus Christ himself, remembering that his victory over sin and death at the cross empowers me to be brave and stand firm.*

SEPTEMBER 25

Finally, be strong in the Lord and in the strength of his might.
—Ephesians 6:10

Understanding how spiritual warfare intersects with common, everyday problems like anger, fear, and escapism starts with remembering that the whole world is in the power of the Evil One (1 John 5:19). The Evil One is a God-mimic. He wants us to be God-mimics too.

How does this play out when we're angry? If we're mimicking God instead of going to God, we become, like Satan, a false judge and accuser (Revelation 12:10). We become self-righteous, condemning, malicious, unfair.

What about fear? Here we see Satan mimicking God as a false prophet. Anxiety as a voice that tells us lies about ourselves, God, our world, and the future: "You have ruined everything." "God doesn't love you." These are not the words God speaks in Scripture to his beloved children.

What about escapism and addiction? The wrong kind of pleasure-seeking shows us that we're looking for something besides God to make us happy or to help us deal with the unpleasant realities of our lives. Satan continually proposes self-salvation schemes to people designed to keep them from the real Savior.

So when we struggle with anger, fear, and escapism, we see all of our enemies at work. This is frightening! But our hope is embedded in what we learn in Ephesians 6: Be strong in the Lord (v. 10).

Take with You: As you read Ephesians 6:10–20, put on the whole armor of God, which will enable us to stand firm (vv. 11, 13). In all circumstances the shield of faith can extinguish all the flaming darts of the evil one (v. 16). Keep alert with perseverance in prayer and the Word of God (vv. 17–19).

SEPTEMBER 26

What causes quarrels and what causes fights among you? Is it not this, that your passions are at war within you? —James 4:1

Here are five questions to ask yourself, and one thing to do to help you meet God when you struggle with anger:

1. *What is happening around me when I get angry*? Make a list of the last five times you got angry. When did you get angry at something that doesn't really matter in God's world? When did you make a good thing more important than God? And when did you get angry because you were truly wronged?
2. *How do I act when I get angry?* Do you express your anger in bitterness? In arguing? In slander? Were there times when anger was an expression of love, not hate, and was expressed constructively?
3. *What were my expectations when I became angry?* This reveals what hijacked God's place in your heart. Your answer will show where you need God's help most.
4. *What message does God, in his Word, have for me that will speak to my anger?* If you remember this is God's kingdom, the way you deal with your anger will change. When you add to that an understanding of your real sins, then you will also see how God, in Christ, is tenderhearted and forgiving to you.
5. *Ask God for help.* You must turn to God for help if your wrong anger patterns are going to change. Turn to the God who loves you. Tell him all about what's making you angry.

Take with You: Take some time to work through these questions. Grab a journal and write if that helps you focus and see patterns. Turn to the Lord for help.

SEPTEMBER 27

Know this, my beloved brothers: let every person be quick to hear, slow to speak, slow to anger; for the anger of man does not produce the righteousness of God. —James 1:19–20

Becoming like God means that when you see a true wrong you will learn to respond in the way God does. God responds constructively toward us by naming our wrongs clearly and then offering us the mercy and grace we do not deserve.

- *God is patient.* God is described in the Bible as "slow to anger" (Exodus 34:6). Learning to be "slow to anger" means living in a world that has things wrong in it and being willing to stay in difficult situations and relationships for the long haul.
- *God is merciful.* Because God is merciful, he sent Jesus to die on the cross for you. His just anger was poured out on Jesus. As you experience God's mercy, you will learn to be merciful.
- *God is forgiving.* God's forgiveness doesn't make what was wrong okay. He names what's wrong and deals with the wrong by paying the price himself. Loving someone who's done wrong is the way to overcome that wrong.
- *God confronts in love.* Because God lovingly confronts, so can you. It's both constructive and loving for wrongdoers to face the consequences of their wrongs. Your anger can be constructively expressed as a clear reprimand and fair consequences.

Take with You: When you feel tempted to angrily judge others, try rolling up your sleeves and helping to right the wrongs you see. Taking a constructive approach means addressing the wrongs you see, but doing it patiently, kindly, and lovingly.

SEPTEMBER 28

All the ways of a man are pure in his own eyes,
but the LORD weighs the spirit. —Proverbs 16:2

Motives matter. The sinfulness or godliness of anger comes from the motive. People motivated by desire for God's glory, for personal conformity to Jesus's model and will, and for the well-being of others will be angry in one way. People motivated by the "desires of the body and the mind" (Ephesians 2:3), by pride and false beliefs, will be angry in a different way. *The simplest question to ask about what underlies anger is, "What do I really want?"* If you are honest, with God's help, you can recognize if you really crave to get even, hurt someone, avoid inconvenience, prove someone wrong, score points, be recognized and appreciated, humiliate, win, or get your way. You're ruled by what the Bible terms "self." And, with God's help, you can also recognize if you really want the Lord of life to be honored in word, deed, attitude, and intention. The counsel of brothers and sisters can help us sort things through when we're blind to something and can't figure it out. Counsel can help us when we deceive ourselves about our motives, dressing up something unsavory as though it were God's will.

One of the delightful things about sorting out our own anger is that the link between root and fruit is so accessible. God is honored not just in the accomplishment of righteousness, but in the struggle toward righteousness. And remember, as you struggle toward righteousness, God gives grace.

Take with You: The next time you're angry, ask yourself, *What do I really want?* Does your answer exalt your "self" or the Lord?

SEPTEMBER 29

But God, being rich in mercy, because of the great love with which he loved us, even when we were dead in our trespasses, made us alive together with Christ—by grace you have been saved. . . . For we are his workmanship, created in Christ Jesus for good works, which God prepared beforehand, that we should walk in them.
—Ephesians 2:4–5, 10

If we truly know God, we will come to know ourselves. Self-esteem is a popular psychological idea. Low self-esteem is a serious problem full of debilitating heartache, broken relationships, discouragement, sense of failure, an overwhelming sense of not belonging. Self-evaluation is a much healthier term, because it combines the picture you have of yourself with the assessment you make of that picture. Is the way you know yourself actually true? Do you understand yourself as you actually are? You can't answer those questions accurately without going to what God says about you.

An accurate self-evaluation means you see yourself as a creature of the living God, dependent on him, while also seeing your sinfulness. In true self-knowledge, you also know you've been loved at the price of the life of the Son of God. You're saved by grace, cared for by the heart of the One who matters. You can then rightly understand both your gifts and limitations. *There's a dignity and joy in knowing what you have to offer and where you need help. True self-knowledge isn't an issue of good or bad self-esteem—but true or false assessment of yourself.* Are you understanding God, the world, sin, and your growth in the right way?

Take with You: Do you struggle with low self-esteem? Shift your focus toward God's picture of you: beloved, saved, created for a purpose.

SEPTEMBER 30

For you have delivered me from death and my feet from stumbling, that I may walk before God in the light of life. —Psalm 56:13 NIV

How are you changing? You're already being transformed: The darkness is not as dark; the light is getting lighter. Redemption is ongoing until the day we die.

While we're all unique, fundamental similarities run through all of our stories as light dawns from deep darkness. The reason for these similarities is that the same Person is at work, with the same fundamental purpose for each one of us, although the details may be completely different in Christ's way of working with you.

There are three simultaneous dynamics in every person's story. Situational evils—things that deceive you and heinous actions committed against you. There is always a challenging, tempting, disorienting situation. And the things that happen to us count. There's also always something going on with you: internal evils, struggles, disturbing emotions, confusion, chosen sins, and disorientation to be reckoned with. The third dynamic at play is that there's always an intervening Savior, a Redeemer on site. He says what he does, and he does what he says. His hand and voice are on hand in each situation.

When these dynamics are knit together, it creates a fourth dynamic: what's changing in you. *The person in the situation (you) changes under the hand of the on-site Redeemer. Your story is not done; it's unfolding. You can have strength, purpose, forgiveness, and courage. You can walk before God in the light of life.*

Take with You: Take a step back and look at your story with a wide-angle lens. What are your situational evils? What are the biggest struggles warring inside you?

OCTOBER 1

"Blessed are the poor in spirit, for theirs is the kingdom of heaven.
Blessed are those who mourn, for they shall be comforted.
Blessed are the meek, for they shall inherit the earth.
Blessed are those who hunger and thirst for righteousness,
for they shall be satisfied." —Matthew 5:3–6

The Beatitudes envision a hard world. And they give us a blueprint for how to live in the midst of a world that has many hardships in it.

The poor in spirit are blessed because the kingdom of heaven is theirs. To be poor in spirit is to know you need help from someone outside yourself. You're fundamentally needy—you aren't independent. You call to the One who can help you. That is the key that opens the door to the very presence of the King of kings.

Those who mourn are blessed because they will be comforted. This is a sorrowful world that needs comforting; it needs strengthening. It needs help, and the King is the only One who can bring that comfort.

The meek are blessed because they will inherit the earth. The meek put their hope in God. The meek want God to tell them who he is and who they are and how they can live and what his promises are.

Those hungering and thirsting for righteousness are blessed because they shall be satisfied. There are many things we wish we could have and keep and treasure, but we only lose them. Hunger and thirst for the one thing that can never be lost.

Take with You: *O Lord, let me find my satisfaction in nothing less than your righteousness, righteousness that will one day make right all of the wrongs of this broken world. You alone can satisfy.*

OCTOBER 2

"Blessed are the merciful, for they shall receive mercy.
Blessed are the pure in heart, for they shall see God.
Blessed are the peacemakers, for they shall be called sons of God.
Blessed are those who are persecuted for righteousness' sake, for theirs is the kingdom of heaven." —Matthew 5:7–10

The merciful are blessed because they will receive mercy again and again. Mercy is not only forgiveness; it's generosity and addressing the needs of all who are broken, needy, struggling, hurting, and confused. The merciful are given even more of the very thing they already have. Now they overflow with mercy and are able to give even more of it away.

The pure in heart are blessed because they will see God. Pure in heart describes our motives and why we do things. It propels us forth into the world with the purposes of mercy, peacemaking, courage, and a willingness to be part of the solution.

The peacemakers are blessed because they will be called the sons of God. The world is full of heartache, war, conflict, hatred, lying, cliques, and competition. We are called to become people who make peace, who are able to live content with who we are and with an eye and a heart for the need in the world around us.

Those persecuted for righteousness' sake are blessed because the kingdom of heaven is theirs. This is a calling to be willing to suffer, to lose, to bear pain, and to go toward what's hard. This is a call to courage.

Take with You: The path of blessing isn't an invitation to an easy life, but it *is* an invitation to an indestructible life oriented toward Jesus Christ and his purposes. Say yes!

OCTOBER 3

"Blessed are the poor in spirit, for theirs is the kingdom of heaven.
Blessed are those who mourn, for they shall be comforted.
Blessed are the meek, for they shall inherit the earth.
Blessed are those who hunger and thirst for righteousness,
for they shall be satisfied.
Blessed are the merciful, for they shall receive mercy.
Blessed are the pure in heart, for they shall see God.
Blessed are the peacemakers, for they shall be called sons of God.
Blessed are those who are persecuted for righteousness' sake, for
theirs is the kingdom of heaven." —Matthew 5:3–10

The eight promises in the Beatitudes are absolutely flooded with the love of God. They promise you a kingdom, comfort, and the earth as your inheritance. They promise satisfaction, mercy, eyes to see God, and that you will be called a child of God.

Within them are contained in seed form everything that the Bible is about—everything that Christ is doing and everything we need for our lives to be transformed into his image. *The Beatitudes are about the transformation of normal people into exceedingly unusual people who live for a different reason, who have a reason for their indestructible hope, in the face of all that is lost.*

Take with You: *Our Father in heaven, grant to us the ability to have a deep care and concern for others. We are your children. We are brothers and sisters, and you intend for us to be a blessing to each other. Let us live in the light of life through Jesus Christ our King. Amen.*

OCTOBER 4

But he said to me, "My grace is sufficient for you, for my power is made perfect in weakness." Therefore I will boast all the more gladly of my weaknesses, so that the power of Christ may rest upon me.
—2 Corinthians 12:9

There are seasons where progress in your spiritual growth is slow. You wonder why you keep struggling with a temper, anxiety, or being clumsy in relationships. But often when we think about growth and transformation, we have an idealized image in our minds. I doubt that most of us picture honest struggles. It's not unusual for life to be difficult. We see things within ourselves we wish would change, but we keep failing in some way. If sanctification means becoming like Christ, then the way we struggle is as much a part of our sanctification as some idealized image of what we hope we would become.

You may be growing in particular ways that you don't even see. Living in weakness doesn't necessarily feel like growth, but your heart may be becoming more generous to other people. You have a growing sense that other people really matter. You can be gracious to them in their shortcomings and their heartaches. Now none of these are splashy transformations. They're just good, quiet, strong, steady fruits of the Lord working in our lives.

If you add these two together—a reality check about the ongoing struggle that makes you need the Lord and then contentment with quiet, unspectacular graces in your life—then sanctification can move forward, even when you're going through a hard patch.

Take with You: Can you think of any small, quiet transformations God is working in your life? If you can't, ask God to show you how he's working. God loves a process.

OCTOBER 5

He who began a good work in you will carry it on to completion until the day of Christ Jesus. —Philippians 1:6 NIV

If you have baggage from a sinful past, you may be wondering how Christ can heal you. You feel shame or grief over past sin, and you wonder if God could really love and accept you. In all hard human questions, the Bible shines, but it particularly shines here because where else in the world is mercy the response to a lot of really bad baggage?

There's a beautiful story of redemption woven throughout Scripture. The Bible is full of people with checkered pasts who were redeemed and restored by God. If you feel humbled and discouraged, understand that is already a work of God's mercy, and he will finish the work he started in you.

There's a grace that deals with the past, a grace that deals in the present, and there's a grace that will deal with us in the future. The gospel tells us of a sin-bearer, the Lamb of God, who takes away the sins of the world and erases them. When you think about why you still feel the stain, the promise of present grace applies: We have the Holy Spirit. We have the promise of presence and power to help in the moment of struggle. Regarding future grace, Christ will come back to finish what he's begun. God's grace and mercy are our foundation and hope at every point.

Take with You: When you're haunted by your sins, remember the three tenses of grace: past, present, and future. Christ has already paid for your sins. The Holy Spirit lives in you right now. Jesus will return to complete what he started.

OCTOBER 6

Blessed is the one whose transgression is forgiven,
whose sin is covered. —Psalm 32:1

We face a choice regarding our guilt and shame. On one hand, if we try to deal with it on our own, we're choosing to experience loss—separation from mercy and lovingkindness, being left alone with our troubles. On the other hand, if we turn to the Lord with our guilt and shame, we have access to all of the Lord's blessings.

All you need to do is ask for the exact help you need from the One who can help you. It's a personal transaction. Recognize that Jesus solves what's most wrong. If you know your guilt, you can be forgiven. If you know your weakness, you can be strengthened. If you know your foolishness, you can be given wisdom. If you know your brokenness, you can be made whole. If you know you have failed, you can be planted by streams of living water and prosper in all you do. If you don't know these things about yourself, you can't be helped. If you don't know you're in trouble, you can't find peace with God. Those who humble themselves will be exalted—it's a wondrous paradox found in our relationship with our Lord. *The humility of knowing your need and asking for help and saying thank you and loving the One who helps you is what the Christian life is about.*

Take with You: As you pray today, practice asking for what you need. You may need to dig a little to get past asking for what you want or for what you *think* you need. When confronted by your guilt and shame, what do you *really* need? Mercy? Healing? Forgiveness? Just ask.

OCTOBER 7

"My son, do not regard lightly the discipline of the Lord,
nor be weary when reproved by him.
For the Lord disciplines the one he loves,
and chastises every son whom he receives." —Hebrews 12:5–6

Our life stories involve countless encounters with God. God is our environment. We are continually dependent, continually colliding with him, continually under observation, continually needing and receiving mercies, continually disciplined. He interrupts us, protects us, lead us, afflicts us, encourages us.

Much of personal change is a matter of slow-forming habits—the slow buildup of new habits of thinking, habits of attitude, habits of response. Much of how we grow happens subliminally, just as a child grows. We grow up in endless daily choice points between good and evil. We receive subtle influences from modeling.

Our lives in Christ take a lifetime of "formation," of learning, unlearning, and relearning. Like any skill, wisdom includes definable, explicit things learned. Wisdom also involves unspoken, implied, caught-not-taught learning. There are ways I've grown that I could never quantify that I don't even see. And the struggle will not cease until I see the face of God.

Your entire Christian life is a series of variations and permutations of the process of sanctification. This is how you grow and live. This is how you minister to others, loving them well in their need. This is how you arrive in heaven, seeing Jesus face-to-face, finding that you have been made like him.

Take with You: Most of your learning right now revolves around academics. What would change in your life if you recognized that your most important learning is sanctification? Commit to becoming a lifelong learner!

OCTOBER 8

For this light momentary affliction is preparing for us an eternal weight of glory beyond all comparison. —2 Corinthians 4:17

God's ways with us do not work according to a formula. No single factor, no one truth, no protocol can capture how and why a person grows into Christ's image. Sanctification is progressive. It comes bit by bit and through multiple factors.

Though our lives involve countless variables, change occurs through the interplay of four factors: You are changed by *God, the Word of Truth, wise people*, and *suffering and struggle*. Each one contributes to how we change. They're present in differing degrees as our lives are rescripted. Grace bears fruit in a change of mind, in turning, hoping, taking refuge, trusting, loving, and obeying. Variants on these four elements intertwine within every story of our discipleship. They appear everywhere in Scripture. The story of your life in Christ is also composed of these elements.

By definition, a person who changes acts. You do something. You believe something. You ask for help, from a friend, from God, from both. You make different choices. You change your mind, attitudes, feelings, goals in life, and the way you treat others.

And you find, sooner or later, that God himself was working all along—within the hardships, amid the sins, by the friendships, through his Word, in you. The farther you walk on this road, the more you realize God is the decisive actor and foundational factor in the drama.

Take with You: What is one action you can take as God works change in your life? Where do you need change the most? How can you invite God, his Word, wise friends, or mentors in to help you change?

OCTOBER 9

May the God of hope fill you with all joy and peace in believing, so that by the power of the Holy Spirit you may abound in hope. —Romans 15:13

God himself changes you. He intervenes in your life, turning you from self-will to the kingdom of life. He raises you in Christ when you're dead in trespasses and sins. He restores hearing when you're deaf and gives sight when you're blind. All good fruit in our lives comes by the Holy Spirit's work. The Holy Spirit continues to do the things Jesus does.

Second, *the Word of Truth changes you.* God communicates messages to us—many messages. Scripture speaks with a true voice into a world churning with false voices. Scripture reveals innumerable features of God's person, purposes, will, promises, and actions. It clarifies every facet of human experience.

Third, *wise people change us.* At the most basic individual level, whoever walks with the wise becomes wise (Proverbs 13:20). The honesty and graciousness, humility and clarity, good sense and convictions of others can radiate like sunlight in your life (James 3:17–18).

Fourth, *suffering, struggle, and troubles change us.* Difficulties make us need God. Hardships make Scripture and prayer come alive. The difficulties awaken a sense of weakness—this is just where the Spirit is working. People change because something's hard, not because everything goes well. Christ enters trouble, lives through trouble, is unafraid of trouble, and speaks and acts into trouble.

Take with You: Godly growth often comes through the gifts and graces of brothers and sisters in Christ. How do your Christian friends help you grow? How do you encourage others with the wisdom God has granted you?

OCTOBER 10

My soul clings to you;
your right hand upholds me. —Psalm 63:8

The Lord describes our relationship with him from many perspectives. Love him. Fear him. Walk in his ways. Entrust yourself to him. Believe his promises. Seek him. Do what he says. Serve him. Yet he knows we tend to get stuck in ruts—I do anyway, and I'm pretty sure you do too. So he keeps coming at us from different directions. Here's one way the Bible puts it that we don't often hear mentioned: *cling* to him. Hold on tight.

Be glued to him. Don't let him go. Hold fast.

What does it mean to cling to Christ by faith when you face something threatening: a cancer diagnosis for yourself or a family member, the sudden loss of a friendship, the disapproval of your parents, or other difficult news? *Faith has two core activities: dire need, then utter joy. The order matters. First, we are weak and need his help. Second, knowing his care, we become strong and joyful.* When loneliness surrounds you, when you feel like you'll never measure up, when your relationships break down, when sickness and death come knocking, you are invited to become aware of your dire need for help. Many psalms cry out to God in need. We cling to Christ. We ask the Lord to save us from our real troubles, real sins, real sufferings, and real anguish.

Take with You: What does clinging to Jesus look like to you? How might you tighten your soul's grasp around the Savior? Do you need a greater sense of your own need or a greater sense of Jesus's readiness and willingness to save?

OCTOBER 11

"It is the LORD who goes before you. He will be with you;
he will not leave you or forsake you. Do not fear or be dismayed."
—Deuteronomy 31:8

When facing crisis or times of fear, you may go to the one who loves you. You may bring your struggles and tell him all about them. Remember who he is. He cares. He's involved. He's a sure and certain presence. He will walk with you through pain. He will strengthen you and give you courage. He will deliver you from your fears. He's your refuge, a safe place amid danger. He will clarify your thinking and anchor your hopes in what can never be lost. He's merciful to you. He will settle you in your true identity.

Many biblical truths will serve and bless you in your struggle, but the simple reality that "God is with you" overarches all. It's a summary of all God's blessings to you. *The promise of God's caring, committed, merciful presence through all of life in every circumstance is a primary strand of biblical DNA. This reality weaves through all of Scripture. It's woven into the life of every one of God's children.* Again and again God repeats to his people, "I will never leave you." He reminds us, "Though you walk through the valley of the shadow of death, I will be with you. Though the mountains fall into the heart of the sea I will be with you. I will not leave you as an orphan. I will come to you" (Psalms 23:4; 46:2; John 14:18, author's paraphrase).

> **Take with You:** How real is God's presence in your life? What would be different for you if you *truly* believed God's promise, "I will never forsake you"?

OCTOBER 12

The Lord is my strength and my shield;
in him my heart trusts, and I am helped;
my heart exults,
and with my song I give thanks to him. —Psalm 28:7

Here are two sets of questions. First, what's your greatest struggle and need right now? Where will you face today's crucial choices? In that moment, in that situation, what will you do? How will you treat people? What will you believe and want? Where will you place (or misplace) your trust? These questions look for the significant, decisive choices in a person's everyday life: "When you face that situation, which way will you turn?"

Second, what does the Lord say that speaks directly into what you're facing? Who is he? What is he doing? What does he promise? What is his will? And what does he call you to believe, need, trust, hope, and obey? These questions explore a person's current perceptions of the God who's there.

Both questions help us to work on the things that count. The first question helps us grasp the environment in which growth (or hardening) takes place daily. It makes discipleship relevant. The second question helps us grasp what we do (or don't) understand about God and how he meets us. *Often, we already know significant truth, but we don't know it in a way that changes our lives. Discipleship does the hard work of kneading truth into how we actually live.*

Take with You: Is God relevant or irrelevant to your daily life? Does knowing God and his Word change how you act, think, and feel in the world? Use these questions as much as you need to help knead the gospel into your life.

OCTOBER 13

Be merciful to me, O God, be merciful to me,
for in you my soul takes refuge;
in the shadow of your wings I will take refuge,
till the storms of destruction pass by.
I cry out to God Most High, to God who fulfills his purpose for me.
He will send from heaven and save me;
he will put to shame him who tramples on me.
God will send out his steadfast love and his faithfulness! —Psalm 57:1–3

Has anyone ever faced a threatening situation more wonderfully and honestly?

Notice all the active verbs. They describe the God I honestly need. Do you have such a straight-on relationship with this God?

So what are you facing today? Anything that threatens you? The psalm makes the experience of danger chillingly specific, but it leaves exact circumstances undefined. That invites us to insert our own details.

Later in the psalm, in the middle of this disturbing and difficult experience, comes the astonishing centerpiece: *"Be exalted, O God, above the heavens! Let your glory be over all the earth!" (v. 5). It is a wonder. Here is the living faith toward which true discipleship aims. Pointedly placed right in the midst of troubles, this is a whole different way of seeing things and responding.* These sentences are where the psalm pivots. You and I don't think this way very often. Threatened people usually react with fear, retaliation, or escapism. They forget the Exalted One. Discipleship aims to help such people remember.

Take with You: It's not natural to turn toward praise when you feel threatened. Are you convinced, like David, that our God rescues, will rescue, and has already rescued us?

OCTOBER 14

"I am the true vine, and my Father is the vinedresser.
Every branch in me that does not bear fruit he takes away,
and every branch that does bear fruit he prunes,
that it may bear more fruit." —John 15:1–2

I'll often say to someone, "The Vinedresser uses pruning shears, not a chain saw. He's not going to work on everything all at once. He's not going to make you face every kind of trouble right now. He's not going to teach you everything about himself. But something about who he is and what he says to you can make a decisive difference in some challenge you are facing right now." When I help others, I am doing nothing more than pursuing the same line of questioning and reasoning that I need myself. God meets you—and me—exactly where we are.

The Word is alive with the love of God in Christ Jesus. He invades our darkness, and his words vividly portray the human struggle. The wise will of God is realistic and relevant, as God shows himself operating in the midst of the worst and best of life and all the muddling in the middle. Scripture is timely, adapted to the varied conditions and experiences of real people, because God is a timely Redeemer.

Take with You: Where is the Vinedresser pruning you right now? What is the one small truth about God that you're learning through the pruning. Dig into the Word with confidence that your timely Redeemer will teach you what you need right now.

OCTOBER 15

Incline your ear, O Lord, and answer me,
for I am poor and needy. . . .

Be gracious to me, O Lord,
for to you do I cry all the day.
Gladden the soul of your servant,
for to you, O Lord, do I lift up my soul. —Psalm 86:1, 3–4

Right now you may be living in a world of despair. You can't see any solution to your problems. You're not looking forward to anything. The future seems empty.

But God's perspective on your life is very different. Your life is precious to him. He knows everything about you—even how many hairs are on your head. He loves you to such a degree that he sent his own Son to die for you (John 3:16).

Your Savior is not surprised or put off by your hopeless feelings. He wants you to bring your despair to him and cry for help right now, in the middle of your darkness and pain. Throughout history God's children have cried to him. He has helped them. Psalm 86 captures for us how David cried out his despair to God thousands of years ago: "In the day of my trouble I call upon you, for you answer me" (v. 7).

Today is your day of trouble. Even so, on this day the living God promises to listen to you and help you. "You will seek me and find me, when you seek me with all your heart" (Jeremiah 29:13).

Take with You: Tell Jesus all your sorrows, all your troubles. Say out loud to God, "Hear my prayer, Lord; listen to my cry for mercy" (Psalm 86:6 niv).

OCTOBER 16

"You are the light of the world. A city set on a hill cannot be hidden. Nor do people light a lamp and put it under a basket, but on a stand, and it gives light to all in the house. In the same way, let your light shine before others, so that they may see your good works and give glory to your Father who is in heaven." —Matthew 5:14–16

A Prayer for Growing in Love for God and People

Father, we do not take for granted that the energies, opportunities, responsibilities, and even the breath we take is a gift of yours to us. I pray that we who tend to be so self-obsessed and so stuck in our limited perspectives would be, by your mercy, mastered in new ways by you. I pray that we would start to wear other people on our hearts and center our lives on you, not self-interest. *I pray that we, who have been so spectacularly loved by Christ, would in some measure, become like him, by the power of your Spirit.*

Lord, we can't anticipate all the contingencies, trials, or tragedies that may come into our lives. But we ask that whatever you bring into our lives, that we would seek and find you. We would grow in knowing you and loving you. And that we would cooperate with your work in us, that through you we would increase the quantum of light that's in this world. And we pray these things in Jesus's name. Amen.

Take with You: You are the light of the world. In what small ways can you cooperate with God's work today and so reflect his light in the world?

OCTOBER 17

The LORD is my rock and my fortress and my deliverer, my God, my rock, in whom I take refuge. —Psalm 18:2

There's always something profound underneath your actions and words, feelings and thoughts—an organizing pattern that drives you. One powerful motive is something we often forget about—*the love of pleasure*. Paul discusses this in his letters to Timothy. Our culture has a lot of ways to invite us into pursing pleasure, even pleasures that become addictive. Pleasure says, "I love feeling good. I'll do anything to keep that feeling going and to forget my troubles."

But think about the fact that in the entire book of Psalms, the leading theme is that God is our refuge in the midst of trouble. You could say most of the Psalms are actually the antidote to what drives people addictively. Life is hard, and I look for something to make me feel good, something to make me forget my troubles. The Psalms say, life's hard and there's a refuge. And it's not what you might decide to turn to. It's not heavy drinking, binge-watching sports or guilty pleasure shows, scouring the internet for pornography. It's not exercising hard so you get endorphins. When these things own you, they become the substitute for seeking and finding the refuge that would actually be life itself. Looking to pleasure to save you from trouble is a form of unbelief. But by going to God, in claiming God as my rock, fortress, deliverer, refuge—we can press into faith instead.

Take with You: Where do you run when life gets hard? Do you try to distract yourself with the pursuit of pleasure or do you run to God?

OCTOBER 18

"For each tree is known by its own fruit. For figs are not gathered from thornbushes, nor are grapes picked from a bramble bush. The good person out of the good treasure of his heart produces good, and the evil person out of his evil treasure produces evil, for out of the abundance of the heart his mouth speaks." —Luke 6:44–45

What is Jesus saying when he describes the person whose heart produces good as opposed to the person whose heart produces evil? *Jesus is saying your situation is significant, but it doesn't determine your response. It's what's inside you that determines how you will respond.*

Imagine that I have a glass full of water. When I hit the glass hard, water will come spilling out of it. Why is there water on the floor? It's not just because it was hit—that's only the external pressure. Water comes out of the cup because there was water in the cup. This illustrates an important biblical truth. When we get hit by life's hardships, what determines our response is what's inside of us. Do we have a good heart that trusts in Jesus? Or do we have an evil heart that trusts in ourselves?

At the end of the day, God searches the human heart, and the true nature of your heart will shine through, regardless of your circumstances. That's why we need a heart that's being transformed to be like Christ. Because of God's mercy and grace, the gift of a new, good heart is ours for the asking.

Take with You: What is in your glass? When the hard things of life hit, what will come spilling out of your heart?

OCTOBER 19

But I say, walk by the Spirit, and you will not gratify the desires of the flesh. —Galatians 5:16

I want to zero in on one particular verb, which is the notion of desire—what we lust for, crave, demand, and believe we need. It all adds up to "I want." Using the language of desires lets you get specific. Desires have an object. It was hugely helpful in my own sense of where I needed to repent to see, for example, that in a conflict I was desiring to be accurately understood and desiring vindication. I became frustrated and obsessed and preoccupied if I didn't get what I wanted in a particular situation.

What is the desire that drives your anger? What do you want? What are your expectations? What are you after? Interpersonal conflict is driven by what we want and aren't getting. The Bible has a rich description of this link between the issue of the heart and our desires. You've got God-centered desires on one side of the equation, and on the other side, the desires of the flesh. *Desires of the flesh are opposed to God's rule over our lives. The fruit of the Spirit expresses submission to the desires of the Spirit.*

Romans 13:12, 14 speaks to this struggle by telling us what to do next: "Let us cast off the works of darkness and put on the armor of light. But put on the Lord Jesus Christ, and make no provision for the flesh, to gratify its desires."

Take with You: *Father God, help me to walk by the Spirit and submit all of my desires to you. Help me to want what you want and nothing else.*

OCTOBER 20

Be not quick in your spirit to become angry,
for anger lodges in the heart of fools. —Ecclesiastes 7:9

One key to getting anger straight is to understand that when you're angry, *you* are doing something. Anger is not an "it." Anger is not just one part of you. Anger does not "happen" to you. You do anger. And it's something *you* do with all your heart, soul, mind, and body. You size something up in a flash and say, "I don't like that!" As your adrenaline surges, your body wakes up, heats up, tightens up. You feel intense emotions, which spill into your tone of voice, decibel level, body language, and facial expression. You think quickly, rehearsing what happened, imagining scenarios, evaluating, planning, and choosing. You go into action. Your desires and expectations are active. You want fairness, to be proved right, to be treated lovingly, to get to your appointment on time, to protect someone, or to get your way.

When anger goes astray, it says something about who's the center of the universe. When anger runs amok, you don't just need a technique to calm yourself down. You don't just need other people to change. Your core motives must change. The god you worship (my will be done, my kingdom come . . . or else) must be overthrown.

The most high God, his higher law, his loving mercies, and his higher purposes transform anger. Something miraculous happens when I no longer say, "My kingdom come, my will be done on earth." *The mercy that humbles us begins to master us, and my universe returns to reality.*

Take with You: *Father, help me to rightly see my anger in all its forms. Your kingdom come, Lord. Your will be done.*

OCTOBER 21

Search me, God, and know my heart;
test me and know my anxious thoughts.
See if there is any offensive way in me,
and lead me in the way everlasting.
—Psalm 139:23–24 NIV

The psalmist asks God to look into his heart and to identify any offensive ways in him. In other words: Search my motives, Lord. Motives are your core values and commitments. They shape and energize your emotions, thoughts, and actions. They determine how you treat people, and how you react to pain, loss, or threat. Your motives are not neutral. They are either God-honoring or self-honoring. This includes how and why you get angry.

Overthrowing the self-serving motives reflected in your anger is not easy. When anger goes bad, it's because your motives are committed to serving you, not God. Changing your motives takes something much deeper than simply learning conflict-resolution skills. It calls for more than altering how you talk to yourself, though that also will change. It takes more than finding some technique, management tool, or medication that works to calm you down. Sure, deep breaths can help your nervous system. But the results will not be lasting.

Motives are the goals and desires around which you organize your life. You need God to help you reform them. *When God's larger purposes are in control, the poisonous evil of anger is neutralized. Anger becomes a servant of goodness.* It becomes just, and its purposes become merciful to all who will turn and work to become conformed to God's image.

Take with You: What motives of yours need work? We all have them. Pray for help and ask a good friend—one who will be honest with you—to tell you where change is needed.

OCTOBER 22

Be angry and do not sin. —Ephesians 4:26a

Anger is the fighting emotion. It's also the justice emotion and the deliver-the-oppressed-from-evil emotion. It stems from love for the needy and those who need protection.

All of us come wired with a sense of justice. It can be bent, for good or ill, but you cannot erase it. It's part of the original equipment in human nature. It's how God made us. You are able to identify when something is wrong and harmful. It matters. You are created to get upset about it. You speak and act forcefully to address the problem. When human beings work this way, it's beautiful. It's constructive. This anger is natural and good. It's a capacity given to you by God so you can be like him in this important way.

If only you and I got angry at the right time and in the right way. But sadly, anger is "natural" in a second way. What was created good is entangled with and corrupted by our fallen self-centeredness, which has also become "second nature" to us. *So to be human means you're created with a capacity for just anger. And to be human means you're fallen, with a bent toward bad anger.* A lot of what makes anger so hard to sort out is our difficulty in figuring out which is which.

Take with You: Ask God to show you when you're expressing bad anger. God knows it's hard to change and wants to help you with this. Seeing your anger and the motives and desires behind it will remind you of your need for Jesus and real transformation.

OCTOBER 23

He does not deal with us according to our sins,
nor repay us according to our iniquities.
For as high as the heavens are above the earth,
so great is his steadfast love toward those who fear him;
as far as the east is from the west,
so far does he remove our transgressions from us. —Psalm 103:10–12

Forgiveness does not ignore or excuse what's wrong. It doesn't pretend that the person didn't really mean what they did or said. Instead, recognizing that a debt is owed, it forgives the debt.

What is the dynamic? Pay close attention to how Psalm 103:8–13 unfolds. It begins by remembering how God described himself to Moses when they met on Mount Sinai: "The LORD is merciful and gracious, slow to anger [patient] and abounding in steadfast love" (v. 8).

These words express the genetic code of the Bible. This DNA comes in the flesh in Jesus Christ. This is who he is and what he is like.

"As far as the east is from the west, so far does he remove our transgressions from us" (v. 12).

His forgiveness is that wide. To know such a Savior is to be in awe of him, love him, to be humbled, and want to be like him. *By receiving forgiveness in our need, we become able and willing to give forgiveness to others.* Is it easy? No. One and done? Rarely. Entirely possible? Yes. Christ shows love to the loveless that they might lovely be.

Take with You: God's forgiveness is an essential part of his love for you. Being forgiven shows us the path to forgiving others—start by loving them.

OCTOBER 24

"Bear fruit in keeping with repentance." —Matthew 3:8

The Christian life is a lifelong "race of repentance."* *Repentance* is the Bible's word for "thorough, deep-seated, genuine change." It means turning from old barren ways to new fruitful ways. You no longer sleepwalk through the world of your desires and fears. Instead, you wake up to find yourself living in God's world. The race of repentance calls for the ongoing reversal of our deepest instincts. It's a process that takes the rest of your life.

A famous theologian once said that coming to vital Christian faith starts a lifelong quarrel inside a person: "You and sin must quarrel, if you and God are to be friends."** Imagine, you must quarrel with yourself if you are to befriend God! To deal firmly with yourself is the hard way, the narrow way . . . and the only good way.

Honest war with yourself comes paired with incomprehensible gifts that help you change. Whatever you do, get this wisdom, this kingdom of God, this Christ! Nothing you could possibly desire compares. The cost is high: your very life. The reward is higher: "What no eye has seen, nor ear heard, nor the heart of man imagined, what God has prepared for those who love him" (1 Corinthians 2:8–10).

Take with You: To bear fruit for God means submitting to his ways and repenting of yours. But he is a gentle gardener. His pruning shears may hurt, but the fruit you bear will be even sweeter.

---

* John Calvin's piercing phrase in *Institutes of the Christian Religion*, Book III 3:9, in John McNeil, ed., *Library of Christian Classics*, Vol. XX (Westminster Press, 1960), 602.

** J. C. Ryle, *Holiness: Its Nature, Hindrances, Difficulties, and Roots* (James Clark, 1952), 70.

OCTOBER 25

"I will not leave you as orphans; I will come to you. . . . Because I live, you also will live." —John 14:18–19

Therefore, preparing your minds for action, and being sober-minded, set your hope fully on the grace that will be brought to you at the revelation of Jesus Christ. —1 Peter 1:13

You might not think very much about the future, especially the events described by the apostle Peter in the verse above. He is referring to the end times when Jesus has promised that he will return for you; he will not leave you as an orphan. Peter wants you to set your hope fully on this promise.

But how do you know that your remaining sin will not prevent this from happening? John makes another amazing promise that when we see Jesus, we will become just like him (1 John 3:2). This means that our change will be complete, and we can go home with him.

And this good news is not simply for the future. What Jesus will do on that day reshapes what we do now. Peter bases the transformational power of our present Christian life on what will happen in the future when he says, "As obedient children, do not be conformed to the former lusts which were yours in your ignorance" (1 Peter 1:14 NASB). How will you hang in over the long haul, growing wiser until the end? *Future grace gives us hope, the Spirit gives us the power to begin the transformation now, and everlasting life awaits.*

Take with You: Jesus is coming back and will finish the job he started in you. While you look forward to that, what is one thing you're hoping Jesus will help you change now?

OCTOBER 26

When the righteous cry for help, the LORD hears
and delivers them out of all their troubles.
The LORD is near to the brokenhearted
and saves the crushed in spirit. . . .
The LORD redeems the life of his servants;
none of those who take refuge in him will be condemned.
—Psalm 34:17–18, 22

God's grace to sufferers demonstrates that he hears the cry of the afflicted. He offers mercy not only to sinners but also to sufferers. Jesus dies for the wicked; he also defends the innocent, feeds the hungry, gives refuge to the broken, and heals the sick. How do you know you're safe? You know you're safe because in Matthew 28:20 he says, "And behold, I am with you always, to the end of the age."

At the center of the Christian life is our need for God's protection. In the past, he showed such mercies, in part to give us hope today (Romans 15:4). He helps, comforts, heals, and encourages. Someday he will act decisively to remove all heartache and bring us joy (Revelation 21:3–4). We are broken, but his mercies to the broken change the way we face what afflicts us.

God's people have been in a posture of waiting, in the midst of suffering, for two thousand years. Watching evil prevail. But take heart: He will put all things right in the end. Delay doesn't mean injustice from God. And we, his people, are called to a fellowship of suffering, of waiting. The Lord hears, delivers, and redeems. You can cry out to him in confidence because of his promises.

Take with You: Are you struggling? Are you lonely or sick or afraid? God is near. Tell him what's on your heart. He offers grace upon grace.

OCTOBER 27

Therefore be imitators of God, as beloved children. And walk in love, as Christ loved us and gave himself up for us, a fragrant offering and sacrifice to God. —Ephesians 5:1–2

God wants us to become imitators of him, but never (never!) by our own willpower or self-effort. Through the Bible, God's Spirit teaches you about him and gives you the grace to learn from him. *And the more you hear and know God's Word, it becomes the environment you live in. His promises become the food you live on. His commands become the life you live out.*

Many people think that emphasizing obedience to God's commands equates with trying to be good based on our own efforts. But it doesn't! When God calls for our obedience and holy life, he's not contradicting the grace of his own gospel. Free grace—past, present, and future—is effective grace. It intends to change our sinful patterns from the inside out. Our gracious Master remakes disciples who do more than act like him; they *become* like him—more honest, constructive, purposeful, and loving.

These are long journeys, but the direction of grace is toward obedience to God's law of love. None of these changes mean perfection until Jesus returns. You will always need mercies to be renewed every morning. But there can be much growth amid the ongoing struggle. It isn't always dramatic. Small choices count. But the Spirit will produce his fruit in us. God's grace never fails.

Take with You: To be obedient to God is not about self-effort or rule-keeping. It's opening your heart to become more like him. It's learning to walk in love, depending on his support to do so.

OCTOBER 28

Therefore, if anyone is in Christ, he is a new creation. The old has passed away; behold, the new has come. —2 Corinthians 5:17

God's truth awakens us to reality.

We must *know* the gravity of our condition as human beings. We are fundamentally flawed. We love the wrong things and sometimes the wrong people. We are traitors to Jesus, every day and in many ways. We need rescue from ourselves, from what we bring on ourselves, from what others do to us. The twin evils of being a sinner and being sinned against aren't a theoretical problem. It's my specific problem, and yours, and the other person's too (Ecclesiastes 9:3).

Sin and suffering are what's wrong. But God's mercies make wrongs right. They help us to become a new creation.

We must know our calling as children of such a Father. Jesus announces his kingdom with the words, "Repent." That simply means, "Change." His grace and truth get about the business of changing us. We are called to bring the kingdom of God onto the stage of history, and into the details of our lives. We are called to change and to change the world. We are called to build a wise community. We run a lifelong race of repentance and renewal, not just individually, but all together. Jesus intends to teach us how to live as "disciples" (changers, learners, students), so that we become his instruments of change in the lives of others.

Take with You: Do you have a friend or an adult in your life who lives as a disciple of Jesus? Ask them about it. And ask them to tell you what it's like.

OCTOBER 29

This is what the LORD says:
"Cursed are those who put their trust in mere humans,
who rely on human strength
and turn their hearts away from the LORD.
They are like stunted shrubs in the desert,
with no hope for the future.
They will live in the barren wilderness,
in an uninhabited salty land." —Jeremiah 17:5–6 NLT

The images here offer a stark picture of what life is like when we put our trust in human strength instead of God: "Cursed are those who put their trust in mere humans, who rely on human strength (v. 5 NLT). In this context, the Lord is speaking to the fact that Israel is being allured by the false worship of the nations around them and are turning to the Assyrians and the Egyptians for military help instead of God. *In your life, this can apply to putting trust in others, in yourself, or trusting in human abilities in general instead of placing all your trust in the Lord.*

What is the sad result? "Stunted shrubs in the desert, with no hope for the future." (v. 6 NLT). The English language can hardly capture this picture of absolute barrenness. This is the graphic image that Jeremiah gives us of the nature of sin and where it ends up.

But words of hope are right around the corner. There is another way. We can turn to the Lord and live a blessed life under his care. Read tomorrow's entry to hear more.

Take with You: Have you ever been to the desert? Did you feel thirsty and wonder how anything survives there? This is the picture of a soul who is not depending on God. Is that where you live?

OCTOBER 30

"Blessed is the man who trusts in the LORD,
whose trust is the LORD.
He is like a tree planted by water,
that sends out its roots by the stream,
and does not fear when heat comes,
for its leaves remain green,
and is not anxious in the year of drought,
for it does not cease to bear fruit." —Jeremiah 17:7–8

In comparison to yesterday's passage, the next part of Jeremiah 17 provides a dramatic contrast: *Blessed.* "Blessed is the man who trusts in the LORD" (v. 7). The person whose trust is in the Lord is blessed with this incredible promise: "He is like a tree planted by water, that sends out its roots by the stream." What a positive situation for a tree, yes? But there's more. The tree "does not fear when heat comes, for its leaves remain green, and is not anxious in the year of drought, for it does not cease to bear fruit" (v. 8). Harsh circumstances are not a problem because the tree has a living connection with the stream.

This is a rich portrayal of the nature of faith. The stream is God; you are the tree. *When you are connected to God, you aren't afraid in the face of difficult situations. Your "leaves remain green"—you are fruitful in the year of drought.* When you're in an extremely difficult, high-heat, high-threat situation, are you a fruit-bearing tree or more like a cactus? The answer will depend on whom you place your trust.

Take with You: To be blessed is to live close to God so you can depend on his "living water" (John 4:13–14). Have you asked him for a drink? He never says no.

OCTOBER 31

If then you have been raised with Christ, seek the things that are above, where Christ is, seated at the right hand of God. Set your minds on things that are above, not on things that are on earth. For you have died, and your life is hidden with Christ in God. —Colossians 3:1–3

What does "being raised with Christ" mean when the hardships of life close in on you? It means that, in a sense, you are already in heaven with Christ, and he will help you face your troubles instead of running away from them. When you move toward a problem, you *will* still be challenged by it, but it's an opportunity to grow in your faith, especially in how you relate to others when the pressure is on. *As you move toward problems and people, God desires that you become able to relate to others with the kind of candor, openness, and genuine listening that reflects Jesus our Lord.* What was impossible before, is now possible. You can become like Jesus, with his help.

But that tension between the old you and the new you still exists. You are still a sinner in the process of transformation. One of the advantages of having the picture of the stunted shrub and the fruit tree in your mind is that it forces you to reckon with how the heat—your suffering—challenges the old you. Do you focus on the heat or on where your roots are planted?

Take with You: How do you normally react when life gets hard? Remember, you have dual citizenship, here and in heaven. Set your mind on things that are above, and you will still bear fruit.

NOVEMBER 1

Repay no one evil for evil, but give thought to do what is honorable in the sight of all. If possible, so far as it depends on you, live peaceably with all. Beloved, never avenge yourselves, but leave it to the wrath of God, for it is written, "Vengeance is mine, I will repay, says the Lord."—Romans 12:17–19

The Bible is realistic about life—there are hard things that happen to us, true wrongs are done to us, and they count. Look at how God describes what's happened when we're wronged. He calls it evil. But the Bible is also realistic about our response to the evil done to us. We often want revenge. There's a benefit to identifying what's wrong in your reactions and realizing you're the one who wants to do it. Yes, you. Nothing and no one makes you respond the way you do. Make this part of your confession. You can name your sufferings and also confess your wrong responses.

The Psalms are full of the prayers of those who are dealing with being sinned against and their responses of bitterness and hostility. Like the psalmists, you too can name your sufferings and sins in one breath. God hears our sorrows and draws near to us despite our sins. *His gracious approach gives us the confidence to confess our sins and leave the evil done to us in his hands.*

Take with You: It's hard not to take revenge on someone who hurts you. You want the other person to pay, and you don't want to look weak. But it's God's way. More evil does not solve the problem of evil. Only he can do that.

NOVEMBER 2

The steadfast love of the LORD never ceases;
his mercies never come to an end;
they are new every morning;
great is your faithfulness. —Lamentations 3:22–23

One of the things I love about the way the Bible portrays God's mercies is that they speak and act in two directions. First, he comes to us in our sorrows and troubles, vulnerability, and weakness. Because he's our refuge, we learn to name our troubles and bring our burdens to him (Psalm 28). Second, he comes to us in our sinfulness, drift, and blindness because he's wondrously "unfair" and does not deal with us as our sins deserve (Psalm 103). We learn to name our failings in confession.

The process of coming to see when we get off track and learning how to reorient ourselves to God is a great gift of wisdom. *We drift, but God teaches us to recalibrate our lives to his mercy. Every morning, we awaken afresh to his strengthening and shielding care. The Lord's mercies are new every day of our lives. So is our need.*

We need his strength, his help, and his comfort. He is a steadfast guide and keeper, and he hears our cries. When you trust in Christ, there's a fundamental sense that a joy, hope, and confidence rests—not in us, the vulnerable and straying—but in the mercy of Another, the One whose love never ceases.

Take with You: If you are young in the faith, you may not realize that every Christian, no matter how long they have walked with God, needs his love and mercy refreshed every day. Believe it. It is the "secret" to their perseverance.

NOVEMBER 3

Know this, my beloved brothers: let every person be quick to hear, slow to speak, slow to anger. —James 1:19

How do you come to know other people? One way is to listen to find out what life is like for them. To do that, *learn to pay attention to their experiences and emotions. These are crucial components of who people are. They are signals that register what's happening to them and within them.*

For example, feeling overwhelmed drives people to God, self-evaluation, and seeking help. It has a cause and a "way of escape" that can be found with God's help (1 Corinthians 10:13). It's a point of entry where a helper's words of truth and deeds of love will hit their mark.

Wise living also involves alertness to your own experiences and emotions too. The goal of such self-awareness is not introspection, rather it's a matter of knowing yourself honestly. Here are two helpful kinds of questions to ask yourself or another:

1. What joys, highlights, purposes, or glad hopes fill you as you think of the past, present, or future?
2. What sorrows, burdens, guilt, struggles, or fears press upon you as you think of the past, present, or future?

These are "feeling-toned" questions that invite people to become honest with themselves and one another. Such questions also set the stage for people to experience more specific love, counsel, encouragement, confrontation, and intercession or praise to God. They are starting points, not stopping points.

Take with You: To get to know people, take time to listen to them. Ask good questions that invite them to tell you how their life is going—not just what is happening—but how it feels to be them.

NOVEMBER 4

Charm is deceitful, and beauty is vain,
but a woman who fears the LORD is to be praised.
—Proverbs 31:30

Beauty is vain? These are not words you read often on social media. Our culture is filled with voices that comment on how we ought to look and the blessings and curses we will receive depending on how we measure up. We are taught the "good and evil" of our appearance by what we hear and see in others. These messages are so frequent and so convincing that we can easily fall victim to them. We can fall under their spell and find ourselves trapped and driven to try to meet these false standards.

But these standards are not from God.

In several places Scripture singles out the issue of beauty in a pointed way. Proverbs 31:10–31 portrays the true beauty of fearing, trusting, and loving the Lord our Redeemer. It comments on charm's deceitfulness and beauty's emptiness. The true and enduring beauty of character, peaceableness, wisdom, trust, and love breathe forth from these proverbs. Similarly, 1 Peter 3:1–6 redefines beauty. It contrasts the cultural image ("external adornment") with the true and imperishable image of God in the heart.

True beauty is fearless; it can never be ravaged by time or affliction; it can never be made insecure. The Word of God abounds with wonderful passages intended to renew minds and hearts, causing us to serve and aim for a different image.

Take with You: Young women, what standard do you judge yourself by? Young men, how do you judge the young women in your church or school? Are you using God's standards or the world's?

NOVEMBER 5

And he said to his disciples, "Therefore I tell you, do not be anxious about your life, what you will eat, nor about your body, what you will put on." —Luke 12:22

There are lots of things to worry about. Money is a common issue to worry about. *How will I pay for college? Will I be able to get a "good" job? Will I be able to afford an apartment, a car, and . . . everything else?* With money, there's always something else to worry about.

All the things we worry about have one thing in common—they're all uncertain. Jesus explains our worries, however, not by pointing to how uncertain life is, but by pointing to something in us. *We lose sight of God because what we want (and worry about) is the only thing we see.* When faith is dying out, greed and worry come to life. When anxious greed comes to life, it kills off faith. A worrier seeks certainty in the world, not in Jesus.

Jesus gets very tender in this sermon: "Your Father knows that you need these things. . . . Don't be afraid, little flock, because your Father has chosen to give . . ." (Luke 12:30, 32 NASB). You can rest on these words. Jesus makes it as personal and as generous as possible. He knows your situation. He knows your personality. Cast your cares on him, because he cares for you (1 Peter 5:7).

Take with You: The only certain thing in this world is God himself, and he both loves you and knows what you need. Ask him to give you his perspective on what worries you. It *will* help.

NOVEMBER 6

For it is God who works in you, both to will and to work for his good pleasure. —Philippians 2:13

What do you crave, want, pursue, wish, long for, hope to get, feel you need, or passionately desire? Your answers cut to the marrow of who you are and what you live for. God sees our hearts as an embattled kingdom ruled either by earthly desires (which can hijack your heart), or by holy passions that express your love for God.

The problem is we don't understand our desires very well. We misinterpret them and don't really want to know the truth anyway. But it's good to ask God to examine our desires because it's one of the most fruitful ways to understand what motivates us.

Which will triumph in our lives: the natural tendency to grasp after temporary, earthly pleasures, or the restored sanity of the desires of the Spirit? We all struggle with these issues and need help to move in the right direction. Only God has the power to change us in the ways we most need changing. *The mercies of God work to forgive and then to change what is deeply wrong within us. The inworking power of his grace qualitatively transforms our very desires. We can be fundamentally rewired by the merciful presence of the Messiah.*

Take with You: Do you need to be "rewired" so you can recognize when your desires are off track? Know that it is God's good pleasure to do so.

NOVEMBER 7

For the word of God is alive and active. Sharper than any double-edged sword, it penetrates even to dividing soul and spirit, joints and marrow; it judges the thoughts and attitudes of the heart. —Hebrews 4:12 NIV

Even at a young age, your heart desires your full attention. You may desire good looks, material things, or certain relationships. And it's easy to let these desires take up too much of your time and attention, squeezing out your relationship with Jesus.

The New Testament writers use the phrase "lusts of the flesh" to describe this sin, and it's good to pay attention to what this means. The Bible says that if you love "all that is in the world, the lust of the flesh and the lust of the eyes and the boastful pride of life," you do not love God (1 John 2:16 NASB).

So are preferences, wishes, desires, longings, hopes, and expectations always sinful? Of course not. The moral issue always turns on whether your desires take on a ruling status in your life. When they do, they create bad "fruit" in our lives, such as anger, grumbling, immorality, and despair. The things people desire are delightful as blessings received from God, but terrible as rulers. They deceive you, promising blessing, but don't deliver.

Take with You: God knows (and judges) what entices you, but don't turn away from him in shame. He is a good Father. His correction may be painful, but he loves you too much to leave you on the wrong path.

NOVEMBER 8

Teach me your way, LORD,
that I may rely on your faithfulness;
give me an undivided heart,
that I may fear your name. —Psalm 86:11 NIV

Can you change what you want? Yes and Amen! This is central to the work of the Holy Spirit. You will always desire, love, trust, believe, fear, obey, value, and serve something. You're motivated when you feel desire. God does not anesthetize us. He redirects us so we will be ruled by different (better) desires. He promises to change what you really want! God insists that he be first, and all lesser loves be radically subordinate.

God challenges the things that everybody, everywhere eagerly pursues (Matthew 6:32). Consider the desires of the body: health, food, clothing, sexual pleasure, and rest. And desires of the mind: happiness, being loved, meaning, respect, success, and control. Can these cravings really be changed? The Bible says yes and promises that God will live in us, indwell us with power, and write the truth on our hearts.

The evil in our desires does not necessarily lie in what we want but in the fact that we want it too much. Our desires for good things seize the throne in our hearts, becoming idols that replace the King. God refuses to serve our earthbound longings and commands us to be ruled by longings for him. *But what God commands, he provides the power to accomplish: he works in us both the willing and the doing of his good pleasure (Philippians 2:12–13).*

Take with You: Have you heard the phrase: "It's just human nature"? It can be used to excuse desires that are contrary to God or to suggest you can't change. But God created human nature, and he knows best.

NOVEMBER 9

"I will sprinkle clean water on you, and you shall be clean from all your uncleannesses, and from all your idols I will cleanse you. And I will give you a new heart, and a new spirit I will put within you. And I will remove the heart of stone from your flesh and give you a heart of flesh." —Ezekiel 36:25–26

Jesus is in the rehab business. When he takes something that's broken into his hands, it begins to work again. That's so of an individual. It's so of a relationship. It's so of a church.

Obviously, this does not mean instant, complete change right now. It's a lifelong process—until the day when we see Jesus face-to-face. Then he will wrap it all up in a flash, at the last trumpet (1 Corinthians 15:51–52; 1 John 3:1–3; Revelation 20–21).

But as he changes us, we are not just restored to a godlier version of ourselves. Instead, we are qualitatively changed in this process of repair. We are redeemed, turned into something new, something better and different from we ever were. We have a new heart, a heart of flesh. And though the changes will not be complete until he returns, *we are marked by the Holy Spirit—and so become able to comfort others whatever their troubles, as we have been comforted in our troubles (2 Corinthians 1:3–4).*

Take with You: Have you ever considered that your faith does more than save you? It empowers the rehab process too. As we are renewed, we are able to love and comfort others. In this, we are Jesus's boots on the ground.

NOVEMBER 10

For by the grace given me I say to every one of you: Do not think of yourself more highly than you ought, but rather think of yourself with sober judgment, in accordance with the faith God has distributed to each of you. —Romans 12:3 NIV

Mostly, we think of ourselves too highly. Change calls for self-knowledge, but we have at least four tendencies that sabotage this process.

First, pride creates self-delusion. My perspective and my way of doing things seem good, even very good! But to know myself as I truly am, I must come to know myself through the eyes of someone outside of myself—God. Second, we're too caught up in our lives. Our day-to-day responsibilities and worries consume us. Entertainment offers us a wide choice of narcotics. Either way, we live mindlessly. Third, some of us are "activists." We're mindful but don't focus on the right things. What's on our minds is the compelling press of all that needs to be done! Such activism does not produce heartfelt patience or the ability to wisely enter another person's struggles. Fourth, some of us are too introspective. We live mindfully—but what's on our minds is the fascinating flood of thoughts about ourselves. These insights do not lead us out into faith and love.

Biblical change, however, makes you into a person who sparkles with patience, kindness, and clarity. You're not self-deluded and self-absorbed. You're both active and self-knowing, but neither activistic nor introspective. True self-knowledge moves you outward toward God in faith, toward others in love.

Take with You: God loves you as you are, but he wants us to have proper judgment about ourselves so we can serve others well. Pray for biblical change today.

NOVEMBER 11

Not that I have already obtained this or am already perfect, but I press on to make it my own, because Christ Jesus has made me his own. Brothers, I do not consider that I have made it my own. But one thing I do: forgetting what lies behind and straining forward to what lies ahead, I press on toward the goal for the prize of the upward call of God in Christ Jesus. —Philippians 3:12–14

The kinds of things I struggle with are similar to the kinds of things you struggle with. The ways Jesus meets me are similar to the ways he meets you. Similar, but not identical. God seems to love variety. You and I do not reduce to a category. Our Father is raising children, and each one of us is unique.

How on earth was I able to change? Because God intervened personally. He gave me words of Scripture to invite me into Christ and a friend who was faithful and honest. And God spoke into my harried, anxious experience. He addressed me pointedly, repeatedly, and patiently over days, months, and years. Truth slowly took root, blossomed, and bore fruit. As I turned from sin to Christ, I was changed.

Your life, too, is lived (and rescripted) in the details. *Your Savior and Shepherd meets you in the particulars of your need for saving and shepherding.* He works in specifics, not in theological generalities. Every person's life is different, and God meets you right there with his gracious, sanctifying purposes.

Take with You: God is looking to change you in the unique ways that will bring you into relationship with him and give you purpose in this world. Welcome him in.

NOVEMBER 12

Be angry, and do not sin. —Psalm 4:4a

When we talk about anger, we're really talking about the problem of evil. There *are* evils in this world worth reacting to. The problem is we react to them in wrong ways. Something displeases us—it matters, and it's wrong—but our response is too destructive, whether it's irritation, bitterness, or outright violence. Overcoming these wrong ways is a long and messy process.

Jesus gets angry in Scripture. Unbelief matters to him, and he stands against it. When people stand in the way of him serving and helping children, women, and the sick, he gets mad. He gets mad when the worship of the one true and living God becomes a sideshow of buying and selling. Because he cares so much, he gets upset at the things that are wrong. You can learn to respond to true wrongs the way Jesus does.

Here's how Scripture tells us to handle our anger: Be slow to anger (James 1:19)—not hot-tempered; and do not to let the sun go down on your anger (Ephesians 4:26)—be quick to resolve things. *Instead of feeding your anger or trying to get rid of it all together, there is a third way forward: get angry differently. Instead of overreacting, seek to react appropriately and constructively.*

Take with You: How do you do with anger? Do you yell and stomp around? Do you say nothing and hold it all in? Either way, you have a problem. Ask a believer who handles their anger well to tell you how they do it.

NOVEMBER 13

Beloved, never avenge yourselves, but leave it to the wrath of God, for it is written, "Vengeance is mine, I will repay, says the Lord." —Romans 12:19

He will send from heaven and save me;
he will put to shame him who tramples on me.
God will send out his steadfast love and his faithfulness! —Psalm 57:3

I wish we'd hear more sermons on how the wrath of God is a good thing—it's something to set our hope on. Part of understanding that God is our refuge and defender is knowing that God's wrath goes to bat for us. He will deal with the wrongs of this life, both the wrongs done to you and the wrongs committed by you.

Concerning the wrongs done to you, God says, "Don't get even. I will repay. I'll take care of it. I'll fix it." You don't have to be about the business of making things right. Instead, you can be about the business of loving.

Concerning your own sin, God has no wrath against you because he already poured it out on Jesus. But he doesn't leave it at that. He's committed to keep contending with you. He contends with your sins, he contends with your unbelief, and he keeps telling you about himself to rattle you into hearing him. It's the most loyal opposition you could ever imagine. *He's willing to oppose you to remake you into his wonderful image. His loving displeasure is our hope.*

Take with You: We're told to stand up for ourselves. That can be good advice, but not if we're filled with wrath. We are to leave that for God to handle. As we do, we will learn from him and become more like him.

NOVEMBER 14

Refrain from anger and turn from wrath;
do not fret—it leads only to evil. —Psalm 37:8 NIV

What "pushes your buttons"? In other words, what makes you angry? It could be something minor or something really big. How do you react? Do you scream or brood, attack or withdraw?

The Bible is exceedingly rich in wanting us to understand what makes us angry, because those reasons always have to do with how you and God are getting along. To get stuck in bitterness, for example, you must forget who God is. This doesn't mean you don't believe in him, but functionally, you're acting as though he doesn't exist.

Over your lifetime, expect to see patterns to your anger. It's into this world of anger buttons, button-pushers, and reactions that the living God speaks and acts. This world has a twofold source of evil—the evil that comes at us and the evil that comes from within us. God steps into that world of double evil and intends to give us a proper sense of perspective to understand our sufferings, provocations, and sins.

As you discover your reasons for anger, this opens the door to an honest relationship with God where you acknowledge your need for mercy and help. In a culture where reacting and anger come easily, let's rebel against what comes easy and do what's hard—whatever small obedience God puts in front of you.

Take with You: Anger feels so right when you're experiencing it—so much so that we often don't realize we sinned until much later (if ever). It's hard to take on your anger. Are you willing to do what's hard?

NOVEMBER 15

For I consider that the sufferings of this present time are not worth comparing with the glory that is to be revealed to us.
—Romans 8:18

If you're angry at God, ask yourself, *What do I want? What do I believe God will give to me?* You will invariably find that your heart is controlled by particular desires and made-up promises, and you become angry when God doesn't deliver. For example, if I crave marriage and believe God will reward my devotion to him with a spouse, my heart sets itself up to be angry at God when the desire is not satisfied.

Nowhere in the Bible do we find a shred of evidence that God fails to fulfill his promises to us. The Bible discusses suffering constantly, but always shows us that any apparent "betrayal" by God must be seen in the context of his larger purposes. But God never promised that in this world we would be free from tears, mourning, crying, and pain—or from the evils that cause them. The interweaving of God's plans for the world and our well-being is far bigger and more complex than people imagine.

To really believe in God's plans for your life is to gain an unshakable trust in him who holds firm in the midst of even hellish torments, let alone the milder pains.

Take with You: Do have specific expectations about how your life will be? Most of us do. But if those expectations are not realized remember this: The most basic promise of God is that he will always be with you. He will not default on that, but most everything else is uncertain.

NOVEMBER 16

Be not far from me, for trouble is near,
and there is none to help. —Psalm 22:11

Losses are a particular kind of hardship. Something or someone you really value, love, and deeply enjoy proves to be fragile. Perhaps it's a good friend who moves away, a pet that dies, or your home is destroyed by fire. In your mind, you would have enjoyed this blessing for a very long time, but it proved to be temporary. Your valued friend, your dog, or your home is gone. And that hurts.

The Bible gives you the exact help you need when you face the loss of any good thing. These good, temporary things will pass away, and the Bible is realistic about that. But the God of the Bible is also committed to entering into and speaking into your pain and meeting you in these realities.

How will you get over it? Are you going to believe your pain is pointless and your life is empty, or are you going to find a hope that's indestructible?

Jesus has hope that's indestructible, though his earthly life was filled with suffering. His earthly father died before he started his ministry, he suffered rejection from many people, even family members, and knew he was going to die a terrible death. He is a man who experienced grief and heartache and anguish, and he managed it by depending on his heavenly Father to care for him. Psalm 22 became his prayer. It can be your prayer as well.

Take with You: Psalm 22 was written by King David during a time of great distress and its cries to God are raw and pleading. Remember this when you face suffering. You don't need to go it alone.

NOVEMBER 17

The Lord is my strength and my shield;
in him my heart trusts, and I am helped;
my heart exults,
and with my song I give thanks to him. —Psalm 28:7

Have you ever faced a severe trial, such as a serious illness or injury? There are many ways to lose the spiritual battle. Will we worry, feel anxious, or be very afraid? Will we obsess about medical intervention? Will we go into denial (*This can't be happening!*)? Will we get irritable with one another, exacerbating the tension by bickering?

Or we could face our troubles the way the Psalms do. For example, Psalm 28 was written by King David. It takes us by the hand and walks us through our battle with the world, flesh, and devil during a difficult time. The first few lines give voice to a sense of utter need and great vulnerability in the face of threat. It cries out to the one able and willing to help. In the next few lines, David grapples with the specific evils facing him. Verses 3 to 5 are about human enemies, but the same pattern of faith applies when we face other grievous circumstances where we need God's strength and shield.

This psalm moves quickly across the emotional register, arriving at joyful peace and trust far more quickly than we tend to. Scripture is giving us a template, not a timetable. David is showing us the direction in which to walk.

Take with You: The Psalms are God's way of showing us how to pray to him, especially when we have no words of our own. Pray Psalm 28 in your time of need and keep praying it until it feels like its words are coming from you.

NOVEMBER 18

But to all who did receive him, who believed in his name, he gave the right to become children of God. —John 1:12

When you come to God through trusting in Jesus, he gives you a new identity. You become part of the family of God. You are his dearly loved child. Listen to what the apostle John says about your identity: "See what great love the Father has lavished on us, that we should be called children of God! And that is what we are!" (1 John 3:1 NIV).

Experiencing Jesus's presence and love will give you the courage to see that the story of your life is bigger than your problems. The difficult things that happen to you are not the last word on who you are and where your life is going. They are a significant part of your story, but they are not the most significant part. They are a chapter of the new story of your life that Jesus is writing.

The Gospel of John closes with this verse: "Jesus did many other things as well. If every one of them were written down, I suppose that even the whole world would not have room for the books that would be written" (John 21:25 NIV). Your life is one of those books that John was talking about. You're continuing the story of what "Jesus did." Jesus showed up and did something—he redeemed you and is still redeeming you so you can love, forgive, and do good to those around you.

Take with You: Being a child of God is the greatest blessing you will ever receive, and it's something that will never be taken away. Once you're adopted into the family of God, it's for always.

NOVEMBER 19

Finally, be strong in the Lord and in the strength of his might. Put on the whole armor of God, that you may be able to stand against the schemes of the devil. —Ephesians 6:10–11

Spiritual warfare is about mounting an *offense,* not playing defense. Popular teaching refers to the protective aspect of the individual weapons of spiritual warfare (Ephesians 6:10–17). But the Bible uses this imagery to portray the Lord overthrowing the evil powers in a darkened world. Christ comes bringing mercy to the humble and mayhem to the haughty.

When Jesus enlists us in his cause, he equips us to join his battle. Spiritual warfare is about light invading darkness. We are God's invading army, and we are on the attack, bringing light into a dark world. We, the army of light, are on the offensive.

Paul talks about how he has the "weapons of righteousness in the right hand and in the left" (2 Corinthians 6:7 NIV). Paul is going to war. The war is not just coming to him. *But what are the weapons he fights with? They are humility, love, truth, courage, faithfulness, goodness, and wisdom. These are unusual weapons. We fight like Jesus did in his earthly ministry. He is the Lord of light, and he calls us to bring the light of his love into this dark world.*

Take with You: Have you ever thought about yourself as a soldier in the army of God? When we come to faith, we are drafted into his service. Old and young, tall and small, we serve together in the army of light.

NOVEMBER 20

Now may the God of peace himself sanctify you completely, and may your whole spirit and soul and body be kept blameless at the coming of our Lord Jesus Christ. He who calls you is faithful; he will surely do it. —1 Thessalonians 5:23–24

Scripture portrays sanctification (growth in holiness and Christlikeness) in a range of colors and shades. But how do people actually change? How are disciples made? Here's my core premise: Ministry "unbalances" truth for the sake of relevance; theology "rebalances" truth for the sake of comprehensiveness.* What I mean is this: You can't say everything all at once—and you shouldn't try. So, *in ministry, when you are speaking to or helping someone, you say one relevant thing at a time.* This is what Jesus did. He gave people what they needed and could handle right then. *By saying one thing, not everything, he purposely "unbalanced" the truth, as if that is all there was to know.* And it *was*—at that time. This nourishes those who are listening. But they will need more at another time.

But in *theology*, the task is different. The goal is to be comprehensive, thereby "rebalancing" truth for the sake of completeness. This balance protects us from exaggerating, ignoring, or overgeneralizing. Every part of God's truth matters. Through it, Jesus claims our loyalty, commands our attention, and elicits our humility as he compels us to grow in him.

Take with You: We need both. We need to learn from those ministering to us the part of God's truth that matters in the moment. At other times, we need to see the whole picture. Together, we learn to become disciples.

---

* I am indebted to Rev. James Petty for this way of putting it.

NOVEMBER 21

Bless those who persecute you; bless and do not curse them. . . .
Do not be overcome by evil, but overcome evil with good.
—Romans 12:14, 21

The experience of being wronged is a door to growing in your faith. Being wronged by another creates a challenging experience. The heat is on high. There are two possible responses to being wronged. Some people respond with the most flagrant sins possible: hatred, murder, and vengeance. But, out of that same struggle, there can come the most beautiful, brightest graces of which a human being is capable: mercy, forgiveness, courage, endurance, and the ability to persevere in hope in the midst of pain and loss.

To be sinned against is expected in a fallen world. It happens to everyone. We are sinners who live among sinners, and we will be wronged. But God's anger is against evildoers, the violent, the hostile, and the treacherous. *In Romans 12, we are promised that God will right all wrongs and will destroy all that is evil. This is the hope of his children who are suffering and it's at the core of why you do not need to be a vengeance-taker.* You do not need to be a vigilante because there's One whom you trust to deal more than fairly, sometimes even mercifully, with evil. Starting with this truth opens the door to overcoming evil with good and with a clear-eyed mercy that gives off the lasting fragrance of heaven.

Take with You: To fight the desire for vengeance—pray. Ask God how to overcome evil with good. It won't make sense to the world, but it will grow your faith.

NOVEMBER 22

No, in all these things we are more than conquerors through him who loved us. —Romans 8:37

There's something about the experience of evil that can actually purify our faith because it can force us to set our hopes on the only person our hopes should be set upon—Christ himself. Then we can help other people in whatever they're facing, because of the way we have received comfort from him. Whether we're facing a relatively mild evil or something heinous, any step, no matter how small, toward the light of God's love can be shared with others.

This section of Romans 8 speaks of how we gain a settled hope in the context of suffering. Our character is formed, and the love of God is poured out into our hearts through the Holy Spirit. It's counterintuitive, but in the context of being wronged, I can learn that God is for me, so who can be against me? The result: a settling of our hope and the transformation of our lives. Over time, there's a purposeful goodness that comes out of the furnace of affliction. *Given the passage of time and the pursuit of a living God, people are actually able to say, "God did work all things for good in my life, even through some very, very hard things that I would never wish to go through again."*

Take with You: What is a settled hope? One that has been and is firmly anchored in God's work in our lives. It's easier to hope for fewer trials, but learning that God is for you even when you face evil is a treasure worth having.

NOVEMBER 23

Though I walk in the midst of trouble,
you preserve my life;
you stretch out your hand against the wrath of my enemies,
and your right hand delivers me. —Psalm 138:7

When you suffer, your greatest need is to hear God talking to you and to experience his purpose at work. When you hear him, take his words to heart. Know that when he's with you, everything changes, even when nothing has changed in your situation. Left to yourself, your troubles obsess you, distract you, depress you. God seems invisible, silent, far away. Threat, pain, and loss cry out long and loud. Faith seems inarticulate. Sorrow and confusion broadcast on all the channels. It's hard to remember anything else, hard to put into words what's actually happening, hard to feel any of the force of who Jesus Christ is.

But God works to reverse this downward spiral into despair. The Holy Spirit powerfully and intimately communicates God's words, presence, and love into our hearts. Sufferers awaken to hear their Father's voice and to see their Savior's hand in the midst of what's happening.

You need to hear what God says and to experience that he does what he says he will do. You need to feel the weight and significance of what he is about. Though you walk through the valley of the shadow of death, you need fear no evil. He is with you. Goodness and mercy will follow you. This is what he's doing. God's voice speaks deeper than what hurts, brighter than what's dark, and more enduring than what's lost.

Take with You: When you need help, use Psalm 138 to cry out to God. He wants to hear from you, and you need to hear from him.

NOVEMBER 24

Oh give thanks to the LORD, for he is good;
for his steadfast love endures forever! —1 Chronicles 16:34

A Thanksgiving Prayer

Father in heaven, we thank you for pouring out many kindnesses upon us—all the blessings of this life, our creation, preservation, and above all, your love in our Lord Jesus Christ. *We thank you today for forgiving our sins, healing our diseases, redeeming us from the pit, and crowning us with steadfast love and mercy so we will soar as on eagles' wings.*

We thank you, our Lord, that you understand our plight. You know we are but dust. We are weak, mortal, prone to sin, and easily baffled. We thank you for invading our lives with light and life. You've come to make us new. You strengthen us for the battle. You give us the grace and hope we need in hard times. You shield us, you grow us, you do not give up on us, and you will complete what you have begun.

We pray that you would look, this day, in us one and all. That we, as your children, would grow in wisdom, in favor with God and man. We would learn to love you more steadily, to hold in our hearts the struggles of other people, that we would be people of genuine kindness. People who are patient, people able to endure, people able to forgive by the mercies of Christ himself.

We pray in the name of this great Messiah. Amen.

Take with You: A good prayer for Thanksgiving; a good prayer for any day. God has given us his kingdom. It's good to thank him for it.

NOVEMBER 25

Therefore, as you received Christ Jesus the Lord, so walk in him, rooted and built up in him and established in the faith, just as you were taught, abounding in thanksgiving. —Colossians 2:6–7

"Thank you."

Simple to say, but strangely hard to do. Of all the valid things that might be said about the ignorance and waywardness of our hearts, Paul singles out ingratitude for special mention: "They didn't thank God" (Romans 1:21, author's paraphrase). When we don't say, "Thank you," it's extremely revealing. It's as if it's *the* transgression that clinches the case against us.

Colossians is a short letter but being thankful pops up seven times. "Thank you" is one of humility's core instincts. So why wouldn't you say thank you? Perhaps you don't feel thankful. Perhaps you feel entitled and don't recognize who's giving you every good thing. You don't want to need help or to depend on anyone. Perhaps you want to take all the credit for your successes.

But when you awaken to who gives you good gifts, you will be grateful. *Gratitude is a primary expression of sanity. First Corinthians 4:7 teaches us to say: What do I have that is not a gift?! James 1:17 teaches us to see that every good gift is from above, coming down from our Father.*

What are you thankful for? Think about that.

Take with You: Practice being thankful to God until it becomes second nature. You will be blessed with growing humility and deeper trust in his will for your life. You will struggle less and be more at peace. More to be thankful for!

NOVEMBER 26

The aim of our charge is love that issues from a pure heart and a good conscience and a sincere faith. —1 Timothy 1:5

In this verse, Paul describes the goal of all ministry: the transformation of both our behavior and motives. This is what holiness looks like *in action.*

Paul charges me to pointedly, freely, and genuinely love others because I am awake to God. *God wants me to stop, care, notice, listen, express candid appreciation, and share my life. And he helps.* This goal has marked my conscious intentions when I've chatted with coworkers, conversed with friends, and come home to my family. Being indifferent, or opinionated, or avoidant, or preoccupied comes easy. But it is a bit of holiness when I am happy to see someone, when I ask a question and mean it, when I listen attentively, when I genuinely affirm, when I push back candidly and constructively.

I have been consciously reflecting and seeking the three ways this command describes our reorientation to God. A pure heart. Father, make me less divided by competing loyalties and agendas, by unruly desires and anxieties. A good conscience. Lord, attune my conscience so I weigh all things the way you weigh them. Fill my conscience with Christ's merciful, redeeming purposes. A sincere faith. Holy Spirit, make me trust you in need, in gratitude, in joy, in dependence.

Take with You: What God asks us to do, he enables us to do. He will help you to have a pure heart, a good conscience, and a sincere faith, if you seek it. Do you want to?

NOVEMBER 27

This I know, that God is for me. —Psalm 56:9b

Learning that God is *for you and with you* is foundational for every Christian. Even the fact that he disciplines us (Hebrews 12:5–14) demonstrates his fatherly love and hands-on commitment to pursue our welfare. God gets our attention when life doesn't go well, or when our conscience rightly stings. He keeps working with us—using both comfort and reproof—so that we learn to "strive for peace with everyone, and for the holiness without which no one will see the Lord" (v. 14). *His chastisement is an essential mercy to us.*

When I directly confess and repent of my sins, what helps me is how Psalm 25:11 brings together a candid sense of need with God's person and promises: "For your name's sake, pardon my guilt for it is great."

But I dare not extrapolate my exact experience of God's mercies to everyone else. One pattern of Christ's working will be different from others. Scripture and the Holy Spirit play a 47-string concert harp, using all ten fingers, and sounding all the notes of human experience. Wise ministry, like growth in wisdom, means learning to play on all the strings, not harping on one note.

Take with You: When hard times come, or God's discipline is upon us, it is especially hard to believe God is *for* you. Yet, that is when his presence is most vivid. The next time you are in peril or in pain, ask him to let you feel his presence and to know that his face shines upon you.

NOVEMBER 28

All Scripture is breathed out by God and profitable for teaching, for reproof, for correction, and for training in righteousness, that the man of God may be complete, equipped for every good work. —2 Timothy 3:16–17

God speaks to all of us together in the public ministry of Word and prayer. We participate in worship. We listen well to faithful preaching and teaching. We humbly receive the Lord's Supper. We pray together to our Father. Psalm 23 becomes a group prayer: "Lord, you are our Shepherd. When we walk in dark places, we fear no evil because you are with us!"

God speaks to each of us in the private ministry of Word and prayer. You read and reflect on Scripture. You meditate and take truth to heart. You journal your insights, concerns, troubles, sins, prayers, joys, and gratitude. You seek the Lord personally. You take thought for how you live wisely this day.

God speaks to you (and through you) in interpersonal ministries of Word and prayer. You seek honest friendships. You ask for help and offer help. You listen well. You engage in the give-and-take of a small group. You seek advice or counsel or offer it to someone else. You seek or offer mentoring. You are intentional about life-on-life caring for one another.

Take with You: Some people think if they go to church once a week that's all God expects of them. False! He expects you to pursue him on your own and to minister to others. God speaks to you in all three of these places. He's equipping you to do good work. Are you willing?

NOVEMBER 29

For whatever was written in former days was written for our instruction, that through endurance and through the encouragement of the Scriptures we might have hope.
—Romans 15:4

The Bible personally applies and addresses the concerns of long-ago people in faraway places, facing problems that no longer exist. They had no difficulty seeing the application. But nothing in the Bible is written directly to you or about what you face. In a sense, we're reading someone else's mail. Yet the Bible repeatedly affirms that these words are also written for us (Romans 15:4). The Spirit reapplies Scripture in a timely way now.

The Bible is about God, not you. The main focus is the triune Redeemer Lord, culminating in Jesus Christ. When Jesus opened the minds of his disciples to understand the Scriptures (Luke 24:45), he showed them how everything written there reveals him. We're reading someone else's biography. Yet that biography demonstrates how he includes us in his story. Jesus is the Word of God applied. As his current-day disciples, we also learn to apply the Bible. The Spirit rescripts our lives by teaching us who God is and what he's doing.

Personal application proves wise when you reckon with these marvels. *The Bible was written to others—but speaks to you. The Bible is about God—but draws you in. Your challenge is always to reapply Scripture afresh, because God's purpose is always to rescript your life.*

Take with You: The way Scripture works in our lives is something of a miracle. It's old, but it's relevant. It's not written to us directly but blesses us beyond measure. It's the food we need to nourish our souls. Are you hungry?

NOVEMBER 30

Your words were found, and I ate them,
and your words became to me a joy
and the delight of my heart. —Jeremiah 15:16a

Let me say two things about how to read Scripture. First, I encourage you to sit with the text. Perhaps on a first reading, it's either strange or feels irrelevant. Sit with it for a while. God's Word is about life and people and a Redeemer and how it all connects. Ask God himself to help you understand it.

Second, if you feel stuck, go somewhere else in Scripture. Most of us have certain go-to passages, and they are there for a reason. Without fail, I can get traction from Psalms 23, 40, and 103, as well as Philippians 4 and 2 Corinthians 1. *There are certain passages of Scripture that are so universally applicable to our daily lives that I can be unashamed to abandon my reading plan and go somewhere familiar, because I know I need the Bread of Life.* I'm perfectly willing to shift gears. I'm not wed to a reading plan, which is simply a tool helping me to access the living God who speaks.

There's a cumulative effect to the way God works. Be sure to read those harder chapters, even if afterward you read something else. Both the long sections and the familiar verses will help you to know God and understand his ways.

Take with You: Scripture is a fountain of life that never runs dry. Read it regularly. Read it with a flexibility that prevents boredom or frustration. Return to passages you've read before, and you will find new and deeper meanings there. Drink deeply and live.

DECEMBER 1

The LORD is merciful and gracious,
slow to anger and abounding in steadfast love.

As a father shows compassion to his children,
so the LORD shows compassion to those who fear him.
—Psalm 103:8, 13

Psalm 103 is a favorite Scripture passage for many people. One reason is that there's tremendous comfort in learning about how our Father loves us and has compassion on us.

This psalm has permeated my soul. I've gone back to it again and again. It covers all of life's terrain, addressing what makes it hard. It speaks of God's love, which is so strong that it sustains us and overcomes our fragility, and it speaks of his goodness, which adorns our lives and makes them sparkle.

Interestingly, all of the major themes in the first chapter of Ephesians are also found in Psalm 103: sonship, adoption, sin, death, steadfast love, and mercy. *In Ephesians we understand how God forgives our sins, redeems our life from the pit, and surrounds us with steadfast love and mercy because of Jesus. In Psalm 103, we see how these themes connect to daily human experience and the hard things we struggle with.* It will do your heart good to climb back into Psalm 103 once you understand what Jesus has done for us in places like Ephesians 1.

> **Take with You:** God speaks to us about the same things in different ways throughout the Bible. Sometimes a story is best; another time it will be a psalm, or the words of a prophet. What types of Scripture passages speak to your soul?

DECEMBER 2

But God, being rich in mercy, because of the great love with which he loved us, even when we were dead in our trespasses, made us alive together with Christ—by grace you have been saved . . . so that in the coming ages he might show the immeasurable riches of his grace in kindness toward us in Christ Jesus. —Ephesians 2:4–5, 7

No one who knows God can stay the same person. But it's also true that no one can truly change without his help. Attempts to change without his grace will fail. Self-manufactured change does not work. It does not dislodge the almighty "me" from the center of my self-manufactured universe. I only act a bit differently, and I end up either praising myself or living in shame.

But in mercy, God gives us himself. Ephesians 2 marvels at the sheer goodness of God and God's grace, what a friend of mine calls "God's thermonuclear goodness." His goodness is of an all-consuming intensity, like the nuclear furnace of the sun. In his presence, we would be incinerated by goodness. But Christ's incalculable grace multiplies goodness times forgiveness times kindness times mercy. Christ carries us into the fiery sun of the living God. *Grace turns you upside down: The self-righteous and destructive become the grateful and constructive.* That is true change.

Take with You: It's a beautiful mercy that God helps us change. He gives us a template in Jesus and the Holy Spirit to help us pursue it. Being turned upside down is good; we all start off facing the wrong way.

DECEMBER 3

Now there are also many other things that Jesus did. Were every one of them to be written, I suppose that the world itself could not contain the books that would be written. —John 21:25

John's Gospel largely consists of scenes selected from Jesus's encounters and conversations with various followers, foes, and undecideds. John takes time to zoom in, slowing everything down, lingering on a snippet of conversation or a situational detail. Watch Jesus interact, person by person, situation by situation. Listen to the questions he asks and how he answers the questions people ask him. He finds a point of engagement. He helps, rattles, invites, irritates, teaches, argues, clarifies, perplexes, saves, warns, and encourages. As Jesus crosses paths with people, he reveals people for who they are. In response to him, people change, either making a turn for the better or for the worse.

These same kinds of interactions occur in our lives, and Jesus aims to catch your ear too. He is looking for a point of engagement. How will you respond? *Truth comes to life at the intersection of Jesus's life and your life.*

It is noteworthy that Jesus never ministers by going through the motions. There is no distilled formula. No abstract generalizations. Because situations and people come unscripted, fluid, and unpredictable, Jesus engages each person and situation in a personalized way. It is no truism to say that Jesus really does meet you where you are. Always.

Take with You: Jesus wants to know you and you to know him. What do you want to ask him about? He is ready to talk.

DECEMBER 4

Then Jesus told his disciples, "If anyone would come after me, let him deny himself and take up his cross and follow me. For whoever would save his life will lose it, but whoever loses his life for my sake will find it." —Matthew 16:24–25

Jesus is a man on a mission. He is on the move, up to something. Did you ever notice the bodyguards for a rock group or an elected official? Their purpose, their call, is to serve the well-being and agenda of the "big person" they were hired to protect. But ultimately, Jesus is this boss, the big person, in your life.

He claims you. He calls you to leave behind everything else you live for and follow him. What are you primarily about? Your possessions? Your friends? Your future? He's come to turn you away from serving yourself to give you someone so much greater—himself.

He calls you to glorify, trust, and love him. Die to what entangles you. *Let every emotion—gratitude, just anger, trusting encouragement—find its fulfillment and truest expression in Jesus Christ, the King of creation and re-creation. Let your every act, from driving, to studying, to serving your family, find its organizing center in what will give glory to God.* Jesus has come to turn you from who you are now to who you are meant to be—a glad worshipper of the living God.

Take with You: Does it seem strange that Jesus "claims" you? The language of possession is not in style, but Jesus, who is God in the flesh, is the one person who has the right to do so. If you lose your life for him, you will be who you are meant to be.

DECEMBER 5

For this is the will of God, your sanctification.
—1 Thessalonians 4:3a

When the risen Jesus gave final instructions to his followers, he commissioned them to make more disciples (Matthew 28:18–20). They were to help bring about the spiritual birth and growth of a new people with a new way of life. We often hear Jesus's words as a call for evangelism with conversion as the desired result. But conversion is the first step in a long salvation. *It's the birth that leads to a lifetime of growing up into Jesus's image. Sanctification is discipleship into his way of life.*

What is his way of life? Jesus is the man of faith and wisdom who fears the Lord. He's the man of righteousness who loves God and neighbor. He is the man of redeeming mercies. He's the servant of the Lord who lays down his life for others. And he calls each new generation of disciples to help others follow him.

The actual unfolding of progressive sanctification (growth in your faith) is no theoretical exercise. Every Christian has a unique story about what was key in helping them when they struggled to believe or to obey God. The stories are so varied! Both Scripture and personal testimony teach us that there's no single formula for the kinds of problems that call for sanctification or for the truths and other factors that produce it. Multiple stories help because they make you realize not everyone is like you.

Take with You: Though the end point is the same, every person's journey of following Jesus is theirs alone. Remember, whatever the question is, the answer is Jesus.

DECEMBER 6

"Blessed are the poor in spirit, for theirs is the kingdom of heaven."
—Matthew 5:3

This verse is the first beatitude of Jesus's Sermon on the Mount. The focus on our spiritual poverty, need, and weakness comes first for a reason: We need what God gives. We need our Father to give the Holy Spirit to us so that Christ dwells in our hearts by faith and, through the love of God, we're ready when the heat is on. Some part of our faith is important and necessary to be able to manage our life—right now.

The Bible models how ministry and life focus on one thing at a time. A good theology book rightly asks: Who's God? And it goes on to fill four hundred pages with truths. But Psalm 121 cries out with beautiful simplicity: "From where does my help come?" It answers with the same essential simplicity: "My help comes from the LORD."

In the Bible's vivid picture, we "turn" to our Father, Savior, and Comforter. He works in us toward one goal: change. The central dynamic of the Christian life has this "From . . . to" movement. *When God calls, you listen. When he promises, you trust and talk back to him in your need. When he loves, you love. When he commands, you obey. You aim your life in a new direction by the power of the Holy Spirit.* In every case, you turn. These are the purposes of the whole Bible, the whole mission of our Redeemer.

Take with You: To admit you are poor—in any way—is hard to do, but the prize is heaven itself. You need God, and to become like him is your life's purpose.

DECEMBER 7

For as we share abundantly in Christ's sufferings, so through Christ we share abundantly in comfort too. —2 Corinthians 1:5

How do we gain wisdom to interact with other people's problems? It's mind-blowing when you think about where the apostle Paul starts as he writes his second letter to the Corinthians. He immediately starts to talk about his own troubles. Paul goes to the hardest things that happened, right down to the fact that Paul explains how he learned wisdom, and not only wisdom, but joy, and the ability to have a persevering faith and endurance that hangs in there through all kinds of troubles.

As he begins talking about his own troubles, the language he chooses to use in 2 Corinthians 1:4–7 is interesting—he uses two words over and over again: "affliction" and "suffering." The word *affliction* literally means you are squeezed, under pressure. There is trouble, big trouble that just weighs heavily on you, it constricts, constrains, and hassles you. Then there's suffering. *Suffering* literally means you hurt. You're under extreme pressure and in pain.

This is the way you get wisdom to help others—through turning to God in your suffering and affliction, and thus sharing both in Christ's affliction and his comfort.

Take with You: When you have a problem, the best help comes from someone who has been through something hard too. This is also true in matters of faith. Paul saw his suffering as a form of instruction from God to teach him perseverance and the wisdom needed to comfort others. God will do the same for you.

DECEMBER 8

If we are afflicted, it is for your comfort and salvation; and if we are comforted, it is for your comfort, which you experience when you patiently endure the same sufferings that we suffer. —2 Corinthians 1:6

To help others suffering, you need to experience suffering yourself, and it needs to be the right kind of suffering. The wrong kind of suffering, by which I mean, the mishandling of suffering, is the way we show ourselves to be the biggest fools on the planet—self-pitying, self-righteous, vindictive, escapist, and so forth. It's only through the right kind that you learn what's absolutely necessary for you to help another person.

As fallen human beings, it's the wisdom of the flesh that people express instinctively in response to pressure and pain. What tends to come out is grumbling, complaining, moaning, and groaning. Grumbling expresses, "*My* kingdom come, *my* will be done in heaven as it better be done on earth." There are so many kinds of things that the flesh intuitively does in the context of suffering and pain. But what do they all lead to, in terms of consequences? The wisdom of the flesh, at minimum, sabotages the possibility of a constructive effect to the suffering you encounter.

God is up to something in your suffering—something good. He always wants to move us from trusting in ourselves to trusting him. He's working to shift our allegiance from ourselves to him.

Take with You: Suffering is hard, and it's beneficial only if it is the "right kind." It's not what's happening to you that determines whether it's the right kind. Rather, it's trusting that—whatever is happening to you—God is up to something good in it.

DECEMBER 9

But that was to make us rely not on ourselves but on God who raises the dead. —2 Corinthians 1:9b

Paul identifies suffering and affliction as the means to shift our fundamental trust from ourselves to God. He wants our deepest allegiance to be to him. That's the path of life and hope. Notice he's calling us to trust in the God who raises the dead. Of all the things that could be said about God, Paul picks out the one thing those facing a death sentence most need to know. He's the God who raises the dead. That's a spectacularly relevant promise because we are all facing a death sentence.

But trust may not be the relational term that speaks to you. There are many different ways of talking about our hearts, both where we go astray and where we are found again. You could also ask yourself: *What do I love? What do I listen to? Who do I serve? Where do I set my hopes? Where do I take refuge?* Trust is just one of the active verbs that relates us to God—trust in God versus trust in myself, money, my ability to run my own life, my pleasure, etc.

Trusting in God blesses us, but that's not its only benefit. It teaches us how to help other people who are under a death sentence too. *We become wise friends and family members by being counseled wisely, effectively, lovingly, ultimately by God himself.*

Take with You: If we trust God and our deepest allegiance is to him, he will help us endure this life and become wise. What we learn from him we can then pass on to others who face death, which is everyone.

DECEMBER 10

"The good person out of the good treasure of his heart produces good, and the evil person out of his evil treasure produces evil, for out of the abundance of the heart his mouth speaks." —Luke 6:45

Anger is a simple emotion. It's an active stance you take to oppose something that you assess as both important and wrong. You notice something, size it up, and say, "That matters . . . and it's not right." Anger always rests on a value judgment. It has rightly been called "the moral emotion" because it makes a statement about what matters.

But anger isn't the only reaction that proclaims what you value. In fact, every time you speak (or don't) you're reacting and thereby broadcasting your values to others. This is what is meant, for example, when Jesus said that "out of the abundance of the heart his mouth speaks" (Matthew 12:36; Luke 6:45). Every word you say—including small talk—tells the hearer something important about you. *What you choose to talk about (or would never say out loud) broadcasts what matters to you.*

Your emotional reactions and your choices always proclaim your values. Stir in a bit of emotion—because you care, because something that matters is going wrong—and you can get the reaction we call anger. Every time you get angry (or don't get angry) you broadcast what matters to you.

Take with You: Do you know what matters to you? Have you noticed that even what you don't say is revealing? Knowing yourself is one of the prerequisites to change so what comes out of your mouth is good, not evil.

DECEMBER 11

Do not say, "I will repay evil";
wait for the LORD, and he will deliver you. —Proverbs 20:22

Because we are sinners, our anger gets messed up, twisted, and perverted. We play at being God and try to run the world, punishing "evildoers" on our own terms. We get mad at things that aren't evil (it's just that our almighty will was crossed). Then we ignore things that really are evil and remain indifferent to suffering and oppression. When we finally do manage to get angry at a real evil, we overreact. We "return evil for evil," and legitimate anger gets expressed destructively.

That's not the end of the story, though. By the grace of God, you and I are redeemable. Whatever is perverse and insulting to God, worthy of his anger against us, can be forgiven and changed. Our consciences can be rewired. *We can and will learn to perceive good and evil in a different way, the way things really are. This restores us gradually to sanity, to the image of Christ.*

The person who had a touchy, sensitive temper becomes slow to anger. Hostility turns to love for enemies. Long-standing bitterness softens into the ability to forgive our debtors. The God who is totally for us and who loves us too much to leave us in our sin is in the business of long, slow progress. He's at work transforming his children so our anger will be reflected in loving action.

Take with You: We are redeemable! God can change a hothead into a thoughtful person who recognizes evil and responds in a measured way. He can change bitterness and hatred into soft-hearted love. This is sanity in the image of Christ.

DECEMBER 12

Do not speak evil against one another, brothers. The one who speaks against a brother or judges his brother, speaks evil against the law and judges the law. But if you judge the law, you are not a doer of the law but a judge. There is only one lawgiver and judge, he who is able to save and to destroy. But who are you to judge your neighbor? —James 4:11–12

Who are you when you judge someone else's behavior? When you judge others—criticize, nitpick, nag, attack, condemn—you are playing God. When you accuse, you act like the devil, and when you fight with a sibling or a friend, your mind becomes filled with accusations. The other person's wrongs and your rights preoccupy you.

In an argument, both people are focused on the offenses of the other, even blaming each other for their own bad behavior: "Yeah, I was wrong to do that, but you. . ." The log remains firmly planted in the eye (Matthew 7:1–5) as each party plays lawgiver and judge. But there's only one Lawgiver and Judge—he who is able to save and to destroy. Who are you that you judge your neighbor? *Here we see that a far more profound conflict burns at the heart of interpersonal conflict. Presumption, pride, demand, and self-will stand at odds with the one true God.*

Take with You: Conflict with other people is inevitable, but if you judge the person you're at odds with, you're playing God and are already in the wrong. Take a break from the conflict and take the log out of your eye before you continue.

DECEMBER 13

What causes quarrels and what causes fights among you? Is it not this, that your passions are at war within you? —James 4:1

James has this wonderful way of revealing the human heart. There's something you want, and it takes you over. What you want seems reasonable to you, but when you don't get it, the result is anger and interpersonal conflict. You desire and don't have, so you fight with others. Scripture tells us what is really going wrong here. We don't always realize how self-centered we are, but think about it. Don't you want to live in a world where your pleasures and what you want reign supreme?

Against this backdrop, James 4:6 is probably one of the most astonishing one-liners in the entire Bible. After his searing analysis of the self-centered human heart, James writes this: *"But he gives more grace."* That is astonishing. As dark as our hearts can be, God gives more grace. He really cares. He loves us! And he wants us to love him. *God desires that just as his intense love has been given to us, we give back to him our loyalty, intensity, focus, and undistracted devotion. He wants us to be his alone and love him utterly in return.*

Take with You: God knows your heart. He knows what you would like to hide from him. But you can't hide, and you don't need to. Despite our demanding selfishness, he gives more grace. He loves you and gives you what you need to change and to love him back.

DECEMBER 14

But he gives more grace. Therefore it says, "God opposes the proud but gives grace to the humble." —James 4:6

Grace describes God's many blessings upon us. Evidence of his grace is woven into the entire Bible from Genesis to Revelation. It's one of the core promises of God. When you look at the unfolding story of Scripture, you see grace everywhere. Take for example, the story of King David. God's grace to David meant that God blessed him, kept him, shone his face on him, and brought him peace. You might say that the shorthand for grace in the life of David is that God was *with him.*

This promise in James 4, "He gives more grace," is the entire basis of your relationship with God. It is the heartbeat of your prayer life. The promise of grace anchors the way that an honest psalm-like prayer says, "Oh Lord, my life is very hard now. Bless me, keep me, don't abandon me. You've promised to keep me. Make your face shine upon me. Be gracious to me. Turn toward me. Give me peace and not trouble. Have mercy upon me." God's grace is what you trust and delight in, it is what you plead for, it is what you sing about, and it is what you're thankful for.

Take with You: God's grace is a gift to you, given because he loves you. There is ample evidence of it in your life. Not sure about that? Read Numbers 6:24–26 and look again. Once you see it, practice looking every day. You will be blessed all the more.

DECEMBER 15

But I say, walk by the Spirit, and you will not gratify the desires of the flesh. For the desires of the flesh are against the Spirit, and the desires of the Spirit are against the flesh, for these are opposed to each other, to keep you from doing the things you want to do. —Galatians 5:16–17

Anger goes wrong when we want a good thing more than we want God. It's not wrong to want your friends to stick up for you. It's not wrong to want your parents to understand you. It's not wrong to want to fit in and be comfortable at your school. But when fulfilling your desires, even for a good thing, becomes more important than anything else, that's when it becomes a sin. You want it too much. When you don't get what you want and believe you deserve, your anger flares up.

As we discussed a couple of days ago, James wrote about where our wrong anger comes from: "What causes fights and quarrels among you? Don't they come from your desires that battle within you? You desire but do not have, so you kill. You covet but you cannot get what you want, so you quarrel and fight" (James 4:1–2 NIV).

Wrong anger creates a big problem between you and God. Anger going wrong testifies to our pride. *When you see yourself as a sinner, instead of focusing on how everyone around you is wrong, then God's grace and mercy is available to you.*

Take with You: Anger isn't a neutral emotion. It's not always a sin, but it's not always innocent either. Listen to the Holy Spirit and let him guide you.

DECEMBER 16

Do not be conformed to this world, but be transformed by the renewal of your mind. —Romans 12:2a

When you trust in Jesus, the Holy Spirit begins to transform what you want and reconfigure your moral universe. You no longer want human approval more than anything, though of course you still get stuck there. But there's been a fundamental change. Take, for example, a young man who very much wants to play on his high school basketball team. In Christ he can say, "I want to make the team, but Lord, please remind me if I don't that you are still with me and have other plans for me."

Francis of Assisi prayed, "Grant that I would not so much seek to be understood as to understand, that I would not so much seek to be loved as to love." His prayer captures that fundamental upside-downness of life in Christ. *The redemption of us in Christ changes what we basically want, even though we still struggle with renegade desires that would take us in a different direction.*

Lord, strengthen and sustain us by your power, and help us live the life you called us to. In the places, Lord, where we are sloppy or dull or blind, give us eyes to see. In the places we are rigid or narrow, soften us. Grow us together in the image of our Savior. Amen.

Take with You: Knowing Jesus turns our world upside down—or maybe it's right side up! We are called to renew our minds so that what we want and how we live reflects his character. Our old ways will still seep through, so pray for Jesus to keep watch over you.

DECEMBER 17

"Observe the Sabbath day, to keep it holy,
as the LORD your God commanded you."

"You shall remember that you were a slave in the land of Egypt, and the LORD your God brought you out from there with a mighty hand and an outstretched arm. Therefore the LORD your God commanded you to keep the Sabbath day." —Deuteronomy 5:12, 15

Why should we rest? In the first giving of this commandment (Exodus 20), we hear how the Creator made all things and then stopped to rest, enjoying all he'd made. But in the second giving of this commandment (Deuteronomy 5), we hear how the Redeemer freed his beloved from the meaningless sweat of slave labor in Egypt and carried them into a place of rest and peace. We serve this Savior by working well and resting well.

Amazing. *To get hard work and rest right is to imitate the One who made you. To get hard work and rest right is to imitate the One who saved you. These two complementary truths draw out and sustain your faith.* They turn off the motors of restless busyness and restless amusement. Reasons outside of yourself give you the inner reason that makes obedience a most sweet endeavor. The Sabbath was made for man, not man for the Sabbath. You lay down burdens and cares. You enter into rest and fun because the God who made you his own does the same.

Take with You: God rested on the seventh day of creation, not because *he* needed to, but because *we* need to. He led the way. And it's not about being prohibited from doing certain things; it's about having time to do other good things like rest, worship, and just having fun.

DECEMBER 18

And so, from the day we heard, we have not ceased to pray for you, asking that you may be filled with the knowledge of his will in all spiritual wisdom and understanding, so as to walk in a manner worthy of the Lord, fully pleasing to him: bearing fruit in every good work and increasing in the knowledge of God. —Colossians 1:9–10

This prayer for the Colossians is specific and personal, as it should be. Our prayers should be intelligent prayers that braid together the real God and real people in real-life situations. If you are alert to both the Redeemer and the real needs of others, you won't ever pray rote prayers. You won't just pray for situations to go well—for health or success. When you carry the welfare of particular people in your heart, your prayers will be warmly personal, inclusive, and caring. You will intercede for them before God in ways that are concrete and immediate.

In my early Christian life, *my pastor's way of praying for people had a profound effect on me. He would never close a conversation by saying, "I'll be praying for you about this." Instead, he would say, "Let's ask God right now to help you."* That made a huge impression. Yes, he also prayed later on, but in the moment, those specific and relevant prayers communicated that God is here, he cares about what's going on with me, and he's up to something in my life.

Take with You: Praying for another person is a privilege. It's an opportunity to bless them in numerous ways at the same time. Be engaged when you do it. Be specific, show compassion, and then follow up with them later on.

DECEMBER 19

I write these things to you who believe in the name of the Son of God, that you may know that you have eternal life. —1 John 5:13

We love stories. That's how God made us. We bear the image of a person whose own story plays out in all that has been made and all that happens. No surprise, that's how his Bible works too.

Think of the Bible as a richly annotated story. God clothes the big themes with events, action, named people, and complications. He doesn't simply summarize truth or provide us with an outline of topics with a list of key points and subpoints. No, his purposes in writing are pastoral, not literary. He wants to change how you understand life. He wants to change how you live.* Its rich pages contain story, worldview, and application rolled into one.

The Bible contains the exact ingredients that our lives need. God intends that we see and hear—witness—what he's all about and what we're about. God has no interest in simply entertaining or inspiring. He has no interest in simply providing information or telling people what to do. Instead, he does and says everything needed to win us out of our self-fascination. He does and says what moves us to need him and love him.

Take with You: The Bible is written so you can know God and live with him forever. It's an old book and is sometimes hard to understand, but the truths it tells are timeless and essential. Your time spent with it is priceless. It will change how you understand life.

---

* I am indebted to Paul Tripp for this insight.

DECEMBER 20

When a man's ways please the LORD,
he makes even his enemies to be at peace with him. —Proverbs 16:7

Critics are God's instruments. None of us likes to be criticized. Whether a critic's manner is gracious or malicious, the very experience of being criticized reveals that you fit in one or more of these categories.

Self-satisfaction: You're content with your recent performance. You think you solved the problems of the day, and maybe you did. But when the problems change, you'd rather rest on your laurels. You want to etch in stone your last best insight or achievement.

Self-justification: You are sure you have done everything well and are arrogant and self-righteous. Yesterday's faithful obedience (or what you thought was such) becomes today's prop for the kingdom of self.

Self-protection: You want to have an easy life. To be criticized is not pleasant, so to protect yourself you avoid, duck, and hide from anyone who wants to speak into your ways.

Real people and real problems are hard to deal with. *But we all need to listen consciously to critics, even to invite criticism. This will help us live in the world God controls, the world in which Christ keeps on working to redeem. Christ uses critics to guard our souls from self-destructive tendencies.*

> **Take with You:** God used a prophet as a critic to confront King David about his sin with Bathsheba (2 Samuel 12). Jesus confronted Peter for saying he did not have to die (Matthew 16:23), and James and John for wanting to call down fire on some Samaritans (Luke 9:54–57). God loves you and will do the same for you. Listen carefully. He's blessing you.

DECEMBER 21

Not only that, but we rejoice in our sufferings, knowing that suffering produces endurance, and endurance produces character, and character produces hope, and hope does not put us to shame, because God's love has been poured into our hearts through the Holy Spirit who has been given to us. —Romans 5:3–5

Grace teaches you courage. When God says, "Fear not," his aim is not that you would just calm down. And he does not say, "Don't be afraid because everything will turn out okay." Instead, he says, "Don't be afraid; I am with you. So be strong and courageous." Do you hear the difference? Your troubles have not gone away. The opposite of fear is not unruffled serenity. It's courage. To "fear not" is to be courageous in the face of fearsome things.

You can always work to lessen your anxiety. But management techniques won't make you fearless in the face of trouble. They won't create that resilient fruit of the Spirit called "endurance," which is a purposeful "abiding under" what is hard and painful and considering others even when you're under great pressure. Grace teaches you to trust God at these times. Your life is a holy experiment as his hands shape you into the image of his Son and change the way you suffer by embedding in it a deeper meaning.

In fact, fearless endurance is for the purpose of wise love. God is making you like Jesus in the hardships of real life.

Take with You: Most of us would prefer God remove our sufferings rather than use them to help us grow. But growth doesn't come when times are easy. In God's trustworthy hands, suffering produces much fruit, which brings him glory and prepares us to serve him well.

DECEMBER 22

Blessed be the God and Father of our Lord Jesus Christ, the Father of mercies and God of all comfort, who comforts us in all our affliction. —2 Corinthians 1:3–4a

Here are eight ways God comforts us when we go through difficulties and suffering.

1. *God comforts us by how he communicates his care in words.* He says "I love you" in many different ways.
2. *God comforts us by what he does.* He demonstrates "I love you" by his actions. He keeps his promises. His love is not a sentiment or a good intention. It is a tangible reality.
3. *God comforts us by his loving presence.* The one who loves you, sticks with you. He never leaves your side.
4. *God comforts us by how other people communicate their care in words.* We are heartened when another person says "I love you," and "You matter to me."
5. *God comforts us by what other people do for us.* Like God, people show their love not only by their words but by their actions.
6. *God comforts us by the loving presence of other people.* All the mercies of God are intended to bring his people near to enjoy peace with each other.
7. *God comforts us when we witness how other people respond to him.* Seeing someone else's responsiveness to God nourishes our joy.
8. *God comforts us as we see a growing stability of faith in ourselves.* He anchors our hope, in part, because we see ourselves growing.

This road is hard but good. It's the only road leading to life and joy.

Take with You: Our God is the God of *all* comfort. Open your eyes to his ways and how he works through others in your life.

DECEMBER 23

Joy to the world, the Lord is come! Let earth receive her King!
Let ev'ry heart prepare Him room, and heav'n and nature sing,
and heav'n and nature sing, and heav'n, and heav'n and nature sing

No more let sins and sorrows grow, nor thorns infest the ground;
He comes to make His blessings flow far as the curse is found,
far as the curse is found, far as, far as the curse is found.
—Isaac Watts, "Joy to the World"

In this wonderful Christmas hymn, we are told that "the Lord is come." That's an odd tense. It basically means the Lord came and he's still here. He's still at work. So this is a great song for any time of the year. It's about the glory and mercy of Jesus Christ. It puts in perspective our twofold struggle with our sins and sufferings.

Christ, our King, comes to make his blessings flow as far as the curse is found. Obviously, we live in the in-between period, where curses can still be found, but this hymn is absolutely filled with joyous awareness of where it's all going. This perspective is key in helping us see past our inward focus on our hurts, hardships, and sins. "Joy to the World" turns our perspective outward. The Savior reigns, the Lord is come, he's the King of the whole earth. The dominant note throughout is a call to living faith, a call to joy, a call to worship, a call to gladness. *It's a great hymn to encourage us to not get stuck in tunnel vision about ourselves and our world.*

Take with You: Receive your King! He comes to make the world right again. Raise your voice and praise him. Hope has arrived, and it's a person!

DECEMBER 24

And the Word became flesh and dwelt among us, and we have seen his glory, glory as of the only Son from the Father, full of grace and truth. —John 1:14

The real gospel is the good news of the Word made flesh, the sin-bearing Savior, the resurrected Lord. This Christ turns the world upside down, rewiring our sense of felt needs. Because the fear of the Lord is the beginning of wisdom, we keenly feel a different set of needs when God comes into view, and we understand that we stand or fall in his gaze. When God comes into view, *my selfish desires are gradually replaced by the growing awareness of my true, life-and-death needs. Here are some of them:*

- I need mercy above all else.
- I want to learn wisdom and unlearn willful self-preoccupation.
- I need to learn to love both God and neighbor.
- I want God's name to be honored, his kingdom to come, his will to be done on earth.
- I need God's mighty and intimate help to do those things that last unto eternal life, rather than squandering my life on what doesn't matter.
- I want to learn how to endure hardship and suffering in hope, having my faith simplified, deepened, and purified.
- I need to learn, listen, worship, delight, trust, give thanks, cry out, take refuge, obey, serve, and hope.

Make it so, Father of mercies. Make it so, Redeemer of all that is dark and broken.

Take with You: What needs on this list spoke to you? Turn them into a prayer and keep praying until you see fruit.

DECEMBER 25

O come, O come, Emmanuel, and ransom captive Israel,
that mourns in lonely exile here until the Son of God appear.
Rejoice! Rejoice! Emmanuel shall come to thee, O Israel.
—"O Come, O Come, Emmanuel," ninth-century Latin hymn

The origins of this hymn go back some 1,500 years. Believers have been singing this for a long time! And we still sing it today at Christmas. It stays fresh. Why?

We're asking God to come in person. This cry gives voice to our greatest need. We need Emmanuel to come. Left to ourselves, we die—captives, sorrowing, alone. But God's presence with us brings life.

Each of the stanzas embodies this same basic structure. *We call on one of the characteristics of the Messiah. We express some aspect of our human struggle. We ask the Lord to intervene. We rejoice. We promise one another that he will come. It is a beautiful and significant pattern.*

Emmanuel embodies the Spirit of wisdom and understanding (Isaiah 11:2–3). We need him to guide us. Emmanuel is the dawning sun (Isaiah 9:2). We need the Light of the World to drive away all that is dark. Emmanuel is the key that opens the door of life (Isaiah 22:22). We need that door to open wide. Emmanuel is the Lord himself, reigning, speaking, and saving (Isaiah 33:22). We need his authority, power, words, and presence.

We've asked the Lord Jesus to come. Now we rejoice, rejoice, rejoice—because he's going to do it. Emmanuel is going to come as he promised.

Take with You: It may seem strange to sing about something that has already happened. Emmanuel has come! But his work is not done until he returns. Praise him for coming and urge him to come back soon.

DECEMBER 26

Beloved, we are God's children now, and what we will be has not yet appeared; but we know that when he appears we shall be like him, because we shall see him as he is. And everyone who thus hopes in him purifies himself as he is pure. —1 John 3:2–3

You might want to do an experiment. Ask people, "Who are you most looking forward to seeing when you get to heaven?" Almost no one says Jesus. But Jesus is the one we're going to see! And when we see him, we'll be like him. That's where the dynamic of change happens—in the light of the destination. We will see him. We will become like him; his name will be on our forehead. He is our destination.

But when it comes to the dynamics of changing to be more like him, it's a matter of direction. Where are you going? Don't be discouraged by your destination's distance from you; instead, use it to stay oriented to where you're heading. No matter how far away it is.

I'll never forget one of the things that my first pastor, Jack Miller, used to say: The glory of God in your life is not some absolute standard of achievement and you only bring glory to him if you reach it. "Here's the ideal Christian, the ideal Christian family, the ideal church." *Instead, the measure of Christ's glory is the difference between what you would be by nature and what you are because of Christ.*

Take with You: How is it even possible that we bring glory to Christ? How is it possible that we become like him? He did all the work, and we receive it as a gift.

DECEMBER 27

Repay no one evil for evil. . . . Beloved, never avenge yourselves, but leave it to the wrath of God, for it is written, "Vengeance is mine, I will repay, says the Lord."

Do not be overcome by evil, but overcome evil with good.
—Romans 12:17a, 19, 21

When wrong things are done to us and we want to return evil for evil, it means we're living for ourselves, not for Jesus. But when the love of God in Christ transforms us, our eyes are opened to our self-centeredness and unbelief. We see how great our need is for God's mercy. *When you understand and know God's mercy, you will be able to grant mercy and forgiveness to others.* This may not happen overnight. But over time, your trust in God and your ability to love others will grow. You will accept that something bigger is going on and that God will make things right. He will repay when evil is done. Your life will no longer be defined by the wrong done to you, but by God's love and mercy.

But if you have been harmed and are walking a difficult path, know you aren't alone. Your faithful Savior is with you, and he will also send people to walk with you who will take seriously the evil that happened to you. They will be compassionate and have a vision of how God can redeem you and your past.

Take with You: When evil is done, God knows exactly what's needed and will implement vengeance justly. By doing so, he's not robbing you of your revenge, he's preventing evil from overcoming you and making room for you to learn how to respond with mercy and forgiveness.

DECEMBER 28

Let all bitterness and wrath and anger and clamor and slander be put away from you, along with all malice. —Ephesians 4:31

Perhaps it makes you feel hopeless to admit that some hard experience you've had will never completely go away. Hear me rightly. I don't mean that the experience will always haunt you. You won't forget what happened, but you do not have to be forever defined by what happened either. There's a way out of the raptor's claws. You can find realistic hope, and realistic hope runs deeper than any hurt. It can take the same experience and offer a different script, a different outcome, and a different meaning.

Deep hurt so easily gets infected—by mistrust, or fear, or rage, or callousness, or avoidance, or addiction. Deep hurt even gets infected by just trying to keep yourself busy and distracted. It turns inward. It turns self-destructive.

But you do not need to endlessly revisit what happened. You do not need to be imprisoned in the complexities and dead ends of your instinctive reactions. Jesus himself walked a hard road; he will care for you. *With his help, hurt and loss can be changed into a deeper good—still fierce, still sorrowing, but now clean. Not only clean but hopeful. Not only hopeful but fruitful.*

Take with You: Do you believe this? Do you think God can give you a script that retells your hurt in a new way? A new way that acknowledges your pain but gives it a deeper meaning and gives you realistic hope? It may be hard to believe, but Jesus wants to and can do this for you. Will you trust him?

DECEMBER 29

"Remember the Sabbath day, to keep it holy. Six days you shall labor, and do all your work, but the seventh day is a Sabbath to the LORD your God." —Exodus 20:8–10a

We are made to love God and our neighbor. The restlessness and drivenness that are pervasive in our lives and culture do not love anyone. It's a failure of love that misuses your time, your choices, your activities, your 24/7/365. In other words, the obsessions that sicken both our labors and our pleasures are addressed by the fourth commandment, which is quoted above.

The Sabbath commandment exposes the imbalance of work and rest. It reorients you with respect to God. He alone brings into focus the complex issues of work and rest. He alone fundamentally changes why you do what you do. He reveals (and alters) the meaning you attach to the basic activities of your life. As you come to love him who loves you, he remakes you—sane.

This commandment has surprising effects. It orients us to a way of seeing many other interconnected specifics. It crystallizes the relationship between all your toils (responsibilities at home, studying, school commitments) and all your pleasures (entertainment, sports, time with friends), revealing life-shaping attitudes. Like all the commandments, it opens a window. *And like all the commandments, it holds out a destination: meaningful work and meaningful rest, sparkling with intelligent faith, love, and purpose.*

> **Take with You:** When most of us are not working, we usually pursue pleasure, but pleasure is not rest. Rest is more than sleep and more than attending a sabbath worship service. It's a time of being content, not striving after anything, quieting your soul. Ask God to show you how to rest.

DECEMBER 30

You make known to me the path of life;
in your presence there is fullness of joy;
at your right hand are pleasures forevermore. —Psalm 16:11

We live in a culture focused on entertainment, amusement, recreation, athletics, vacation, adventure, excitement, fashion, sex, convenience, technology, and whatever else feels good. We choose from an endless array of enticing distractions, things to watch, things to buy, things to do. Desire is the highest god. Limits are the only sin.

What do we make of this? We could rant and complain about how bad "the world" has become. But there is a better path. For starters, let's consider that the Lord made our capacity for pleasure as part of his image: very good. And Eden is a "paradise": literally, a pleasure garden. Let's consider that God doesn't erase pleasure or say that it's irrelevant or suspect or downright bad. He redeems pleasure. Grace and truth take the perversity out and restore the joy. Only what's wrong must go. Then pleasure becomes simple again, and it's a pleasure.

Christian truth cuts against the grain of a culture by offering something better. It's the sane alternative both to self-indulgence and to fussy religiosity. *Pleasure isn't the problem. It's the abuse of a good gift from God that's the problem. Jesus said, "I came that they may have life and have it abundantly" (John 10:10).*

Take with You: The answer isn't restricting all pleasure. The answer is to reclaim this gift and find pleasure as God intended. The Bible says many positive things about sleep, feasting, the beauty of the created world, and even marital love. Check it out.

DECEMBER 31

For I know that nothing good dwells in me, that is, in my flesh.
For I have the desire to do what is right, but not the ability to carry it out.

For I delight in the law of God, in my inner being, but I see in my members another law waging war against the law of my mind and making me captive to the law of sin that dwells in my members. Wretched man that I am! Who will deliver me from this body of death? Thanks be to God through Jesus Christ our Lord!
—Romans 7:18, 22–25a

The apostle Paul is describing his struggle with sin. Even great people of faith still struggle with it. What sins do you wrestle with? See if anything here describes you. Forgetting God? Believing life centers on you? Defensiveness and pride? Laziness or drivenness, or both? Irritability, judgmentalism, and complaining? Immoral impulses and fantasies? Obsessive concern with money, food, or your appearance? Fear of what others think about you? Envy of good things that someone else has?

I can identify with each one, and I suspect you can too. Our Father is at work in us and is not done. *He loves us with mercies new every morning and more numerous than the hairs on your heads.* He's good and he does good. He has chosen to love us. And we love him back—as street children he has rescued and adopted. He says, "You are mine. So take heart. I will complete what I have begun."

Take with You: The sins listed above are pretty bad, but once God starts his work in you, he never gives up—ever. He will complete what he has begun and will bring you safely home.

SOURCE INDEX

January 1. "The Right Kind of Weakness," *JBC* 33, no. 2 (2019): 3.

January 2. CCEF 2016 Regional Conference: Everyday Worship: How God Brings the Bible to Life, Session 2: "Learning to Ask the Right Questions."

January 3. *Life Beyond Your Parents' Mistakes: The Transforming Power of God's Love* (New Growth Press, 2010), 18 and 13—in that order.

January 4 *I Just Want to Die: Replacing Suicidal Thoughts with Hope* (New Growth Press, 2010), 18.

January 5. *Breaking the Addictive Cycle: Deadly Obsessions or Simple Pleasures?* (New Growth Press, 2010), 25–27.

January 6. *Breaking the Addictive Cycle*, 29–30.

January 7. CCEF 2016 Regional Conference: Everyday Worship: How God Brings the Bible to Life, Session 2: "Learning to Ask the Right Questions."

January 8. *Speaking Truth in Love: Counsel in Community* (New Growth Press, 2005), 123.

January 9. "Slow Growth," *JBC* 32, no. 3 (2018): 5–7.

January 10. *Speaking Truth in Love: Counsel in Community* (New Growth Press, 2005), 14–15, 17.

January 11. *Good and Angry: Redeeming Anger, Irritation, Complaining, and Bitterness* (New Growth Press, 2016), 164–65.

January 12. *Good and Angry*, 138–39.

January 13. *Good and Angry*, 94–95.

January 14. *Safe and Sound: Standing Firm in Spiritual Battles* (New Growth Press, 2019), 42.

January 15. *Overcoming Anxiety: Relief for Worried People* (New Growth Press, 2010), 8–9.

January 16. *When Cancer Interrupts* (New Growth Press, 2015), 16–17.

January 17. *Speaking Truth in Love: Counsel in Community* (New Growth Press, 2005), 42.

January 18. *Speaking Truth in Love*, 83–85.

January 19. CCEF 2016 Regional Conference: Everyday Worship: How God Brings the Bible to Life, Session 4: "Other People Make a Difference."

January 20. *Facing Death with Hope: Living for What Lasts* (New Growth Press, 2008), 7–8.

January 21. *I Just Want to Die: Replacing Suicidal Thoughts with Hope* (New Growth Press, 2010), 10–11.

January 22. "Let's Celebrate This Golden Anniversary," *JBC* 32, no. 2 (2018): 3–4.

January 23. "The God of All Comfort," *JBC* 31, no. 3 (2017): 3–4, 6.

January 24. "How Does Sanctification Work?" Part 3, *JBC* 31, no. 1 (2017): 9–10.

January 25. "How Does Sanctification Work?" 25, 27.

January 26. "What Can You Do When God Seems Far Away?" *JBC* 30, no. 3 (2016): 4.

January 27. CCEF 2016 Regional Conference: Everyday Worship: How God Brings the Bible to Life, Session 3: "Martin Luther's 3 Masters."

January 28. *Safe and Sound: Standing Firm in Spiritual Battles* (2019), 21–22.

January 29. *Good and Angry: Redeeming Anger, Irritation, Complaining, and Bitterness* (New Growth Press, 2016), 23–25.

January 30. *Good and Angry*, 57–58.

January 31. *Good and Angry*, 190–91.

February 1. *Overcoming Anxiety: Relief for Worried People* (New Growth Press, 2012), 10–11.

February 2. "An Invitation to Speak Up!" *JBC* 29, no. 3 (2015): 2–4.

February 3. "What Is Your Calling?" *JBC* 28, no. 3 (2014): 82.

February 4. "'I'll Never Get over It'—Helped for the Aggrieved," *JBC* 28, no. 1 (2014): 11–12.

February 5. "In It for Good," *JBC* 26, no. 2 (2012): 2.

February 6. Taken from *God's Grace in Your Suffering* (Crossway, 2018), 35–36. Copyright ©2018. Used by permission of Crossway, a publishing ministry of Good News Publishers, Wheaton, IL 60187, www.crossway.org.

February 7. CCEF 2011 "Dynamics of Biblical Change" video course (filmed at Westminster Theological Seminary), Lecture 3.

February 8. "Dynamics of Biblical Change," Lecture 4.

February 9. "Dynamics of Biblical Change," Lecture 10.

February 10. *Good and Angry: Redeeming Anger, Irritation, Complaining, and Bitterness* (New Growth Press, 2016), 191.

February 11. *Good and Angry*, 146–48.

February 12. *Safe and Sound: Standing Firm in Spiritual Battles* (New Growth Press, 2019), 44–45.

February 13. *Safe and Sound*, 51.

February 14. *Good and Angry: Redeeming Anger, Irritation, Complaining, and Bitterness* (New Growth Press, 2016), 53–54.

February 15. CCEF 2016 Regional Conference: Everyday Worship: How God Brings the Bible to Life, Session 1: "What Makes Words Relevant?"

February 16. *Overcoming Anxiety: Relief for Worried People* (New Growth Press, 2012), 19–20.

February 17. "What Do You Feel?" *JBC* 10, no. 4 (1992): 50–51, 53–54.

February 18. *Speaking Truth in Love: Counsel in Community* (New Growth Press, 2005), 118–19.

February 19. *I Just Want to Die: Replacing Suicidal Thoughts with Hope* (New Growth Press, 2010), 12–14.

February 20. "A Man's Identity," *JBC* 34, no. 1 (2020): 79–80.

February 21. "How Does Sanctification Work?" Part 3, *JBC* 31, no. 1 (2017): 10–12.

February 22. "How Does Sanctification Work?" 28–29.

February 23. "Getting Oriented," *JBC* 30, no. 1 (2016): 2–3.

February 24. "What Is Your Calling?" *JBC* 28, no. 3 (2014): 82–83, 85–86.

February 25. "The Personal God," *JBC* 28, no. 2 (2014): 3.

February 26. "'I'll Never Get over It'—Helped for the Aggrieved," *JBC* 28, no. 1 (2014): 17.

February 27. "Resisting Idols of the Heart and Vanity Fair," *JBC* 27, no. 3 (2013): 37–38.

February 28. *Safe and Sound: Standing Firm in Spiritual Battles* (New Growth Press, 2019), 53–54.

February 29. *Good and Angry: Redeeming Anger, Irritation, Complaining, and Bitterness* (New Growth Press, 2016), 71–72.

March 1. CCEF 2015 National Conference: Side by Side: How God Helps Us Help Each Other, Session 6: "Why We Pray and How We Pray."

March 2. CCEF 2015 National Conference: "Why We Pray and How We Pray."

March 3. "To Take the Soul to Task," *JBC* 12, no. 3 (1994): 1.

March 4. CCEF 2011 "Dynamics of Biblical Change" video course (filmed at Westminster Theological Seminary), Lecture 5.

March 5. CCEF 2017 National Conference: Family: Embracing the Blessing, Facing the Brokenness, General Session 1: "Familial by Design."

March 6. CCEF 2011 "Dynamics of Biblical Change" video course (filmed at Westminster Theological Seminary), Lecture 6.

March 7. "Talk Incessantly? Listen Intently!" *JBC* 15, no. 3 (1997): 2–4.

March 8. CCEF 2011 "Dynamics of Biblical Change" video course (filmed at Westminster Theological Seminary), Lecture 13.

March 9. *Safe and Sound: Standing Firm in Spiritual Battles* (New Growth Press, 2019), 49–50.

March 10. *Controlling Anger: Responding Constructively When Life Goes Wrong* (New Growth Press, 2012), 16–17.

March 11. *Controlling Anger,* 11–12.

March 12. *Renewing Marital Intimacy: Closing the Gap Between You and Your Spouse* (New Growth Press, 2008), 9–10.

March 13. *Grieving a Suicide: Help for the Aftershock* (New Growth Press, 2010), 12–13.

March 14. *Grieving a Suicide*, 5–7.

March 15. *I'm Exhausted: What to Do When You're Always Tired* (New Growth Press, 2010), 13–14.

March 16. CCEF 2011 "Dynamics of Biblical Change" video course (filmed at Westminster Theological Seminary), Lecture 17.

March 17. "Dynamics of Biblical Change," Lecture 16.

March 18. "Dynamics of Biblical Change," Lecture 16.

March 19. "Dynamics of Biblical Change," Lecture 14.

March 20. "Dynamics of Biblical Change," Lecture 13.

March 21. "Dynamics of Biblical Change," Lecture 1.

March 22. "How Does Scripture Change You?" *JBC* 26, no. 2 (2012): 26.

March 23. "'I'll Never Get over It'—Helped for the Aggrieved," *JBC* 28, no. 1 (2014): 17–18.

March 24. "The Personal God," *JBC* 28, no. 2 (2014): 2–3.

March 25. "An Invitation to Speak Up!" *JBC* 29, no. 3 (2015): 4–5.

March 26. "How Does Sanctification Work?" Part 3, *JBC* 31, no. 1 (2017): 30.

March 27. "How Does Sanctification Work?" 12–13.

March 28. "The God of All Comfort," *JBC* 31, no. 3 (2017): 6–7.

March 29. "A Man's Identity," *JBC* 34, no. 1 (2020): 79.

March 30. *I Just Want to Die: Replacing Suicidal Thoughts with Hope* (New Growth Press, 2010), 22–23.

March 31. *Safe and Sound: Standing Firm in Spiritual Battles* (New Growth Press, 2019), 77–79.

April 1. CCEF 2015 National Conference: Side by Side: How God Helps Us Help Each Other, Session 6: "Why We Pray and How We Pray."

April 2. CCEF 2017 National Conference: Family: Embracing the Blessing, Facing the Brokenness, Session 1: "Familial by Design."

April 3. CCEF 2015 Regional Conference: Anxiety: How God Cares for Stressed People, Session 4: "Where Do We Go from Here?"

April 4. "Who Is God?" *JBC* 17, no. 2 (1999): 23.

April 5. "Counsel the Word," *JBC* 11, no. 2 (1993): 3–4.

April 6. *Controlling Anger: Responding Constructively When Life Goes Wrong* (New Growth Press, 2012), 7–8, 10.

April 7. *Controlling Anger*, 3–4.

April 8. "What If Your Father Didn't Love You?" *JBC* 12, no. 1 (1993): 5–6.

April 9. CCEF 2007 National Conference: Running Scared, Breakout Session: "Facing Death."

April 10. "Pray Beyond the Sick List," *JBC* 23, no. 1 (2005): 2–5.

April 11. Taken from *God's Grace in Your Suffering* (Crossway, 2018), 38–39. Copyright ©2018. Used by permission of Crossway, a publishing ministry of Good News Publishers, Wheaton, IL 60187, www.crossway.org.

April 12. Taken from *Seeing with New Eyes* (P&R Publishers, 2003), 44–45. ISBN 9780875526089. Used with permission from P&R Publishing Company, P.O. Box 817, Phillipsburg, NJ, 08865.

April 13. "Reading Scripture with David Powlison," CCEF *On the Go* podcast, April 11, 2018, https://www.ccef.org/podcast/reading-scripture/.

April 14. "A Personal Liturgy of Confession," *JBC* 29, no. 2 (2015): 47–49.

April 15. *Overcoming Anxiety: Relief for Worried People* (New Growth Press, 2012), 12–13.

April 16. *Safe and Sound: Standing Firm in Spiritual Battles* (New Growth Press, 2019), 26–27.

April 17. *Safe and Sound*, 28.

April 18. CCEF 2011 "Dynamics of Biblical Change" video course (filmed at Westminster Theological Seminary), Lecture 1.

April 19. "Dynamics of Biblical Change," Lecture 3.

April 20. "Dynamics of Biblical Change," Lecture 4.

April 21. "In It for Good," *JBC* 26, no. 2 (2012): 2–3.

April 22. "Intimacy with God," *JBC* 16, no. 2 (1998): 2–3.

April 23. *Good and Angry: Redeeming Anger, Irritation, Complaining, and Bitterness* (New Growth Press, 2016), 125.

April 24. *Good and Angry*, 89–90.

April 25. *Overcoming Anxiety: Relief for Worried People* (New Growth Press, 2012), 15–16.

April 26. "How *Does* Sanctification Work?" Part 3, *JBC* 31, no. 1 (2017): 16–17.

April 27. "How *Does* Sanctification Work?" 22–23.

April 28. CCEF 2015 Regional Conference: Anxiety: How God Cares for Stressed People, "Six Ways to Help an Anxious Person."

April 29. CCEF 2013 National Conference: Not Alone: The Relational Core of Life and Counseling, General Session 1: "All Relationships Are Intentional."

April 30. CCEF 2013 National Conference: "All Relationships Are Intentional."

May 1. CCEF 2008 National Conference: The Addict in Us All, General Session 2: "Escape to Reality."

May 2. "X-ray Questions: Drawing Out the Whys and Wherefores of Human Behavior," *JBC* 18, no. 1 (1999): 2–3.

May 3. CCEF 2003 National Conference: Hope for the Suffering, Breakout Session: "Psalm 119: God and Your Hardships."

May 4. CCEF 2005 National Conference: Redeeming Anger in a World Gone Mad, General Session: "Redemption: A Merciful Anger."

May 5. CCEF 2007 National Conference: Running Scared, Breakout Session: "Facing Death."

May 6. "A 'Moderate' Makeover," *JBC* 26, no. 3 (2012): 2–3.

May 7. "Why Do We Pray?" CCEF blog, January 13, 2017, https://www.ccef.org/why-do-we-pray/.

May 8. "Straight Talk," CCEF blog, April 4, 2016, https://www.ccef.org/straight-talk/.

May 9. "When Suffering Won't Go Away, Parts 1–3," CCEF *Help and Hope* podcast, September 2–4, 2016, https://www.ccef.org/podcast/when-suffering-wont-go-away-part-1/; https://www.ccef.org/

podcast/when-suffering-wont-go-away-part-2/; https://www.ccef.org/podcast/when-suffering-wont-go-away-part-3/.

May 10. "Anger Part 1: Understanding Anger," *JBC* 14, no. 1 (1995): 53.

May 11. "Getting to the Heart of Conflict: Anger, Part 3," *JBC* 16, no. 1 (1997): 42.

May 12. "The Fear of Christ is the Beginning of Wisdom," *JBC* 17, no. 2 (1999): 50.

May 13. "What If Your Father Didn't Love You?" *JBC* 12, no. 1 (1993): 1–3.

May 14. "Queries and Controversies," *JBC* 12, no. 3 (1993): 45.

May 15. "How the Bible Gets Personal," *JBC* 29, no. 2 (2015): 4–6.

May 16. "An Open Letter to the Suffering Christian," CCEF blog, March 21, 2018, https://www.ccef.org/open-letter-suffering-christian/. Originally published in Crossway article, "An Open Letter to the Suffering Christian." Published and used by permission of Crossway, a publishing ministry of Good News Publishers, Wheaton, IL, 60187, www.crossway.org.

May 17. "An Open Letter to Those Who Are Apathetic about Their Sanctification." CCEF blog, June 12, 2017, https://www.ccef.org/open-letter-apathetic-sanctification/.

May 18. "Anger Part 1: Understanding Anger," *JBC* 14, no. 1 (1995): 41.

May 19. "Getting to the Heart of Conflict: Anger, Part 3," *JBC* 16, no. 1 (1997): 32–34.

May 20. "Getting to the Heart of Conflict: Anger, Part 3," 34–37.

May 21. CCEF 2015, Regional Conference: Anxiety: How God Cares for Stressed People, Session 2: "Practical Steps toward Change."

May 22. CCEF 2012 National Conference: Guilt & Shame, Breakout Session: "Low Self-Esteem."

May 23. CCEF 2012 National Conference: "Low Self-Esteem."

May 24. CCEF 2009 National Conference: Sex Matters, General Session 3: "Jesus Our Redeemer."

May 25. "X-ray Questions: Drawing Out the Whys and Wherefores of Human Behavior," *JBC* 18, no. 1 (1999): 3, 8.

May 26. "X-ray Questions," 4, 7.

May 27. CCEF 2008 National Conference: The Addict in Us All, Breakout Session: "Addicted to Religion."

May 28. "Think Globally, Act Locally," *JBC* 22, no. 1 (1999): 2–3.

May 29. "Think Globally, Act Locally," 3–4.

May 30. "How *Does* Sanctification Work? Part 1," *JBC* 27, no. 1 (2013): 61.

May 31. *Controlling Anger: Responding Constructively When Life Goes Wrong* (New Growth Press, 2012), 20–21, 23.

June 1. CCEF 2011 "Dynamics of Biblical Change" video course (filmed at Westminster Theological Seminary), Lecture 11.

June 2. "Dynamics of Biblical Change," Lecture 7.

June 3. "Dynamics of Biblical Change," Lecture 6.

June 4. "Dynamics of Biblical Change," Lecture 6.

June 5. "Dynamics of Biblical Change," Lecture 9.

June 6. "Dynamics of Biblical Change," Lecture 13.

June 7. "Dynamics of Biblical Change," Lecture 17.

June 8. "Dynamics of Biblical Change," Lecture 19.

June 9. *I'm Exhausted: What to Do When You're Always Tired* (New Growth Press, 2010), 8–9.

June 10. *I'm Exhausted*, 17–18.

June 11. *Recovering from Child Abuse: Healing and Hope for Victims* (New Growth Press, 2008), 21–24.

June 12. *Grieving a Suicide: Help for the Aftershock* (New Growth Press, 2010), 8–10.

June 13. "Anger Part 1: Understanding Anger," *JBC* 14, no. 1, (1995): 42.

June 14. "Intimacy with God," *JBC* 16, no. 2 (1998): 4.

June 15. CCEF 2016, Regional Conference: Everyday Worship: How God Brings the Bible to Life, Session 1: "What Makes Words Relevant?"

June 16. CCEF 2016 Regional Conference: Session 3: "Martin Luther's 3 Masters."

June 17. Taken from *Seeing with New Eyes: Counseling and the Human Condition through the Lens of Scripture* (P&R Publishers, 2003), 46–47. ISBN 9780875526089. Used with permission from P&R Publishing Company, P.O. Box 817, Philipsburg, NJ, 08865.

June 18. *Good and Angry: Redeeming Anger, Irritation, Complaining, and Bitterness* (New Growth Press, 2016), 194–95.

June 19. *Good and Angry*, 73–74.

June 20. *Good and Angry*, 77–78.

June 21. *Good and Angry*, 84–85.

June 22. *When Cancer Interrupts* (New Growth Press, 2015), 11–13.

June 23. *Overcoming Anxiety: Relief for Worried People* (New Growth Press, 2012), 11–12.

June 24. *Overcoming Anxiety*, 13–15.

June 25. *Speaking Truth in Love: Counsel in Community* (New Growth Press, 2005), 42–43.

June 26. *Speaking Truth in Love*, 33–34.

June 27. *Speaking Truth in Love*, 35.

June 28. *Speaking Truth in Love*, 57–58.

June 29. CCEF 2011 "Dynamics of Biblical Change" video course (filmed at Westminster Theological Seminary), Lecture 17.

June 30. "Dynamics of Biblical Change," Lecture 19.

July 1. *Safe and Sound: Standing Firm in Spiritual Battles* (New Growth Press, 2019), 29–30.

July 2. *Safe and Sound*, 30–31.

July 3. *Safe and Sound*, 32–33.

July 4. *Safe and Sound*, 33–34.

July 5. *Safe and Sound*, 36–37.

July 6. CCEF 2016 Regional Conference: Everyday Worship, Session 4: "Other People Make a Difference."

July 7. CCEF 2015 Regional Conference: Anxiety, Session 2: "Practical Steps toward Change."

July 8. CCEF 2015 Regional Conference: Anxiety, Session 4: "Where Do We Go from Here?"

July 9. CCEF 2013 National Conference: Not Alone, General Session 1: "All Relationships Are Intentional."

July 10. CCEF 2013 National Conference: Not Alone, Breakout Session: "How Can Talking about Yourself Help Someone Else?"

July 11. CCEF 2008 National Conference: The Addict in Us All, General Session 2: "Escape to Reality."

July 12. CCEF 2008 National Conference: "Escape to Reality."

July 13. CCEF 2003 National Conference: Hope for the Suffering, Breakout Session: "Psalm 119: God and Your Hardships."

July 14. Taken from *God's Grace in Your Suffering* (Crossway, 2018), 15. Copyright ©2018. Used by permission of Crossway, a publishing ministry of Good News Publishers, Wheaton, IL 60187, www.crossway.org.

July 15. "How the Bible Gets Personal," *JBC* 29, no. 2 (2015): 3–4.

July 16. *Speaking Truth in Love: Counsel in Community* (New Growth Press, 2005), 99–101.

July 17. *Facing Death with Hope: Living for What Lasts* (New Growth Press, 2008), 9–10.

July 18. *Facing Death with Hope*, 13, 18.

July 19. *Breaking the Addictive Cycle: Deadly Obsessions or Simple Pleasures?* (New Growth Press, 2010), 25–27.

July 20. "Counsel and Counseling," *JBC* 32, no. 1 (2018): 3.

July 21. "What Can You Do When God Seems Far Away?" *JBC* 30, no. 3 (2016): 2–3.

July 22. "What Can You Do When God Seems Far Away?" 5.

July 23. "Resisting Idols of the Heart and Vanity Fair," *JBC* 27, no. 3 (2013): 37–38.

July 24. "Resisting Idols of the Heart and Vanity Fair," 41.

July 25.	CCEF 2011 "Dynamics of Biblical Change" video course (filmed at Westminster Theological Seminary), Lecture 1.
July 26.	"Dynamics of Biblical Change," Lecture 2.
July 27.	"Dynamics of Biblical Change," Lecture 2.
July 28.	"Dynamics of Biblical Change," Lecture 2.
July 29.	"Dynamics of Biblical Change," Lecture 18.
July 30.	"Dynamics of Biblical Change," Lecture 3.
July 31.	"Dynamics of Biblical Change," Lecture 3.
August 1.	"Dynamics of Biblical Change," Lecture 4.
August 2.	"Dynamics of Biblical Change," Lecture 4.
August 3.	"Dynamics of Biblical Change," Lecture 5.
August 4.	"Dynamics of Biblical Change," Lecture 6.
August 5.	*Good and Angry: Redeeming Anger, Irritation, Complaining, and Bitterness* (New Growth Press, 2016), 86–88.
August 6.	*Good and Angry*, 90–91.
August 7.	*Good and Angry*, 67, 69.
August 8.	"A Man's Identity," *JBC* 34, no. 1 (2020): 80–81.
August 9.	"The Right Kind of Weakness," *JBC* 33, no. 2 (2019): 4–5.
August 10.	"The Right Kind of Weakness," 3–4.
August 11.	"What Can You Do When God Seems Far Away?" *JBC* 30, no. 3 (2016): 5–6.
August 12.	"Sex, Truth, and Scripture," *JBC* 13, no. 3 (1995): 2–3.
August 13.	CCEF 2016 Regional Conference: Everyday Worship: How God Brings the Bible to Life, Session 1: "What Makes Words Relevant?"
August 14.	CCEF 2016 Regional Conference: Session 2: "Learning to Ask the Right Questions."
August 15.	CCEF 2016 Regional Conference: Session 3: "Martin Luther's 3 Masters."
August 16.	CCEF 2016 Regional Conference: Session 4: "Other People Make a Difference."

August 17. CCEF 2015 Regional Conference: Anxiety: How God Cares for Stressed People, General Session: "Six Ways to Help an Anxious Person."

August 18. "'Peace, Be Still:' Learning Psalm 131 by Heart," *JBC* 18, no. 3 (2000): 2–3.

August 19. "'Peace, Be Still:' Learning Psalm 131 by Heart," 3–5.

August 20. CCEF 2007 National Conference: Running Scared, Breakout Session: "Gripping Fears."

August 21. "Don't Worry," *JBC* 21, no. 2 (2003): 55, 59, 61, 63.

August 22. "Don't Worry," 64–65.

August 23. "How *Does* Sanctification Work? Part 2" *JBC* 27, no. 2 (2013): 41–43, 48.

August 24. "How the Bible Gets Personal," *JBC* 29, no. 2 (2015): 6–8.

August 25. "Why Do We Pray?" CCEF blog, January 13, 2017, https://www.ccef.org/why-do-we-pray/.

August 26. "Should We Really Call It a 'Quiet' Time?" CCEF blog, April 14, 2016, https://www.ccef.org/should-we-really-call-it-quiet-time/.

August 27. "Should We Really Call It a 'Quiet' Time?" https://www.ccef.org/should-we-really-call-it-quiet-time/.

August 28. "Straight Talk," CCEF blog, April 4, 2016, https://www.ccef.org/straight-talk/.

August 29. Taken from *Seeing with New Eyes* (P&R Publishers, 2003), 121. ISBN 9780875526089. Used with permission from P&R Publishing Company, P.O. Box 817, Philipsburg, NJ, 08865.

August 30. "Resisting Idols of the Heart and Vanity Fair," *JBC* 27, no. 3 (2013): 42.

August 31. "Resisting Idols of the Heart and Vanity Fair," 43–44.

September 1. *Safe and Sound: Standing Firm in Spiritual Battles* (New Growth Press, 2019), 80–81.

September 2. Taken from *God's Grace in Your Suffering* (Crossway, 2018), 115–16. Copyright ©2018. Used by permission of Crossway, a publishing ministry of Good News Publishers, Wheaton, IL 60187, www.crossway.org.

September 3. *I Just Want to Die: Replacing Suicidal Thoughts with Hope* (New Growth Press, 2010), 20–21.

September 4. *Breaking the Addictive Cycle: Deadly Obsessions or Simple Pleasures?* (New Growth Press, 2010), 14–15.

September 5. "How *Does* Sanctification Work?" Part 3, *JBC* 31:1 (2017): 13–14.

September 6. "How *Does* Sanctification Work?" Part 3, 15–16.

September 7. "How *Does* Sanctification Work?" Part 3, 16.

September 8. "How *Does* Sanctification Work?" Part 3, 19–20.

September 9. "How *Does* Sanctification Work?" Part 3, 20–22.

September 10. "Getting Oriented," *JBC* 30, no. 1 (2016): 6–7.

September 11. "An Invitation to Speak Up!" *JBC* 29, no. 3 (2015): 5.

September 12. CCEF 2011 "Dynamics of Biblical Change" video course (filmed at Westminster Theological Seminary), Lecture 2.

September 13. "Dynamics of Biblical Change," Lecture 12.

September 14. "Dynamics of Biblical Change," Lecture 5.

September 15. "Dynamics of Biblical Change," Lecture 5.

September 16. "Dynamics of Biblical Change," Lecture 7.

September 17. "Dynamics of Biblical Change," Lecture 7.

September 18. "Dynamics of Biblical Change," Lecture 15.

September 19. "Dynamics of Biblical Change," Lecture 16.

September 20. "Dynamics of Biblical Change," Lecture 17.

September 21. "Dynamics of Biblical Change," Lecture 18.

September 22. "Dynamics of Biblical Change," Lecture 18.

September 23. "Dynamics of Biblical Change," Lectures 19 and 20.

September 24. *Safe and Sound: Standing Firm in Spiritual Battles* (New Growth Press, 2019), 12–14.

September 25. *Safe and Sound*, 47–49.

September 26. *Controlling Anger: Responding Constructively When Life Goes Wrong* (New Growth Press, 2012), 17–20.

September 27. *Controlling Anger*, 12–14.

September 28. "Anger Part 1: Understanding Anger," *JBC* 14, no. 1 (1995): 52.

September 29. CCEF 2012 National Conference: Guilt & Shame, Breakout Session: "Low Self-Esteem."

September 30. CCEF 2009 National Conference: Sex Matters, General Session: "Jesus Our Redeemer."

October 1. CCEF 2014 National Conference: Loss: Finding Hope That Lasts When Life Falls Apart, General Session 1: "All Is Lost."

October 2. CCEF 2014 National Conference: "All Is Lost."

October 3. CCEF 2014 National Conference: "All Is Lost."

October 4. "An Open Letter to Those Frustrated by Their Progress in Sanctification," CCEF blog, June 5, 2017, https://www.ccef.org/on-sanctification-part-1/.

October 5. "How Can Christ Help Me Overcome My Sinful Past?" CCEF *Help and Hope* podcast, July 10, 2016, https://www.ccef.org/podcast/how-can-christ-help-me-overcome-my-sinful-past/.

October 6. CCEF 2012 National Conference: Guilt & Shame, General Session 3: "Guilt & Shame with Jesus."

October 7. "How *Does* Sanctification Work? Part 2," *JBC* 27, no. 2 (2013): 45, 50.

October 8. "How *Does* Sanctification Work? Part 2," 45–47, 50.

October 9. "How *Does* Sanctification Work? Part 2," 47–48.

October 10. *When Cancer Interrupts* (New Growth Press, 2015), 13–14.

October 11. *When Cancer Interrupts*, 10–11.

October 12. *Speaking Truth in Love: Counsel in Community* (New Growth Press, 2005), 55–56.

October 13. *Speaking Truth in Love*, 58–59.

October 14. *Speaking Truth in Love*, 56–57, 61.

October 15. *I Just Want to Die: Replacing Suicidal Thoughts with Hope* (New Growth Press, 2010), 3, 7–8.

October 16. CCEF 2011 "Dynamics of Biblical Change" video course (filmed at Westminster Theological Seminary), Lecture 1.

October 17. "Dynamics of Biblical Change," Lecture 3.

October 18. "Dynamics of Biblical Change," Lecture 9.

October 19. "Dynamics of Biblical Change," Lecture 16.

October 20. *Good and Angry: Redeeming Anger, Irritation, Complaining, and Bitterness* (New Growth Press, 2016), 46, 54, 58.

October 21. *Good and Angry*, 54–55, 57, 59.

October 22. *Good and Angry*, 63–64.

October 23. *Good and Angry*, 80–82.

October 24. *Speaking Truth in Love*, 36.

October 25. *Speaking Truth in Love*, 43.

October 26. *Speaking Truth in Love*, 43–44.

October 27. *Speaking Truth in Love*, 44–45.

October 28. *Speaking Truth in Love*, 167–68.

October 29. "Dynamics of Biblical Change," Lecture 5.

October 30. "Dynamics of Biblical Change," Lecture 5.

October 31. "Dynamics of Biblical Change," Lecture 5.

November 1. CCEF 2011 "Dynamics of Biblical Change" video course (filmed at Westminster Theological Seminary), Lecture 5.

November 2. "Dynamics of Biblical Change," Lecture 19.

November 3 "What Do You Feel?" *JBC* 10, no. 4 (1992): 58–60.

November 4. "Your Looks: What the Voices Say and the Images Portray," *JBC* 15, no. 2 (1997): 39, 42–43.

November 5. "Don't Worry," *JBC* 21, no. 2 (2003): 55, 57–58, 63–64.

November 6. "The Sufficiency of Scripture to Diagnose and Cure Souls," *JBC* 23, no. 2 (2004): 4.

November 7. "The Sufficiency of Scripture to Diagnose and Cure Souls," 5–6, 11.

November 8. "The Sufficiency of Scripture to Diagnose and Cure Souls," 11–13.

November 9. "I Am Making All Things New," *JBC* 24, no. 4 (2006): 2.

November 10. "I Am Making All Things New," 2–4.

November 11. "How *Does* Sanctification Work? Part 2" *JBC* 27, no. 2 (2013): 37–39, 44.

November 12. CCEF 2005 National Conference: Redeeming Anger in a World Gone Mad, General Session 2: "Creation (A Just Anger) and Fall (A Corrupt Anger)."

November 13. CCEF 2005 National Conference: Redeeming Anger in a World Gone Mad, General Session 3: "Redemption—A Merciful Anger."

November 14. CCEF 2005 National Conference: Redeeming Anger in a World Gone Mad, General Session 4: "Sanctification: A Transforming Anger."

November 15. "Anger Part 2: Three Lies about Anger and the Transforming Truth," *JBC* 14, no. 2 (1996): 13–14.

November 16. CCEF 2014 National Conference: Loss: Finding Hope That Lasts When Life Falls Apart, General Session 1: "All Is Lost."

November 17. *Safe and Sound: Standing Firm in Spiritual Battles* (New Growth Press, 2019), 55–58.

November 18. *Recovering from Child Abuse: Healing and Hope for Victims* (New Growth Press, 2008), 4–5, 7–8.

November 19. *Safe and Sound: Standing Firm in Spiritual Battles* (New Growth Press, 2019), 23.

November 20. "How *Does* Sanctification Work? Part 1" *JBC* 27, no. 1 (2013): 53–55.

November 21. "Dynamics of Biblical Change," Lecture 17.

November 22. "Dynamics of Biblical Change," Lecture 17.

November 23. Taken from *God's Grace in Your Suffering* by David Powlison, Copyright ©2018, pp. 27–28. Used by permission of Crossway, a publishing ministry of Good News Publishers, Wheaton, IL 60187, www.crossway.org.

November 24. "Dynamics of Biblical Change," Lecture 16.

November 25. "Thankfulness," CCEF blog, November 21, 2016, https://www.ccef.org/thankfulness/.

November 26. "How *Does* Sanctification Work? Part 1," *JBC* 27, no. 1 (2013): 56–58.

November 27. "How *Does* Sanctification Work? Part 1," 65–66.

November 28. "Counsel and Counseling," *JBC* 32, no. 1 (2018): 6.

November 29. "How the Bible Gets Personal," *JBC* 29, no. 2 (2015): 2–3.

November 30. "Reading Scripture with David Powlison," CCEF *On the Go* podcast, April 11, 2018, https://www.ccef.org/podcast/reading-scripture/.

December 1. "Psalm 103," CCEF *On the Go* podcast, April 5, 2017, https://www.ccef.org/podcast/psalm-103-david-powlison/.

December 2. Taken from *Seeing with New Eyes: Counseling and the Human Condition through the Lens of Scripture*, pp. 48–49, ISBN 9780875526089. Used with permission from P&R Publishing Company, P.O. Box 817, Philipsburg, NJ, 08865.

December 3. "How *Does* Sanctification Work? Part 2" *JBC* 27, no. 2 (2013), 35–36.

December 4. Personal journal entry, 1/1/1998, supplied by Nan Powlison.

December 5. "How *Does* Sanctification Work? Part 1," *JBC* 27, no. 1 (2013): 49, 51–52.

December 6. *Speaking Truth in Love: Counsel in Community* (New Growth Press, 2005), 65.

December 7. CCEF 2011 "Dynamics of Biblical Change" video course (filmed at Westminster Theological Seminary), Lecture 7.

December 8. "Dynamics of Biblical Change," Lecture 7.

December 9. "Dynamics of Biblical Change," Lecture 7.

December 10. *Good and Angry: Redeeming Anger, Irritation, Complaining, and Bitterness* (New Growth Press, 2016), 39, 41–42.

December 11. *Good and Angry*, 121–22.

December 12. *Good and Angry*, 130.

December 13. "Dynamics of Biblical Change," Lecture 12.

December 14. "Dynamics of Biblical Change," Lecture 12.

December 15. *Controlling Anger: Responding Constructively When Life Goes Wrong* (New Growth Press, 2012), 6–10.

December 16. "Dynamics of Biblical Change," Lecture 16.

December 17. "Innocent Pleasures," *JBC* 23, no. 4 (2005): 22–23.

December 18. "Who Is God?" *JBC* 17, no. 2 (1999): 14–15.

December 19. "Doing 'Wicked Good' Practical Theology," *JBC* 24, no. 1 (2006): 2–3.

December 20. "Does the Shoe Fit?" *JBC* 20, no. 3 (2002): 2–3.

December 21. Taken from *God's Grace in Your Suffering* by David Powlison, Copyright ©2018, pp. 82–83. Used by permission of Crossway, a publishing ministry of Good News Publishers, Wheaton, IL 60187, www.crossway.org.

December 22. "The God of All Comfort," *JBC* 31, no. 3 (2017): 7–13.

December 23. "Dynamics of Biblical Change," Lecture 16.

December 24. "The Therapeutic Gospel," *JBC* 25, no. 3 (2007): 3–4.

December 25. "Emmanuel Shall Come to You," CCEF blog, December 21, 2016, https://www.ccef.org/emmanuel-shall-come/.

December 26. "Dynamics of Biblical Change," Lecture 1.

December 27. *Recovering from Child Abuse: Healing and Hope for Victims* (New Growth Press, 2008), 16–18, 20–21.

December 28. "'I'll Never Get over It'—Helped for the Aggrieved," *JBC* 28, no. 1 (2014): 10–11.

December 29. "Innocent Pleasures," *JBC* 23, no. 4 (2005): 22.

December 30. "Innocent Pleasures," 25.

December 31. Taken from *God's Grace in Your Suffering* by David Powlison, Copyright ©2018, pp. 78–79. Used by permission of Crossway, a publishing ministry of Good News Publishers, Wheaton, IL 60187, www.crossway.org.

DAVID'S FAVORITE HYMNS

"Alas! and Did My Savior Bleed" by Isaac Watts (1707)

"Be Still, My Soul" by Katharina von Schlegel (1752)

"Be Thou My Vision" by Dallán Forgaill (sixth century)

"Come Thou Fount of Every Blessing" by Robert Robinson (1757)

"Fairest Lord Jesus" (Anonymous)

"Great Is Thy Faithfulness" by Thomas Chisholm (1923)

"How Firm a Foundation" by John Rippon (1787)

"I Bind unto Myself Today" (St. Patrick's Hymn) by St. Patrick

"It Is Well with My Soul" by Horatio Spafford (1873)

"Joy to the World" by Isaac Watts (1719)

"Love Divine, All Loves Excelling" by Charles Wesley (1747)

"My Song Is Love Unknown" by Samuel Crossman (1664)

"None Other Lamb" by Christina Rossetti (1892)

"O Come, O Come, Emmanuel" (Anonymous, ninth-century Latin hymn)

"O, the Deep, Deep Love of Jesus" by Samuel Trevor Francis (1875)

"Rock of Ages" by Augustus Toplady (1776)

"Take My Life and Let It Be" by Frances R. Havergal (1874)

"Wake, Awake, for Night Is Flying" by Catherine Winkworth and Philipp Nicolai (1599)

"We Rest on Thee" by Edith G. Cherry (1895)

SCRIPTURE INDEX

PROVERBS

ECCLESIASTES

ROMANS

1 CORINTHIANS

2 CORINTHIANS

1 PETER

2 PETER

1 JOHN

REVELATION

ccef

CCEF is committed to restoring Christ to counseling and counseling to the church. They seek to accomplish this mission through resources, courses, events, and counseling.

To learn more or explore CCEF's resources, visit **ccef.org**.